AF543111

The desire to be a champion, to be a winner, to be better than others is an instinct almost as deeply ingrained as the instinct for survival. And this instinct is best manifest in all its positive attributes in the arena of games and sports where, from times immemorial, man has pitted himself against man to prove he is swifter and stronger than others. Over the years many rules and regulations, and even rewards of several games have changed but what has not changed is the human passion. It is this passion which defines the champion, which makes men and women strive to run that one last step, to jump that much higher or to swim that one more lap.

Presented in this book are the inspiring stories of the lives and the struggles of those Indian sportspersons-men and women - who have proved themselves worthy of being crowned champions.

INDIAN CHAMPIONS

Profiles of Famous Indian Sportspersons

Chitra Garg

rajpal

Price : Rs. 450.00 (Rupees Four Hundred Fifty)

Edition : 2010 © Publisher
ISBN : 978-81-7028-852-7
Indian Champions : Profiles of Famous Indian Sportspersons
by Chitra Garg

RAJPAL & SONS
Madarsa Road, Kashmere Gate, Delhi-110 006
website : www.rajpalpublishing.com
e-mail : mail@rajpalpublishing.com

Contents

BOXING

CHESS

CRICKET

Dedicated to
All Aspiring Champions

ARCHERY

Since centuries archery has been a flourishing sport in India. The two great Hindu epics — the *Ramayana* and the *Mahabharata* — have described in detail the artistry and the perfection achieved by the Indian archers. Who amongst us would not have read in the *Ramayana* about Lord Rama breaking the bow to marry Sita or Arjuna aiming at a fish with his eyes focused on the shadow cast in a bowl of water placed below the target in the *Mahabharata*?

Archery first appeared as a sport in the 1900 Olympic Games in Paris and was held in 1904, 1908 and 1920 as well. However, international rules had not yet been developed and the host country used its own format. As a result, archery events in the early Olymic Games varied widely. Because of the lack of uniform international rules, archery was then dropped from the Olympic Games. The Federation Internationale de Tir a l'Arc (FITA), the international governing body of the sport, was founded in 1931 and it implemented standardised rules for the competitons. It allowed the first World Championship to be held the same year. After all the countries had adopted the new rules, archery returned to the 1972 Olympic Games in Munich. Initially, only the individual competition took place but in 1988, team competition was also introduced.

Four archery events are held at the Olympics — men's individual, women's individual, men's team and women's team. The archers used to shoot a double FITA round of 288 total arrows, with the championship decided by the highest total score. In the 1992 Olympics, the format was changed to head-to-head elimination for the top 64 competitors in order to make the game more exciting.

The bow limbs are generally made of man-made materials, such as fibreglass; the bow handles are made of aluminium alloys and are machined for strength. Most bow strings are made of either fast flight, a hydrocarbon product and arrows are made of either aluminium or carbon graphite. Aluminium arrows are more uniform.

Modern Olympic archery came to India in 1975, soon after archery had been chosen as part of the Olympic Games, held in Munich, West Germany in 1972. The first National Meet in archery was organised in New Delhi in 1973 when more than 50 archers participated. They used bamboo bows and arrows made in Meghalaya and West Bengal. The Bengal archers were in the forefront with their superior techniques.

Efforts were made to build up a team of excellent archers who could participate in international events. India organised the first Asian Meet in Calcutta in 1980. The game progressed in fits and starts until the mid-eighties when it received a shot in the arm with most archers provided with modern sophisticated equipment. Gradually arose a number of talented and promising archers on the national scene, though mainly from the rural belt of India — like Limba Ram and Shyam Lal who performed well in the Olympic Games at Barcelona. The game of archery is making rapid strides in India with more and more sportspersons taking to it. Since then, great progress has been made by the Indian archers in the game which kindles ample hope for the future.

Archery

Dola Bannerjee

Date of Birth : 2nd June 1980

Dola Bannerjee is the first Indian shooter to have ever qualified for the Olympics. She won the 18th Golden Euro Grand Prix Tournament (Antalya) and a gold medal in the SAF Games of 2006. She was honoured with the Arjuna Award in 2005.

The credit for earning fame as the first woman shooter (archery) at the national level goes to Dola Bannerjee. In India, where shooting is predominantly considered to be a man's game, Dola not only participated in the game, but also acquired success at the international level.

Dola Bannerjee was born on 2nd June 1980. She formally learnt archery at the Tata Archery Academy, Jamshedpur. She holds the distinction of being the first successful archer at the national level. She proved successful at the 42nd World Outdoor Target Archery Championship held in New York by becoming the first Indian woman shooter to qualify for the Olympics. This, however, did not come as a surprise to people who were already familiar with her success story.

In the year 2005, she created history after she won the 18th Golden Euro Grand Prix Tournament in Turkey (Antalya). There she defeated Tatyana Dorokhova a third seeded player from Ukraine.

In 2006, Dola defeated her opponent Rina Kumari to win a gold medal in the Women's Archery Competition at the SAF Games held in Colombo. In recognition of her achievements, the Government of India honoured her with the Arjuna Award in 2005.

Achievements

- ☆ *Dola Bannerjee became the first Indian woman archer to qualify for the Olympics.*

- ☆ *She is a successful national-level player to have earned success at the international level as well.*
- ☆ *She is the first Indian woman archer to have earned this distinction.*
- ☆ *The Government of India honoured her with the Arjuna Award in 2005.*
- ☆ *She won a gold medal in the 2006 SAF Games held at Antalya in Colombo.*

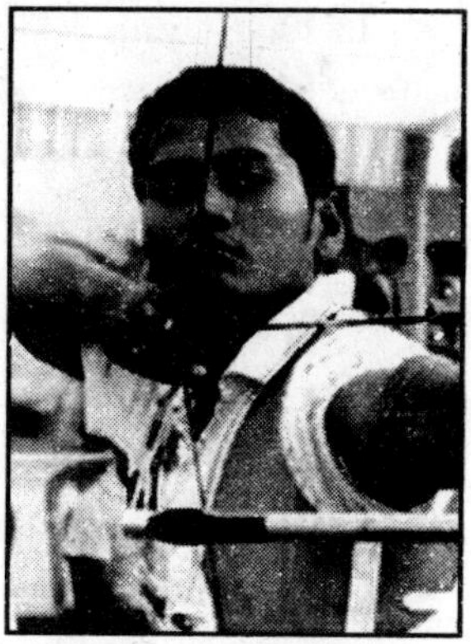

Jayant Talukdar

Date of Birth : 1987

Jayant Talukdar is the first archer from India to be ranked number one in archery in the world in 2006. He enhanced the country's reputation with his victory. He is the first Indian archer to have won a gold medal in the FITA Meteksan Archery World Cup. He won a gold medal at the Colombo SAF Games in 2000.

Jayant Talukdar is one of India's topmost archers. He gave ample proof of his immense potential with a series of scintillating performances in the international field.

Jayant Talukdar was born in 1987 in Guwahati. He is the youngest son of a quarry owner. He was picked up by his coaches at a talent hunt camp in archery organised at Guwahati. He was imparted strenuous training to hone his skill at the training camp held at the Tata Archery Academy. He impressed his coaches with his physical strength, right focus and concentration.

Jayant emerged as the top performer of the Indian team when his team made history by winning the silver medal at the Junior World Championship in Britain in 2004. It was the first medal for India at a world championship.

In 2005, Jayant became the brightest archer when he defeated seasoned players at the 25th Senior National Championship held in Kochi. The very same year he created history when he became the first Indian archer to win a gold medal at the FITA Meteksan Archery World Cup at Porec, Croatia.

Jayant Talukdar is currently ranked second, behind Italy's Ilaris di Buo in the world rankings for the individual recurve event.

In 2006, Jayant defeated his rival Tarundeep Rai and bagged the men's individual recurve gold in archery at the SAF Games held in Colombo. He became the first Indian archer to qualify for the World Cup final and was honoured with the Arjuna Award in 2006.

Achievements

- ☆ *Jayant Talukdar is hailed as the brightest star in Indian archery and one of the topmost archers of the world.*
- ☆ *He created history when he won a gold medal in the FITA Meteksan Archery World Cup at Porec, Croatia in 2005 and became the first Indian archer to attain this feat.*
- ☆ *He won the National Championship in 2005 at Ernakulam (recurve individual event) and in 2006 at Kolkata.*
- ☆ *In 2006, he was a member of the bronze medal-winning Indian team at the Doha Asian Games.*
- ☆ *His team won the silver medal in 2003 at Yangon and a silver medal in 2005 at New Delhi.*
- ☆ *He was a member of the Indian team, which won a silver medal at Madrid in 2005.*
- ☆ *He was a member of the Indian team to have won a silver medal at the Junior World Championship in Britain.*
- ☆ *He is ranked number two in the world in the 'recurve event'.*
- ☆ *He won a gold medal at the 2006 Colombo SAF Games.*
- ☆ *He was awarded the Arjuna Award in 2006.*

Archery

Limba Ram

Date of Birth: 24th September 1971

Limba Ram is the most well-known archer of India. He led the Indian challenge in numerous international events for over a decade and half. He made a world record and won a gold medal in the Beijing Asian Championship in 1992. He missed the medal by one point in the Barcelona Olympics held in 1992.

Limba Ram is one of the most celebrated Indian archers. He was born in Saradit, a relatively unknown village of Udaipur district and belongs to the Ahari tribe of Rajasthan. He has indeed travelled a long way since his days of game hunting in the jungles of Udaipur. He was selected in a talent scouting trial conducted by the Sports Authority of India that groomed him under the Special Area Games Programme.

Limba Ram was selected along with three archers in 1987. In fact, the Sports Authority of India picked him up during its national talent search programme along with the Arjuna Award-winning archer, Shyamlal. In the same year he set up a national record at the Senior National Archery Championship in the 50-metre and 30-metre events.

After stamping his name in the national circuit, Limba Ram reached the international level to win world acclaim. He equalled the world record in the Beijing Asian Championship held in 1992 in the 30-metre event to bag a gold medal.

After remaining unemployed for a few years, Limba Ram was offered a job as sports officer by the Punjab National Bank.

Achievements

- ☆ *Born in Ahari tribe, Limba Ram proved his talent at the national level.*
- ☆ *He represented India in three Olympics, two Asian Games, two World Cup events and many more regional and international meets.*
- ☆ *He equalled the world record in the Beijing Asian Championship in 1992 in the 30-metre event to bag a gold medal.*
- ☆ *He is the first archer from India to have won international fame in archery.*
- ☆ *He was honoured with the Arjuna Award in 1991.*
- ☆ *In less than six months of training he became the junior national champion at Bangalore in 1987.*
- ☆ *The same year (1987) he entered the Senior National Championship at New Delhi and won two gold medals — in the 50-metre and the 30-metre-distance events. He won a silver medal in the 70-metre and a bronze in the National Championship.*
- ☆ *In 1988, he became the national champion at Amaravati and was declared the best archer of the meet. He was then selected for the Seoul Olympics.*
- ☆ *In 1989, he led the team to the Beijing Asian Games where the Indian team won the gold medal, defeating South Korea which got the silver medal.*
- ☆ *He won a gold medal in the overall championship in 1991 at Calcutta; a gold medal in 1992 at Jamshedpur in the overall championship; three gold, one silver and one bronze medal in the Gurgaon Games in 1994; two gold medals, one silver in the Kolkata Games in 1996; a gold in the team and overall championship in the Jamshedpur Games in 1997 and two golds in 2001 at the Amravati Games.*

- ☆ *He won four gold and two silver medals in the National Games at Pune.*
- ☆ *He helped the Indian team to win a bronze in the prestigious Spring Arrow Championship in Moscow (USSR) in 1988.*
- ☆ *The other international meets he won include the one at Sukkhumi, Georgia in 1989 (bronze); Moscow, in 1992 (bronze); Federation Cup in New Delhi in 1990 (team gold); Kolkata in 1991 (gold in team and individual events); in New Delhi in 1995 (gold in individual and silver in team).*
- ☆ *His team won the gold medal in the three-nation international meet in 1990.*
- ☆ *He won a gold medal in the individual and a silver medal in the team event in the international meet held in 1992 at Beijing.*
- ☆ *He won a gold medal each in the team and individual events in 1993 at Bangkok.*
- ☆ *He was given the Maharana Pratap Award in 1990.*

ATHLETICS

Athletics include a variety of sport events and are the oldest forms of organised sport, having been a part of the ancient Olympic Games (776 BC to AD 393). Modern events include distance-running competitions (100-metre dash, mile race, marathon, etc.), relay race, hurdles, steeplechase, high jump, pole vault, long jump, triple jump, shot put, discus throw, hammer throw, javelin throw, decathlon, pentathlon and hepathlon, cross-country runs and walking as adjuncts of track-and-field athletics. Events are held both indoors and outdoors and each event is recorded separately.

The general standard of competition in athletics in India can best be described as mediocre, despite the improvement in terms of facilities, general infrastructure and coaching facilities. A redeeming feature of athletics in India is the increase in the number of women participants in the game, who are elevating the country's status of sorts at the Asian level, if not on the world scene. In the eighties, it was the entry of P.T. Usha in the field of women athletics where the sport reached a very high standard. One of the reasons for women participitating in sports is that more and more women are shedding their inhibitions to enter the track-and-field events, particularly in cities like Bangaluru and Chennai, which have contributed generously by producing some well-known women athletes, like Valsamma in hurdles and Shiny Abraham in the 800-metre race events. The other important state is Kerala, which has contributed excellent athletes in sprints and jumps.

Indian athletes like Milkha Singh, Gurbachan Singh and Sriram Singh had left an indelible mark in Olympics and at the Asian level in the early days but today, the overall standard has not shown much improvement.

Anju Bobby George

Date of Birth: 19th April 1977

Anju Bobby George did India proud by winning the bronze medal in the long jump event in the World Athletics Championship at Paris in September 2003. This happened to be India's first international athletics award. Anju George, at the age of 25 years, became the first Indian athlete to be awarded at a world athletics event in 2003. Her incredible performance at this world platform gave a new direction to Indian athletics and she became a role model for sportspersons to follow in her footsteps. It is notable that prior to Anju's award-winning stint in this event, India's name was synonymous with 'miss at the last lap' in the athletics field. She was awarded the prestigious 'Rajiv Gandhi Khel Ratna' Award in the year 2004, in recognition of her spectacular performance.

Anju was born on 19th April 1977, in a small town called Cheeranchira, in the Kottayam district of south-central Kerala. She went to St. Ann's Girls' School in Changanassery during her initial schooling years. She started displaying an interest in athletics from the delicate age of five, when she started to participate in athletics in her school. Fortunately, for Anju, her parents — her father, T. Markos and mother, Gracy — on seeing her avid interest in the sport, gave their complete support to her and encouraged her to move ahead in that line. Her father run a furniture business.

Anju's school too, on its part, gave her sufficient opportunities to practice by making an exclusive itinerary for long jump, throw and athletics for her. After a while she went to pursue her schooling in the C. K.

Keshwaran Memorial High School, where her teacher, 'Thomas Sir', honed her skills to perfection and she made an invaluable contribution towards winning the 'Overall Performance Trophy' for her school. At that time she concentrated essentially on high jump, long jump, hephthalon and other such events. P.T. Usha, the ace athlete, was her role model.

In the year 1960, the 'Flying Sikh', Milkha Singh, could not win a medal despite setting a world record in race at the Rome Olympics. Later in 1976, Shriram Singh too, ranked seventh, could not win any medal despite setting a national record in Montreal. The misfortune repeated itself in the case of Gurbachan Singh Randhawa. In 1984, at Los Angeles, P.T. Usha too missed her medal by one-hundredth part of a minute.

Anju broke this trend by winning the first bronze medal for India at an international forum like the World Athletics Championship in Paris in September 2003. A lot of hard work and toil went into reaching this level. Her coach is her husband, Robert Bobby George, who also holds a world record in the long jump event. A healthy sports atmosphere prevails in both her parents' as well as her in-laws' house. Her husband Bobby George gave up his career in triple jump so that he could devote all his time in coaching Anju. Undoubtedly, Anju gives the complete credit for her success to her life partner.

Anju's words after winning the bronze medal at the World Athletics were, "I am feeling extremely proud on winning this medal for my country, thereby earning a name for my India in the world. I dedicate this medal to my motherland."

Anju's performance was laudable also due to the fact that she had won the medal from amongst 210 participating countries. This was the most outstanding performance put in by an Indian athlete. While discussing the secret behind her success, Anju said, "One should always believe in the thing that one does. If near-impoverished countries can perform to world standards, then why can't India? If I can take the 6.74 metre jump twice, so can you."

Anju Markos (her maiden name) in the year 1999 had felt that she would never be able to play in her entire life. She could almost see her sports career coming to an end at that time when she suffered a major injury on her ankle in the South Asian Athletics Championship, where she also won a silver medal. She had to abstain from participating in the Sydney Olympics in the year 2000 and shun all sports activities for a period of two years.

Anju resurfaced in the year 2001 and made a record in the 6.74 long jump event. Her career took a new turn when she enrolled in Vimala College, Trichur where her name started emerging at the national level as well. It was during this period that she was selected for the National Coaching Camp and in the year 1998, she left the Indian Railways to join Chennai Customs.

She came into contact with triple-jump national champion, Bobby George and gained expertise from him. After some time their association grew and they decided to get married. Anju won a bronze medal in the Commonwealth Games in Manchester and made a respectable name for herself among other veteran Indian sportspersons. She was the first woman athlete to have won this medal for India by jumping 6.49-metres.

Thereafter she left a mark with her excellent performance by winning the gold medal in the Asian Games held at Busan. Here she managed a jump of 6.53 metres at the rate of 1.8m/sec. She went ahead to get trained by the veteran athlete, Mike Powell who imparted rigorous training to her in America. Anju holds a maximum record of 6.74-metre long jump. She ranked 13th in the world and secured the 7th place for herself in the World Championship.

She won a bronze medal with her 6.70-metre jump in the World Athletics Championship in Paris in August 2003. Prior to this, Seema Antil, an Indian athlete, had won a medal in the World Junior Athletics, but she had to return back the medal on being tested positive in the dope test. Thus, Anju remains the only sportsperson to have won recognition at this level.

Anju owes a major part of her success to her coach and world record-holder in long jump, Mike Powell. He made a world record with his golden 8.95-metre jump at Tokyo in 1991.

The Indian Olympic Union and Samsung India Limited decided to sponsor Indian sportspersons for the Athens Olympics of 2004. Samsung constituted an Olympic fund, offering sponsorship to top Indian athletes. Anju B. George was one among the chosen five athletes, who were provided various facilities and training with this fund.

Anju's training with Mike Powell commenced in March 2003 and continued till the Athens Olympics. Her performance level showed considerable improvement, so much so that it drew the attention of an American sports management company, HIS, towards Anju and they introduced her to gold-medal winners of Olympics in the 100-metre run — Morris Greene, Allan Johnson and many other veterans. Association with such stalwarts translated into an opportunity for good performance.

Thus came a time when the players managed to cross the 7-metre mark in the jump event. However, the bar returned back to normal after the players started succumbing to the dope test. Anju has been rated as one amongst the world's eight best athletes. Hence it was hoped that she would be successful in winning a medal in the Athens Olympics.

In May 2004, during her training tenure, Anju managed to increase her long jump to 6.9 metres. Then her coach-husband raised her bar to the level of 7.20 metres by August 2004. At this time Anju rose higher and became the world's number four athlete.

The honour of holding the Indian national flag at the Athens Olympics of August 2004 was bestowed on Anju. Initially Karnam Malleswari's name was being considered for this honour, apart from the names of top sportspersons like Leander Paes, Dhanraj Pillai and Anjali Bhagwat. However, ultimately the honour of holding the Indian national flag and leading the Indian team at the Olympics went to Anju Bobby George.

Indian hopes rose high on Anju for winning the medal for India. She participated in the long jump event with 30 other athletes and entered the finals with a jump of 6.69 metres. A minimum jump of 6.65 metres was a mandatory condition for entering the finals. A total of 12 competitors reached the finals. However, Anju was unsuccessful in winning a medal.

Nevertheless, in the first attempt itself Anju created a national record by making a jump of 6.83 metres. However, Russia's Tigdi took a jump of more than 7 metres, thereby dashing India's hopes of winning a medal. In the end, Anju managed a sixth position for herself.

In the year 2004, the names of 13 sportspersons were proposed for the nation's topmost sports honour, the 'Rajiv Gandhi Khel Ratna' Award. Anju's name emerged at the top and she was selected for this honour on the basis of the bronze medal she had won at the Paris World Championship, the previous year. This award is given to distinguished sportsper-sons on the basis of their performance in the previous year.

Her coach-husband, Robert Bobby George, was honoured with the Dronacharya Award. Anju and her husband received these awards on 21st September 2004 from the President of India. Apart from the trophy, she was also given a cash prize of five lakh rupees.

The year 2005 did not prove to be a very eventful year in Anju's professional career. However, in the year 2005, the Hero Honda Academy nominated her as the Best Athlete for the Year 2004. In the year 2006, as Anju's performance showed a downslide, her ranking in the I.A.A.F. women's long jump category slumped to number six from number four.

In the Doha Asian Games, in December 2006, Anju was not able to repeat her best performance. She made a jump of 6.52 metres and was successful in winning a silver medal. This also happened to be the best of the season. She was happy that she had managed to win the medal by her performance. She was also content that on her sixth last attempt, she was able to jump up to 6.52 metres, otherwise, the silver would have been bagged by Kazakhstan's athlete for her 6.49-metre jump. Anju had to be satisfied with a bronze. She won a gold medal in the Busan Asiad.

Achievements

- ☆ *Anju is the first Indian athlete to have won a medal in world athletics. In 2003, she won a bronze medal in the World Athletics Championship in Paris.*
- ☆ *In 1999, she won a silver medal in the South Asian Athletics Championship.*

- ☆ *In 2001, she made a record in the long jump with a 6.74-metre jump.*
- ☆ *She reached the 13th position in the world. In the World Championship, she was ranked seventh.*
- ☆ *She won a bronze medal in the Manchester Commonwealth Games.*
- ☆ *She won a gold medal in the 2002 Busan Asiad.*
- ☆ *In the 2004 Athens Olympics, she was given the honour of being the flagholder for India.*
- ☆ *In 2004 she was honoured with the 'Rajiv Gandhi Khel Ratna' Award.*
- ☆ *In 2005, the Hero Honda Academy nominated Anju as the best sportsperson in athletics.*

Athletics

Gurbachan Singh Randhawa

Date of Birth: 6th June 1939

Gurbachan Singh Randhawa, who is popularly known as G.S. Randhawa, is one of the best athletes of India. He had an inborn hidden sports talent, which helped him to perform well in any game that he chose to play. Randhawa is the first track-and-field athlete to be chosen for the Arjuna Award in 1961. He was a national champion in athletic games like long jump, javelin throw and the hurdle race.

Gurbachan Singh Randhawa was born on 6th June 1939 in a small village called Nangli in the Amritsar district of Punjab. Recognised as the most talented athlete of India, he was six feet tall, lithe of build and strong of limb. He completed his education from Khalsa College at Amritsar. He started displaying his successful stint in sports in his school and college days itself.

During his college days, he was a star athlete of Punjab University and a champion in long jump, hurdle race and decathlon. He first tasted success in the National Games at the age of 21 years. In the National Games, held at New Delhi in 1960, Randhawa broke the national record of C.M. Muthaiyya.

Gurbachan Singh Randhawa's family has been associated with sports. His father was a well-known athlete of his time. He too started paying serious attention to the hurdle race to follow in the footsteps of his father J.C. Randhawa, whose efficiency can be seen from the fact that he tried his hand at many athletic events at the same time. It was said that Randhawa was so talented that he could shine in just about any game that he chose.

At first he chose to train in decathlon, then the hurdles before aiming for the Olympic medal.

Randhawa came into sports when Cheemu Muthaiyya was the all-round athlete of the time. In a matter of few years, he gave a new dimension to athletic events, like decathlon. He was a naturally talented player and on top of that, with the pressure of his employers, the Central Reserve Force, on him, he performed to his best capability and became the national champion in javelin, the long jump, the high jump and the hurdles along with the ten-in-one decathlon.

In the 1962 Asian Games in Jakarta, he participated in the hurdle race and completed the race in 15 seconds. He was fifth in the race. After that he took part in the Olympics in the same event and finished fifth again. In the javelin throw event he stood fifth after throwing the javelin to a distance of 59.61 metres. In the midst of these two events, he participated in the decathlon competition and won a gold medal with 6,739 points. At that point of time there was no other sportsperson who had the guts to take part in so many events at the same sports meet and win.

Gurbachan was the second Indian to participate in the Olympic Games final. At the Olympic Games in Tokyo, in 1964, he participated in the 110-metre hurdle race and set an excellent record by finishing the race in 14 seconds. Even though he finished fifth, he set up a record in India.

Randhawa was the first track-and-field athlete of India to be chosen for the Arjuna Award in 1961.

Achievements

- ☆ *Gurbachan was the national champion in all athletic events like javelin, long jump, high jump, hurdle race and 'ten-in-one decathlon'.*
- ☆ *He was the second Indian to participate in the final of the Olympic Games in Tokyo in 1964.*
- ☆ *At Tokyo again he participated in the 110-metre hurdle race and set a record by finishing the race in 14 seconds. This record of 14 seconds could not be broken for 40 years in India.*

- ☆ *In the 1962 Asian Games in Jakarta, he participated in the decathlon competition and won a gold medal with 6,739 points.*
- ☆ *In the 1962 Asian Games in Jakarta, he participated in the hurdle race and completed the race in 15 seconds.*
- ☆ *He was given the Arjuna Award in 1961 and won the first track-and-field event.*

Athletics

Jyotirmoyee Sikdar

Date of Birth: 11th December 1969

In the 1998 Bangkok Asian Games, when Indian sportspersons were disappointing the country, at that time Jyotirmoyee Sikdar brought the word 'victory' to India. She saved the Indian team from a total disaster by winning two gold and one silver medal. Her victory not only sparked the enthusiasm of her sports fraternity but also put a full stop to the criticisms of sportspersons and officials by the media. Her victory sent waves of happiness among the Indians. Recording her career's best performance in the Games, she took 2:09:00 seconds to complete the 800-metre run and won a gold medal followed by another gold in an excellent performance in the 1,500-metre race in 04:12:82 seconds. In the 4 x 400 metre team relay, she won a silver medal.

Jyotirmoyee was born in Debogram village of Nadia district in West Bengal in December 1969. With the help of her father, she built up her stamina by practicing in the open grounds so that she could go in for long runs later. Simultaneously, she continued with her studies and graduated in physics. Initially she started participating in 400-metre runs before going on to 800-metre and 1,500-metre races.

Jyotirmoyee started her career at the national level by winning a silver medal in the 800-metre race in the All India Open Meet held in 1992. The very next year she won a gold medal in the National Open Championship and was included in the Indian squad to participate in the South Asian Federation Games (SAF) held in Dhaka in 1993. In these Games, Jyotirmoyee won a silver medal in the 1,500-metre long run.

Then in 1993, she won a gold medal in the Singapore Open. She broke the national record in 1994 in the 1,500-metre race. In the Asian Games at Hiroshima in 1994, she was unable to score any victory and secured a fourth position.

In the Bangkok Asian Games in 1998, Jyotirmoyee Sikdar won two gold and one silver medal. She gave her best performance in the 1,500-metre and 800-metre run and won two gold medals, apart from a silver medal in the 4 x 400 metre relay race.

When 29-year-old Jyotirmoyee returned to India after her victory, she was given a rousing welcome. She was taken around in an open jeep bedecked with flowers and was given the name — the 'New Golden Girl'. For this victory, she was given the 'Most Valued Performance Award' by Samsung and a cash prize of 13 lakhs.

Jyotirmoyee was honoured with the Arjuna Award in the year 1995 and became the first athlete to be bestowed the 'Rajiv Gandhi Khel Ratna' award in 1998.

At present she is working as a superintendent in the Eastern Railways and is married to her former coach, Avtar Singh.

Achievements

- ☆ *In the year 1994, Jyotirmoyee won a gold medal in the 4 x 400 metre relay at the World Railway Meet, London.*
- ☆ *In the year 1995, in the Asian track-and-field meet held in Jakarta, she won a gold medal in the 800-metre run and a silver medal in the 4 x 400 metre relay.*
- ☆ *In the year 1995, in the 800-metre race, she set up a national record.*
- ☆ *In the year 1996, at Taipei, she won a gold medal in the 400 metres.*
- ☆ *She participated twice in the international ITC meet and won a bronze in 1995 and a silver medal in 1997.*
- ☆ *In the year 1997, in the Asian track-and-field meet held at*

Fukuowa in Japan, she won a bronze medal in the 800 metres and in the 1,500 metres race; in the 4 x 400 relay, she won a silver medal.

☆ *She works as a superintendent with the Eastern Railways. She has married her former coach, Avtar Singh.*

☆ *She was awarded the Arjuna Award in 1995.*

☆ *In 1998 she became the first woman athlete to be awarded the 'Rajiv Gandhi Khel Ratna' award.*

Athletics

K.M. Binamol

Date of Birth: 15th August 1975

K.M. Binamol's name came into news after she won two gold and one silver medal at the Busan Asian Games in October 2002. She won a gold medal in 800-metre race and repeated the victory with a gold in the 400-metre relay race. She won great name and fame in the sportsworld after again winning a silver medal in the 400-metre race.

K.M. Binamol hails from a small village called Kombidinnjal from Idukki district of Kerala and belongs to a peasant family. This village is huddled among the hills, about 20 kilometres away from Aadimali of Idukki district. Most of the village inhabitants are agriculturists who had come and settled here from the plains a few decades earlier.

Bina was inclined towards sports from a fairly young age. At the time when she was studying in Parathod High School, her coach Raju recognised her talent and thus began the exercise to groom her raw talent by hard work and regular practice. She trained under Purushottam, a coach from the G.V. Raja Sports School, Thiruvananthapuram, between 1990-1996.

She came into notice for her performance at the National School Meet held in 1991 and the Asian Junior Meet held in 1992. Thereafter she set a national record and was selected to represent India in the Sydney Olympics in 2000. Here she managed to reach the semi-finals and shattered the record of 400 metres set up by the 'sprint queen' P.T. Usha in Jakarta.

Bina's winning streak continued and she won acclaim for winning two gold and one silver medal at the Busan Asian Games. Her entire village celebrated her spectacular achievement with sweets and crackers. The village is extremely proud of their Binamol and now the road from the village bus stand to Binamol's house is known as Binamol Road.

In the Busan Asian Games, Binamol's brother K.M. Binu also won a silver medal in the 800-metre race.

After the Busan Asian Games, she was selected for the Samsung 'Most Valued Performance Award' and was thus gifted the complete range of Samsung products as part of the prize. She was selected for this award by a jury of five press reporters, present at the Busan Asian Games.

Binamol had huge expectations of herself from the Athens Olympics in 2004. However, she was unable to win a medal there.

She participated in the 4 x 400 metre relay in the Athens Olympics. Rajvind Kaur, Chitra Somen, Manjit Kaur and K.M. Binamol were the participants in the heat event. This team made it to the finals after winning the relay. In Athens, the team managed to secure a seventh place for itself, while in Colombo it reached the twelfth place.

Binamol's brother K.M. Binu put up a better performance in the 400-metre race in the Athens Olympics to reach the semi-finals. Incidentally, this was Binu's first race outside the Asian boundaries. Binu moved ahead undeterred and managed to break Milkha Singh's record with his spectacular performance.

Binamol's initials, K.M. stand for Kalaythumkzhi Mathews, hence the name, K.M. Binamol.

Achievements

- ☆ *Binamol made headlines with her performance when she participated in the National School Meet in 1991.*
- ☆ *She participated in the Asian Junior Meet in 1992.*
- ☆ *She was selected for the Sydney Olympics in 2000 and managed to reach the semi-finals and broke P.T.Usha's 400-metre record.*
- ☆ *She won two gold and one silver medal at the Busan Asian Games in 2002.*
- ☆ *She was awarded the 'Rajiv Gandhi Khel Ratna' award for 2002-03.*

Athletics

Milkha Singh

Date of Birth: 8th October 1935

Milkha Singh is a renowned Indian runner and athlete who participated in the 1960 Rome Olympics. However, he lost his chance to win a bronze medal by a mere one second. He is rated as one of the greatest sportspersons of India. Milkha Singh is popularly known as the 'Flying Sikh'. He was awarded the Padma Shri by the Government of India. After his retirement he took up employment in Punjab in the capacity of Director of Sports. Milkha Singh is one of those exemplary sportspersons who gave a splendid performance despite having never received any formal training or financial assistance.

Milkha Singh was born in Lyalpur, in Pakistan on 8th October 1935. He lost his parents in the India-Pakistan partition riots and crossed over to India in a train that was carrying refugees from Pakistan. So he had only a brother and a sister in the name of a family to support him.

Milkha Singh's name shot into prominence when he broke the 200- and 400-metre record in the National Games at Cuttack. In the year 1958, he won a gold medal in the 200-metre and 400-metre race in the Asian Games at Tokyo, breaking the Asian record. In that very year, he won a gold medal in the Commonwealth Games at Cardiff (Great Britain). It was owing to these astounding successes that he was awarded the Padma Shri by the Government of India in 1958.

A very interesting story is nararated about how he came to be called the 'Flying Sikh'. While participitating in the Indo-Pakistan sports meet, he left behind Asia's famous runner, Pakistan's Abdul Khaliq in the 200-metre event and marched ahead at lightning speed. It was then that people observed that 'Milkha Singh was far from running; he was flying'. Thereafter he came to be known as the 'Flying Sikh'.

Milkha Singh has demonstrated his sports ability at many occasions. He broke the Olympic record in the Rome Olympics in 1968 in the 400-metre race by reaching the finishing line and shattering the previous Olympic record of 59 seconds.

This achievement of his is recollected and narrated as a fairy-tale in Punjab and has become a part of Punjab's rich heritage. At that time many Olympic sportspersons had broken records and established new ones. Many world-renowned outstanding athletes participated with him then.

In the Rome Olympics of 1960, Mikha Singh stood second (with 47.6 seconds) in the first heat of the 400-metre race. Then in the semi-finals, he clocked 45.9 seconds, thereby defeating an American athlete to finish second again. In the finals, he left behind all the athletes to race ahead. When he slowed down a bit, because of his lead, he ended up in a loss as the other athletes caught up with him, and sped past him. Even though he put in a lot of force at that time, he was unable to race ahead of them. Two American athletes — Ottis Davis and Kaufman — came to be ranked first and second at 44.8 seconds respectively. South African athlete, Mel Spence was ranked third for recording 45.6 seconds. Milkha Singh clocked 45.6 seconds and lost his chance of winning a bronze medal by a mere 0.1 second.

Milkha Singh realised later that slowing down his speed initially had proved fatal for him. He lost out in this competition with leading athletes and could not win even the bronze medal.

Milkha Singh became an extremely successful athlete at a time when no facilities and formal training arrangements were available. Today, after so many years, no athlete has been successful in winning a medal at the Olympics. Milkha Singh became so popular at the Rome Olympics that he was always given a standing ovation whenever he entered the stadium. Even though he was not a top athlete, his name was undoubtedly among the excellent athletes. His long flowing beard and his long hair was another reason for his popularity.

At that point of time, people were not much aware about Sikhism as a religion, so people took him for a saint and appreciated a saint running so well. Also, since there was no trend for a *patkha*, he used to tie a kerchief. Yet another reason for Milkha Singh's popularity was that he had already defeated many reputed athletes in Europe and so, even before he reached Rome, his popularity had preceded him.

Two incidents are extremely important in Milkha Singh's life — the first is the India-Pakistan Partition in which his parents and many relatives were killed and the second is the Rome Olympics, where he missed his medal. It was because of this that when he was invited to participate in an athletic competition in Pakistan, he was not very excited, but was somehow persuaded to run with Asia's best athlete. At that time Abdul Khaliq was Pakistan's best athlete who had won in the 200-metre race in many Asian sports competitions.

As soon as the 200-metre race began, it seemed as if Milkha Singh was literally flying instead of running. He left Abdul Khaliq far behind and the people could just watch him with awe. At that time it was announced that Milkha Singh was flying instead of running and thus he won the nickname, the 'Flying Sikh'. At that time even Pakistan's President, General Ayub, was watching the race. After the victory, Milkha Singh was taken into the special V.I.P gallery to meet him.

Milkha Singh donated his trophies, medals, shoes (the ones with which he broke the world record), blazer, uniform, etc. to the National Sports Museum located in the Jawaharlal Nehru Stadium. He won a gold medal at the Asian Games held in 1962. After his retirement from sports, he joined the Department of Sports, Youth and Education in the capacity of Additional Sports Director in Punjab. He is married to Nirmal, a former international sportsperson and has been blessed with a son and three daughters. His son, Chiranjeev Milkha Singh (also known as Jeev Milkha Singh) is one of the top golf players of the country and has won many prizes in national and international events. He participated in the Asian Games held at Beijing in 1990.

Milkha Singh's ardent wish is that an Indian should win a medal in athletics in the Olympics — a medal, which he missed due to his minor mistake. After his retirement, Milkha Singh hopes to start an academy for athletics in Chandigarh or nearby so that he can train good athletes.

It was because of Milkha Singh's iron determination that he was able to achieve the position where he is today and where it is difficult to reach without any formal training.

Achievements

- ☆ *In 1957, Milkha Singh set a new national record by finishing the 400-metre race in 47.5 seconds.*
- ☆ *In 1958, in the Third Asiad held in Tokyo, Japan, he set two new records in the 400-metre and 200-metre races.*
- ☆ *In the Fourth Asiad (1959) held in Jakarta (Indonesia), he bagged a gold medal in the 400-metre run.*
- ☆ *The Government of India bestowed on him the Padma Shri in 1959 for his achievements.*
- ☆ *In 1960, he set a new record in the 400-metre race at the Rome Olympics.*
- ☆ *He won a gold medal in the Asian Games of 1962.*

M.D. Valsamma

Date of Birth: 29th October 1960

M.D. Valsamma, whose full name is Manthoor Devasia Valsamma, is the winner of a gold medal in the Asian Games. She earned her title in front of the home crowd at the Jawaharlal Nehru Stadium in the Asian Games of 1982. She won a gold in the 400-metre hurdles race and the Arjuna Award in 1982 followed by the Padma Shri in 1983. The Kerala government awarded her the G.V. Raja cash award.

M.D. Valsamma is fondly adderssed as Valsui by her friends and relatives. She was the third player to win an Asian gold medal. Earlier Kamaljit Singh Sandhu (won it for 400 metres in 1974) and Geeta Zutshi (for 800 metres in 1978) had achieved this feat. Valsamma's performance that fetched her the gold was enacted in front of the home crowd at the Jawaharlal Nehru Stadium in 1982. She won a gold medal in the 400-metre hurdles, which had been included in the Asian Games for the first time. Valsamma set a trend in the sub-continent.

M.D. Valsamma was born on 29th October 1960 at Ottathai in Cannore district of Kerala. Her athletic career began during her school days and became her life when she moved to Mercy College, Palghat for graduation. She won her first medal for Kerala in the 100-metre hurdles at the Inter-University Championship in 1979.

She got a job in the Southern Railways and was being coached by A.K. Kutty. She came into prominence when she won five gold medals at the Inter-State Meet at Bengaluru in 1981 for the 100-metre and 400-metre hurdles, 400-metre race and two relay races. This performance catapulted her into the Railways and the national team. In 1982, Valsamma became the national champion in 400-metre hurdles race when she set a new record, which was even better than the Asian record.

In the Asian Games at Delhi in 1982, she set a new national and Asian record of 58.47 seconds in the 400-metre hurdles event. She later won a silver medal in the 4 x 100-metre relay race. Her brilliant performance at the Asiad fetched her the Arjuna Award in 1982. She was awarded the Padma Shri in 1983. The Kerala government honoured her with the G.V. Raja cash award.

As a member of the Indian team, she participated in the Malaysian Open and won a silver medal in the 400-metre race and a gold medal in the 4 x 100-metre relay race. She participated in the Spartakiad 1983 at Moscow. In 1983, she won a bronze medal in 100-metre race in the South Asian Federation Games (SAF) at Islamabad, a silver medal in the 200 metres and a gold in the 4 x 100 metre relay.

In the Beijing Asian Games of 1990, she picked up a silver medal, both in the 4 x 100 metre and 4 x 100 metre relay races.

In her career spanning about 15 years, Valsamma took part in World Cup meets at Havana, Tokyo, London, the Asian Games of 1982, 1986, 1990 and 1994, all the Asian track-and-field meets and the SAF Games. The special aspect was that she left a mark in each and every competition.

Achievements

- ☆ *Valsamma won her first medal for Kerala in the 100-metre hurdles at the Inter-University Championship in 1979.*
- ☆ *She left a great impact at the Inter-State Meet in Bengaluru in 1981 by winning five gold medals.*
- ☆ *In the Asian Games at Delhi, in 1982, she set a new national and Asian record of 58.47 seconds in the 400-metre hurdles.*
- ☆ *In the Malaysian Open, she won a silver medal in the 400 metres and a gold in the 4 x 400 metres relay race.*
- ☆ *She won a silver medal in the Asian track-and-field meet at Delhi in 1982 in the 4 x 400 metre relay.*

- ☆ *She won a bronze in 100 metres, silver in 400 metres and gold in the 4 x 400 metre relay in the SAF Games at Islamabad.*
- ☆ *She won a silver medal each in the 4 x 100 metre and 4 x 400 metre relay in the Beijing Asian Games in 1990.*
- ☆ *She was presented the Arjuna Award in 1982.*
- ☆ *She received the Padma Shri in 1983.*
- ☆ *The Kerala government honoured her with the G.V. Raja cash award.*

Athletics

Neelam Jaswant Singh

Date of Birth: 8th January 1971

Neelam Jaswant Singh is one of the best athletes of the country who proved her excellence first at junior level and then at senior level. She enjoys the rare distinction of being the natioal champion for the longest time. In 1998, the Indian Government honoured her with the 'Arjuna Award'.

Neelam Jaswant Singh has been one of the foremost playeers of discus throw in India. She was born at Julana in the Jind district of Haryana.

Her sporting career started in 1986 when she first won the athletics championship at junior level. She also won championship at senior level. Even today she is active in sports at national level.

Neelam received her early education in a government school of Julana. She joined Government Women's College in Patiala for further studies. She rose to eminence for the first time in 1986 when she made record in school level sports competition held in Delhi. Later, she won gold medal in junior national game in Hissar. Neelam won a bronze medal in Asian Track and Field Meet in Jakarta.

Neelam always attempted to improve her performance in every sports event. In 1988, for the second time she participated in Asian Junior Track and Field Meet, Singapore. In 1989, she participated in A.T.F. senior category in Delhi and was ranked fourth. The same year she participated in Islamabad SAF Games and won a gold medal.

The secret of Neelam's success lies in her determination and courage. It is these qualities which helped her to excel in every competition. In the beginning, her best score was 50m which she improved to 50.66m in 1997.

In 1995 SAF Games of Chennai, Neelam's highest score was 50.96 which was three metre further than her previous record.

In 1998, Neelam continued to give an improved performance and scored 57.94 metres in discus throw. She gave her best performance in the Asian Championship, held at Fukoko in Japan. In 1998, Neelam won bronze medal in Bangkok Asian Games. The same year in 1998 she won gold in Kasanova International Athlete Meet, Almaaty (Kazakhstan). In 1999 Natioanl Games, held in Trivandrum, Neelam improved to score 60.28 metres in discus throw.

In August 2000, Neelam won a gold in Asian Track and Field in Jakarta but she gave a dismal performance in Sydney Olympics where she scored merely 55.26 metre.

Neelam married her coach Jaswant Singh. Now she is working in Railway Coach Factory, Kapurthala. In 1996, she was awarded by the Punjab Government and in 1998, she was honoured with the 'Arjuna Award'.

Achievements

- ☆ *Neelam Jaswant Singh is considered one of the best players in discus throw.*
- ☆ *In 1986, she made a new record at junior level in Delhi.*
- ☆ *In 1986, she won gold medal in Hissar Junior National Championship.*
- ☆ *Neelam won bronze in Asian Junior Track and Field Meet in Jakarta.*
- ☆ *Neelam won gold in Islambad SAF Games by scoring 50.96 in discus throw.*
- ☆ *She won silver in Fukoko Asian Championship held in Japan by scoring 59.19 in discus throw.*
- ☆ *She won gold in Kasanova International Athlete Meet, Almaaty (Kazakhastan).*
- ☆ *In 1999, she improved her performance and made a new record by scoring 60.28 in Trivandrum.*
- ☆ *In 1998, she was honoured with the 'Arjuna Award' by Indian Government.*

Athletics

P.T. Usha

Date of Birth: 27th June 1964

P.T. Usha has been honoured with many national honours in a bright sports career of over 20 years. She was awarded the Padma Shri in 1984 and the Arjuna Award in the very same year. From 1984-1989, P.T. Usha, 'the golden girl' dominated the hearts of not only India, but also of entire Asia. She had the honour of being declared the 'Best Athlete of Asia' for five consecutive years.

The 'flying girl', 'the Payyoli Express', 'the golden girl' — many such nicknames have been conferred on a woman who, in her heydays, was the country's glory and the source of inspiration for scores of women. But Pilavullakandi Thekkeparambil Usha, or P.T. Usha, favours the term her husband, V. Sreenivasan uses for her — 'the greatest'.

She has won 102 international medals and this is a rare distinction that she shares with world-class athletes, like Merelene Ottey and Carl Lewis. She has won over 1,000 medals and trophies on the national and state-level meets. Usha, at 43, today lives with the sorrow of not having won an Olympic medal, which always eluded her despite her sustained efforts. No one but she knows what is the value of one-hundredth part of a minute. This miniscule fraction of time can make all the difference for an athlete. It is 0.01 seconds if you want to know it in numerals and ask P.T. Usha about it, for who else can know it better than her?

At the Los Angeles Olympics in 1984, she smoothly cleared 10 of the 2' 6" inches high hurdles for 400 metres. For the first time this event was being conducted for women at the Olympics. She clocked 55.42 seconds as the Asian record, but this wasn't good enough to put her on the victory podium, even for the third place. Cristina Cojocaru of Romania edged her out by that one-hundredth of a second.

That's how near Usha was to the coveted goal and yet so far away from the elusive Olympic medal. Freestyle wrestler Kashaba Jadhav won an Olympic medal in 1952 at Helsinki; tennis ace Leander Paes won it in 1994 at Los Angeles; and weightlifter Malleswari in 2000. Apart from these few and far between beacons of individual accomplishments, the Indian hockey team has done India proud by winning an assortment of golds and silvers.

Pilavullakandi Thekkeparambil Usha is an athlete with a name as long as her legs — legs that have raced her to glory at various stadia in Asia. She dominated the Indian athletic scene for more than two decades and firmly registered the presence of Indian women athletes on the international scene. At the Asian Games in Seoul in 1986, she gathered four gold and one silver medal. She may well have won a fifth, if Filipina Lydia de Vega hadn't pipped her to the tape in the 100 metres.

She was born on 27th June 1964 and was the second of the six children to Paithal, a cloth merchant and his wife, Lakshmi in Payyoli village, of Kozhikode, Kerala. Usha was fond of facing difficult things, like jumping a high fence. Her informal initiation into the game came when she was in Standard IV. "My drill master, Balakrishnan, one day made me run with a Standard VII champion and I outran her," recalls P.T. Usha.

When P.T. Usha reached Standard VII, she made a formal beginning in sub-divisional athletics and emerged the district winner. She came first in four and second in one event. At that time, G.V. Raj Sports Institute had been established in Kerala, in which a sports department was created exclusively for women. She braved opposition to join the Sports Department in Cannore. Her coach O.M. Nambiyar worked very hard to make her a champion.

It's been a long journey for her from the Cannore sports hostel. As a gangly sprinter who came under the shrewd tutelage of the supercoach O.M. Nambiar, she redefined the limits of Indian sprinting. 'Flying Sikh' Milkha Singh had attained instant immortality at the Rome Olympics in 1960 but could manage only the fourth place. That was the best performance by an Indian until P.T. Usha happened.

And the phenomenon, who came to be known as the Asian 'sprint queen', happened in spite of the system — a system that cannot identify, groom and help an athlete to hold his or her own against the fastest in the world. Usha and Nambiar worked in tandem to smash records and inspire a whole generation of speedsters from South India, particularly Kerala.

P.T. Usha, on her own, has no complaints except that India does not have a sports culture. "Why is it that our children don't have sports icons, except in cricket? I believe most sportspersons, barring cricketers, are from poor families. And to many, any sport is a ticket to a job quota. This must change," she once lamented.

Her Rs 40-crore project — the Usha Athletic Academy — takes up most of her time today as she hopes to give state-of-the-art track and facilities to upcoming athletic champions of the country. Nothing quells her determination. In reply to the false allegations made against her by the Sports Authority of India (SAI) saying that she consumed drugs, she said, "All my major achievements were in the international arena. No honour would come without the dope test. And those who cast aspersions on me are unaware that in the year in question, I had not participated at all!"

In her house at Payyoli, Usha reveals that she nurtures the ambition to retrieve the Olympic medal she had narrowly missed a decade-and-a-half ago. One thing her juniors or her own son, Ujjwal, would not do is to commit the mistake that she did — not lunge forward at the tape and lose a bronze by one-hundredth of a second in the Los Angeles Olympics.

P.T. Usha started her international career in 1980 with the Moscow Olympics and participated only in the 100-metre race. After that she had won two silver medals at New Delhi in the Asian Games in 1982, she participated next year in the Asian track-and-field meet in Kuwait and won a gold medal in the 400-metre and a silver medal in the 200-metre race.

But she can never forget the Olympic bronze that she missed at Los Angeles in 1984 by one-hundredth of a second despite setting a national record of 55.24 seconds in the 400-metre race. In 1985, when she won five gold medals at Jakarta in the Asian track-and-field meet, she earned the name 'golden girl'. After this memorable golden performance, Usha never looked back and continued the trend of winning gold at almost every international event. At Jakarta, she won four gold medals, one each in the 100-metre, 200-metre, 300-metre and the 400-metre race and one gold medal in the 400-metre relay race, astounding the sports community. The race of medals wasn't over yet. She managed to get a bronze medal for the Indian team which was lagging behind in the 4 x 400 metre relay race in the very last lap. In the 1986 Asian Games, she won three gold medals and one silver medal in the 100-metre race. The gold medals were for the 100-metre, 400-metre hurdle race and 4 x 400 metre relay race.

In the 1987 Asian track-and-field meet in Singapore, P.T. Usha again repeated her performance with four gold medals in the 200-metre, 300-metre and 400-metre race, the 4 x 400 metre relay race and one silver medal in the 100-metre race. In the hurdle event she managed to win a silver medal for the women athletes' team with a spectacular struggle in the last lap.

Her record performances in 1984, 1985, 1986 and 1987 gave the impression that she would more than make up for the loss of the 1984 Olympic medal at the forthcoming Seoul Olympic Games in 1988. However, unfortunately due to a heel injury, she lost in her favourite 400-metre hurdle race in the heat only.

However, P.T. Usha resurrected her 'golden girl' image when she won four gold medals in the Asian track-and-field meet in 1989 at New Delhi. She won gold medals in the 200-metre, 400-metre race, the 400-metre hurdle race and the 4 x 400 metre relay but had to satisfy herself with silver medals in the 100-metre race and the 4 x 100 metre relay. She tried hard to push the limits of her resources in 1998, as this was her second comeback. She had taken a break from sports, married Srinivasan in 1991, given birth to a baby boy named Ujjawal, before deciding to get herself a new coach. She continued with her practice and made a comeback, aspiring to win a medal again and give a new direction to Indian sports. She had come refocussed and recharged for the Fukuoka Championship, but had to be satisfied with two bronze medals in the 200-metre and the 400-metre relay races.

P.T. Usha hoped to repeat the performance of the last Asian Games in Beijing in 1990 but was sorely disappointed to win only a silver medal in the 400-metre race.

In 1996, she was highly hopeful of winning a medal in the Atlanta Olympics. She participated in the 4 x 400 metre relay but could not go beyond the heat competition round. In the 1998 Bangkok Asian Games too she made it to the finals of the 400-metre and the 4 x 400 metres for the last time.

However, before her farewell ceremony, she managed to win two bronze medals at Fukuoka city of Japan in the Asian track-and-field meet in tfhe 200- and 400-metre race. She finished the 200-metre race in 23.27 seconds — her own national record — and won a bronze. In the 400 metres, the team won a gold medal.

In the last few years of her sports career, she trained under a new coach, Jaswinder Singh Bhatia. She worked very diligently for winning a medal at least in the forthcoming competitions, staying away from her husband and son for long spells so as to regain her stature as the best athlete.

P.T. Usha desires her son Ujjawal to take her name forward as she retired from active sports in 2000. To a journalist's query: "You had come back on the track after taking retirement earlier; any similar plan to make a comeback?" Usha's answer was, "This is my final decision and there is no question of turning back. I don't want to leave my son alone any more."

Usha had only one grudge — the mass media's criticism of her from time to time. She believes that if she had been in a European country or America, she would have definitely won an Olympic medal with better training, nourishment, facilities and encouragement.

Achievements

- ☆ *P.T. Usha set a national record in the State Athletic Meet in Kottayam in 1977.*
- ☆ *She came into limelight when she registered a win as a junior athlete in the National Inter-State Competition in Kollam in 1978.*
- ☆ *In 1980 she was selected to represent the nation in the 18th Pakistan National Games in Karachi.*

- ☆ *She is the first Keralite and the first Indian woman sportsperson to reach the finals of Olympic Games.*
- ☆ *At the age of 16, she was the youngest athlete to participate in the Moscow Olympic Games.*
- ☆ *She participated in the 1982 Asian Games in Delhi and won the first gold medal. She won silver medals in the 100-metre and the 200-metre races.*
- ☆ *In 1983, in Kuwait, she took part in the 400-metre race in the Asian track-and-field meet (which came to be known as the Asian Championship later), where she met with her first success at the international level.*
- ☆ *In 1984, she completed the 400-metre hurdle race with an Asian record of 55.42 seconds at Los Angeles.*
- ☆ *In 1985 in the Jakarta Asian Athletic Meet she won five gold medals and one silver medal to justify the name of Asian 'sprint queen'.*
- ☆ *In 1986 she put up a marvellous performance at the Seoul Olympics and won four gold medals and the title Asian 'sprint queen'.*
- ☆ *She participated in all the Olympic Games from 1980 to 1996 (Atlanta). However, she was unable to take part in the 1982 Barcelona Olympics.*
- ☆ *She holds a world record of winning 102 international medals.*
- ☆ *She has won more than 1,000 medals and trophies at the national and state levels.*

Athletics

Shiny Abraham Wilson

Date of Birth: 8th May 1985

Shiny Abraham Wilson has participitated in the world athletic meets more than 75 times. In 1996 she was awarded the 'Birla Award'. In 1998 she was honoured with the Padma Shri. As she is one of the topmost athletes of Asia, she was honoured with the 'China Journalist Award' in 1991.

Shiny Abraham was the national champion in the 800-metre race for 14 years. She represented India more than 75 times. In all likelihood she is probably the only athlete who has participated in the Asian Games as many as six times.

Shiny was born in Kerala in the Thodupuzha village of Idukki district of Kerala on 8th May 1965. Right from her childhood, she had a strong inclination towards sports, with a special interest in athletics. She took training at the Kerala Sports Department of Kottayam to hone her sports abilities. Actually, it was in the same Kerala Sports Department in different cities of Kerala where athletes like P.T. Usha and M.D. Valasamma had been trained. After their initial training, they all were coached by P.J. Devesla of the National Institute of Sports.

Subsequently, Shiny Abraham took her lessons at the J.V. Raja Sports School at Thiruvananthapuram, before joining the Alphosa College at Palai for further education. Her career ran alongside that of P.T. Usha's at that time. In the Asian Games of 1982 in New Delhi, both P.T. Usha and Shiny represented India. In 1981, in the 800-metre race, Shiny became the national champion. After this, she kept winning one or the other medal in whatever competition she participated.

Shiny will never forget the Los Angeles Olympics of 1984 in which she was the first woman athlete to reach the semi-finals at the Olympics level. She participated in four Olympics — the first in Jakarta, in 1985 and subsequently she continuously participated in six Asian track-and-field meets. Along with good experience, Shiny had to face some sour times also. In the 1986 Asian Games held in Seoul, when she was about to reach the finishing line, all of a sudden, she changed her track and started running in the inner lane, as a result of which she was disqualified.

Shiny was also a part of the relay team, which set a new Asian record. After this record, the performance of the relay team became much better.

The Asian track-and-field meet in 1989, at New Delhi, became a very memorable competition, because in spite of being pregnant, Shiny was able to secure the second position in the 800-metre race, while China's Sun Sumei came first. But with Sumei testing positive in the dope test, Shiny was declared the winner. In those days, Shiny's coach was Shri Ram Singh under whom she was being trained.

The year 1992 brought Shiny a lot of cheer. In the Barcelona Olympics, it was an extremely proud moment for Shiny when she became the first Indian woman athlete to hold the Indian national flag at the Olympics.

Shiny Abraham's biggest achievement was that even after the birth of her child, she was able to run fast in the competitions that followed. In the South Asia Federation Games held in Chennai in 1995, after the birth of her daughter Shilpa, she set a new record in the 800-metre race when she clocked a timing of 1:15:8. It was for the first time that she had succeeded in clocking below two minutes in the 800-metre race.

She participated in four World Cup competitions and is the only sportsperson to participate in six Asian track-and-field meets. She started this trend at Jakarta in 1985. In these Asiad competitions, Shiny won seven gold, two silver and two bronze medals. She participated seven times in the South Asian Federation Games, where she won 18 gold and two silver medals.

Shiny married the world-famous swimmer and Arjuna awardee, Cherian Wilson and Shiny's full name became Shiny Abraham Wilson. She is working as a Deputy Manager (Sports) in the Food Corporation of India. She was honoured with the Arjuna Award in 1985, the 'Birla Award' in 1996 and in the year 1998, she was conferred the 'China Journalist Award'. She was given this award in 1991 for being one of the 10 topmost Asian athletes.

Achievements

- ☆ *Shiny remained the national champion in the 800-metre race for 14 years.*
- ☆ *She represented India in different countries of the world for more than 15 years.*
- ☆ *She participated in the Asian track-and-field event six times and won seven gold, five silver and two bronze medals.*
- ☆ *Shiny participated in the SAF Games seven times and won 18 gold and two silver medals.*
- ☆ *In the Los Angeles Olympics in 1984, she reached the semi-final stage.*

Sunita Rani

Date of Birth: 12th April 1979

Sunita Rani is a renowned Arjuna awardee in athletics. In the Busan Asian Games of 2002, she became infamous for testing positive in the dope test after winning the gold medal in the 1,500-metre race and a bronze medal in the 5,000-metre race. Subsequenlty she continued to be in the headlines in all leading newspapers and news channels for many days to come. After she tested positive, her medals were taken away and all the records she had made were declared null and void. However, all the lost glory (medals, et al.) was returned back to her after she was proven 'not guilty'.

Sunita Rani belongs to a middle-class background. Her father is Ram Sarup who retired from the post of a village *patwari* and now runs a small sports goods store. Sunita is the proud recipient of the Arjuna Award from the former President, K.R. Narayanan.

Sunita's sports career began in school itself in 1994. Born in Sunam, in Sangrur district of Punjab, this 15-year old used to think that only a naturally talented person could earn a prize in the races. A senior student at her school, Goldie Rani asked her to work hard to win the race. Her senior's words greatly inspired her and she came second after Goldie in the 3,000-metre race in the under-18 category at a district-level sports event. Here she also won the first prize in the under-16 category and earned great praise for the same.

After this there was no looking back. She participated in a number of competitions with the help and support of her father and her brothers. She came to the notice of sports officers in 1995 after winning the Federation Cup.

Sunita engrossed herself in preparing diligently for the Sydney Olympics. She aspired to develop her capacity for the 5,000-metre event rather than the 10,000-metre one. Simultaneously, she kept practicing for the 800-metre race to maintain her speed as well. She was confident that if only she could rectify her timing a bit, she could definitely win a medal. However, she was unable to participate in the Sydney Olympics due to some unavoidable reasons.

In the 2002 Busan Olympics, she managed to break her own national record and win a gold medal in the 1,500-metre race. She covered the distance in 4:06:03 minutes and broke the Asian record by 6 seconds. She was ahead of the other competitors by 6 seconds.

However, all this fame was not there to stay, perhaps! Sunita was reduced to a very despicable state after she tested positive in the dope test. She was getting criticised and ostracised from all quarters. The Athletics Federation and National Olympic Union did far from helping her prove innocent. In fact, they gradually started distancing themselves from her for fear of being dragged in the muck. During this period, Sunita was slowly fading into oblivion.

When Sushantika Jayasinghe of Sri Lanka and Linford Christie of England found themselves in a similar situation, their countries made all possible attempts to safeguard their career, but not the Indian counterpart.

It was Sunita's bad luck. At that critical time no one stood by this 23-year-old athlete in her hour of need. It is said that many state-sponsored doping programmes came to be run in the country after 1998 so that players and sportspersons can perform to medal-winning standards. However, no one yet knows if this is 'the truth'.

On 24th December 2002, the Indian Olympic Union declared that International Olympic Medical Commission had taken back the doping allegations against Sunita, who welcomed the news as her New Year gift.

No one can ever forget the day Sunita had walked into the Jawaharlal Nehru Stadium to place her case before the Salwan Committee. She had to be escorted by security personnel to safety so as to avoid the media *gherao*. She was in the headlines at that time because of failing in the drug test. In the end, however, Sunita was given a clean chit and the medals were returned to her. The Olympic Council of Asia had confiscated her medals earlier.

Ultimately the Doping and Biochemistry Committee of the Olympic Council of Asia detected some discrepancies in the Seoul test laboratory and decided to shut the case for good. Hence it was decided to retain the records set by Sunita.

This was the first time in the history of Asian Games that the results of the dope test were modified. The chairman of the Indian Olympic Union, Mr. Suresh Kalmadi had also made efforts to absolve Sunita of the blame put on her.

Sunita Rani returned back to the tracks after a long interval. This athlete, who works for Punjab police, won a gold medal in the 10,000-metre race at the National Athletic Circuit Meet in May 2005 by completing the race in 34:57:42 seconds.

In a sensational comeback, Sunita secured the first position in the 1,500-metre race in 4:20: 63 seconds. In the Federation Cup Athletics organised at the Jawaharlal Nehru Stadium in New Delhi, she recorded 12 seconds more than her national record.

What is the Dope Test?

The dope test or drug test is conducted on the blood samples of various sportspersons. In actual practice the Asian Olympic Council introduced a ban on the use of certain steroids and drugs, which can influence the player's performance for a temporary period of time and enable him or her to win a medal. This ban on steroids and drugs holds good for almost all sports competitions held at the international level. The drugs induce a sudden spurt of energy in the player which is uncommon to see in a normal individual. A chemical compound called Nandrolin, if found in the blood sample after the dope test, confirms the use of the banned medicines/drugs. This had been the case in Sunita's blood sample as well. However, in the blood test at Seoul, there was a great discrepancy seen in her test report.

Nandrolin is a compound which has inflicted bans and punishments on players who are found guilty of consuming it. According to medical reports, the consumption of this drug stimulates the functions of the human body.

The Indian Athletic Union absolved Sunita of the blame and declared her innocent. In the issues raised by the Union, they had said that there was a difference of around 250 per cent in the quantity of Nandrolin in the 'A' and 'B' samples. They also raised the issue of malpractices in the Busan laboratory. This decision was extremely important for India as following this incident, the international media projected Indian sportspersons as common users of drugs.

Achievements

- ☆ *Sunita Rani won a gold medal in the 1,500-metre race in the Busan Asian Games.*
- ☆ *She won a bronze medal in a 5,000-metre race in the Busan Asian Games.*
- ☆ *She won a gold medal in the 10,000-metre race at the AFI national athletics meet in May 2005.*
- ☆ *She won the first position in the 1,500-metre race in June 2005.*

Athletics

T.C. Yohanan

Date of Birth: 19th May 1947

His full name is Thadathuvilla Chandaipillai Yohanan. He set up a new record in the Teheran Asian Games of 1974 when he cleared a distance of 8.07 metres in the long jump event. This was a new Asian Games and continental record. It became a seminal moment in Indian athletics and remained an Indian record for 30 years. Finally, in 2004, Punjab's player Amritpal Singh eclipsed this record with a spirited effort of 8.08-metre jump. Yohanan was honoured with the Arjuna Award in 1974. He is recipient of many other awards also.

For years to come T.C. Yohanan will be known for the new dimension he gave to long jump in India in the Teheran Asian Games in 1974 — that one leap gave Yohanan a permanent place not only in the records book of Indian athletics but also in the hearts of sports lovers.

T.C. Yohanan was born on 19th May 1947 at the Kundara village of Quilon district in Kerala. He is a diploma holder in mechanical engineering and presently works as Assistant Public Relations Officer with the automobile giant, TELCO.

Yohanan had his early feel of athletics in the Inter-School Meet for the Ezhukone *panchayat* in 1964. After joining the public sector Bhilai steel plant, he represented his department in the Steel Plants Sports Meet in 1969. He had his first taste of athletics at the national level in the same year, i.e. 1969. He finished fourth in the long jump and fifth in the triple jump events. He continued his efforts and became successful in securing the second spot in the long jump event at the National Games in 1970.

He established a national mark of 7.60 metres in Patiala in 1971. After his performance, he was selected to represent India in international games. He won gold medals in both long and triple jumps in the Singapore International Meet.

In 1972, Yohanan added the national triple jump title to his bag. In 1973, he made a new national record with a 7.78-metre jump. This fabulous effort of 8.07 metres in the Teheran Asian Games of 1974 put him into Asian and national limelight.

His achievements of 1974 fetched him the Arjuna Award in 1974. His fabulous leap brought him instant recognition and he was invited to Japan the next year. He won gold medals in competitions held at Tokyo, Hiroshima, Kobe and then repeated his success in championships organised in the Philippines and Sibu City.

His last appearance in international competitions was at the Montreal Olympics in 1976, after which he hung up his shoes. Besides national honour, he has received numerous awards which include a merit award from the Kerala government. He was conferred the title Telco-Veer by his employers and honoured by the Bombay and Chennai Sports Journalists Association, Lions Club, *Sportsweek* (magazine) and Tata Sports Club, Mumbai.

Achievements

- ☆ *T.C. Yohanan is considered one of the best athletes India has ever produced.*
- ☆ *He set a national record of 7.60 metres at Patiala in 1971.*
- ☆ *He was the national champion in triple jump in 1972.*
- ☆ *He created a new national record of 7.78 metres jump in 1973.*
- ☆ *In the 1974 Teheran Asian Games, he cleared a distance of 8.07 metres to set a new Asian record. This record made a mark in the record books of India. This remained an Indian record for 30 years and was broken in 2004 by a Punjab athlete, Amritpal Singh who jumped to 8.08 metres.*

- ☆ *In 1974, he won gold medals in Tokyo, Hiroshima, Kobe and then in Philippines and Sibu City.*
- ☆ *In 1974 he was given the Arjuna Award by the Government of India.*
- ☆ *The Kerala government has also honoured him.*
- ☆ *He was honoured by the Mumbai and Chennai Sports Journalists, Lions Club, Tata Sports Club, Mumbai.*

BADMINTON

The modern game of badminton is possibly a derivation of the popular children's game of battledoers and shuttlecocks that was played in medieval England, supposedly in 1873 and was brought to India by British officers posted here. The game was introduced in India in the 19th century when the British players and some of their Indian companions introduced a net and played it competitively in the city of Pune. Funnily enough, the game was also known as 'Poona' at that time as Poona was also the name of the city, now known as Pune.

Another story says that some of the British officers went home and introduced the new game in Britain during the early 1870s. It is also said that badminton owes its name to the Duke of Beaufort's country palace, which was called Badminton, where the game was played at a lawn party hosted by the Duke.

It is a racquet game played by either two opposing players (singles) or two opposing pairs (doubles), who take positions on opposite halves of a rectangular court that is divided by a net. It is played on a cement court or on the lawn with light racquets and a shuttlecock, which is volleyed across the net. The shuttlecock is a feathered projectile whose unique aerodynamic properties cause it to fly differently from the balls used in most racquet sports.

Badminton tournaments are played indoors primarily to protect the shuttlecock against winds. The game consists of hitting the shuttlecock back and forth without letting it touch the ground.

It was in the 1920s that the game of badminton acquired a regular structure in India and All India Tournaments came to be organised in the thirties. The best known tournament in the world for badminton is the All England Championships. It was in 1992 that badminton came to be included for the first time in the Olympics, where five competitive disciplines — men's and women's singles, men's and women's doubles and mixed doubles, in which each pair is a man and a woman — are played. The sport demands excellent fitness — stamina, strength and speed. It is also a technical sport, requiring good motor coordination and development of sophisticated racquet skill.

Despite originating in England, international badminton has traditionally been dominated by a few Asian countries apart from Denmark in Europe. China, Indonesia, South Korea and Malaysia are among the nations that have consistently produced world-class players in the past few decades with China dominating the game in recent years.

Badminton

Aparna Popat

Date of Birth: 18th January 1978

Aparna Popat is one of the best badminton players of India. She has been the National Women's Champion for eight years continuously. She won the women's singles title in the French Open in 1998. She was honoured with the Arjuna Award in 2005.

Aparna Popat is considered the most expert shuttler in the country. She was born on 18th January 1978 at Mumbai. She has attained fame on both national and international levels.

Aparna won her first national (senior category) title in 1998, after which she won the National Women's Championship in singles for eight years continuously. She won the last national title in February 2005 at Jamshedpur in the 69th Senior National Badminton Championship.

In addition to her hold over the national-level game, she made a name for herself with her excellent performance at the international level as well. She was the runner-up at the 1996 World Junior Championship in Denmark.

Aparna has a lot of sporting talent but she is yet to earn her due at the international level where Chinese players have dominated the scene for a long time. Aparna will have to work hard to conquer them.

She was honoured with the Arjuna Award in 2005.

Achievements

- ☆ *Aparna has been the National Women's Champion for eight years continuously.*

- ☆ *She was the runner-up at the 1996 World Junior Championship in Denmark.*
- ☆ *She won the women's singles title in the French Open in 1998.*
- ☆ *In the year 1998, she won a silver medal at the Commonwealth Games in Kuala Lumpur.*
- ☆ *She has been honoured with the Arjuna Award in 2005.*

Badminton

Pullela Gopichand

Date of Birth: 16th November 1973

India's star shuttler, Pullela Gopichand wrote a new history in the Indian sports world after he won the All England Badminton Championship on 11th March 2001. Nearly 21 years before him, Prakash Padukone had touched the heights of badminton in India.

Pullela Gopichand was born on 16th November 1973 at Nagandla in Prakasam district of Andhra Pradesh to parents Pullela Subhash Chandra and Subba Ravamma. His initial education was at St. Paul's School in Hyderabad and he completed his graduation from A.V. College, before acquiring a degree in public administration. Pullela won his first match at the age of 12 years under the National Talent Search Programme in New Delhi and since then he has never looked back.

He started playing for the country in 1991 when he was selected to play against Malaysia. After this he represented India three times in the Thomas Cup and many times in other world championships.

He made India proud by winning many tournaments at the international level. He won gold medals in the SAARC Tournaments in Vijayawada in 1996 and at Colombo in 1997. He won silver and bronze medals at tough competitions in the Commonwealth Games. He won acclaim when he entered the final of the Grand Prix competition in Delhi in 1997, after defeating many veteran players. However, he could not win in the finals. In the Sydney Olympics of 2000, his name was included in the Indian badminton players' list. After the retirement of Prakash Padukone, there was no badminton player of international standard. So, with the arrival of Pullela Gopichand, unlimited possibilities came to be seen for India in badminton.

Pullela Gopichand is the only player from India after Prakash Padukone to shine on the international circuit. After he reached the finals of the Thomas Cup, it was predicted that India was moving ahead in the world of sports. By the time Gopichand won the All England title in 2001, as many as six Indian players had made a name in the top hundred players of the world, but now only three Indian players are in the top hundred. In 2001, Gopichand reached fourth in the world ranking.

India's star shuttler, Pullela Gopichand wrote a new history in the Indian sports world after he won the All England Badminton Championship on 11th March 2001, nearly 21 years after Prakash Padukone had touched the heights in badminton in India. Inflicting defeat on the world number one player in the quarter-finals, semi- finals and then in the finals of World Badminton Championship is like a dream which happens to only heroes of Indian films. But this turned into a reality in Gopichand's life.

He made a steady progress and won the 'K.K. Birla Foundation Award' in 1998. He was conferred on the title of 'Player of the Decade' by the Andhra Pradesh government in 2000. He was honoured with the 'Rajiv Gandhi Khel Ratna' award in 2001.

Pullela Gopichand works as Assistant Manager in the sales department of Indian Oil Corporation. He played for the German Club for three months in a year to improve his game. In his sports career of 10 years, he has defeated many world-level players, including Olympic champions Ellen Budi Kusuma and Larsen.

Achievements

- ☆ *Pullela Gopichand was the champion at the National Championship in New Delhi in 1998.*
- ☆ *He became the champion at the B.P.L. All India Competition in Bengaluru in 1998.*

- ☆ *He won silver and bronze medals in tough competitions in the Commonwealth Games in Kuala Lampur in 1998, while being the runner-up at the Australian Open.*
- ☆ *He became the champion for the third time at the National Championship in New Delhi in 1999.*
- ☆ *In the National Games in Imphal in 1999, he won two gold and one silver medal.*
- ☆ *He was the champion for the fifth time at the B.P.L. All India Competition in 1999.*
- ☆ *He won the badminton championship in the Scottish Open at Edinburgh and also at the Toulouse Open Championship. He was the first Indian player to win both these competitions.*
- ☆ *He was the champion at the Asian Satellite Games in 1999.*
- ☆ *In the National Games at Imphal in 1999, he became a champion again.*
- ☆ *He reached the finals of the Thomas Cup in 2000 in Kuala Lampur. This was the best performance after 12 years as no other player had reached the finals so far.*
- ☆ *He was honoured with the Arjuna Award for his excellent performance in 2001. In this year he was given the world ranking of 10th, which had only been attained by Prakash Padukone till then.*
- ☆ *He reached the pre-quarter finals of the Sydney Olympics in 2000.*
- ☆ *He was the All England Champion in 2001. In this competition, Gopichand defeated Chen Hong of China in 14-12, 14-6 sets. In the finals he defeated the world number one player, Peter Gade Christiansen, while at the semi-finals he defeated Olympic gold-medallist G. Giping in the quarter-finals. This way he won the All England Championship in England after a gap of 21 years.*

- ☆ *In June 2003, he was appointed the national badminton coach. This was done with the intention that India would win at least one gold, two silver and some bronze medals in the 2010 Commonwealth Games to be held in New Delhi. His comment on this was, "This responsibility is a big honour and very challenging for me."*
- ☆ *Apart from this, he is also running an extremely successful academy at Hyderabad where his student Saina Nehwal has earned a name for India in the world of badminton.*
- ☆ *In 2009, Gopichand was honoured with the Dronacharya Award. He enjoys the rare distinction of being the first person to have all the three sporting honours—Rajiv Gandhi Khel Ratan Award, Arjuna Award and Dronacharya Award.*

Badminton

Prakash Padukone

Date of Birth: 10th June 1955

It will not be an exaggeration to call Prakash Padukone the best badminton player of India till date. He won recognition for India in the international arena in the year 1980, when he became the number one in the world. In the year 1972 he was given the Arjuna Award. He has been the national champion for nine years continuously.

Prakash Padukone has impressed sports lovers across India and the world with his outstanding game. He became the national junior champion at the age of 15 years.

Prakash Padukone was born on 10th June 1955, at Bengaluru in Karnataka. He learnt the nuances of badminton from his father Ramesh Padukone who was Secretary of the Mysore Badminton Association for many years. Prakash started his career in 1970 when he became the national junior champion. In the next year in 1971 he performed a marvellous feat by winning both the senior and junior national titles. After this he never turned back and continued his journey of success.

He was the national champion from 1970 to 1978 for a period of nine years continuously. He made his first international impression in 1974 in the Asian Games. Prakash won a bronze medal at the Asian Games in Teheran. In the year 1974, he participated in the Commonwealth Games at Christchurch in New Zealand and reached the quarter-finals.

In the 1975 World Invitation Cup at Kuala Lumpur also he reached the quarter-finals. He continued to work hard to maintain his position. Prakash made a place for himself in the semi-finals of the Asian Badminton

Confederation Championship in Hyderabad in 1976.

In 1977, Prakash Padukone left for training at Indonesia so that he could perform well at international competitions. Abroad there was more emphasis on 'short sprint' and jumping whereas in the training in India, stretch exercises and jogging, etc. were given more importance. The training at Indonesia honed Prakash's skills further. He managed to clinch a gold medal at the Commonwealth Games held at Edmonton in Canada. This medal earned him international fame. At the Commonwealth Games, he defeated Ray Talbot of Britain in straight sets in the men's singles championship and won a gold medal.

Thereafter he won the English Masters Championship held at the Royal Albert Hall in London in 1979. In 1980 Prakash won the Mini Grand Slam in badminton followed by the Danish Cup. In this very year he also won major competitions like the Swedish Open and the All England Championship in 1980. In these competitions Prakash defeated master champions like Morten Frost, Rudy Hartono and Liem Swie King respectively. He was in such a great form in these matches that the surprised King had to admit that Prakash had 'mesmerised' him.

Prakash had reached the number one ranking after winning the All England Championship. He was the first Indian to reach such a high position in this racquet game.

After this, Prakash's golden performance started declinging. Two months after winning the All England Championship, he could not win a gold medal at the World Championship in Jakarta. He was defeated in the quarter-finals by Hadiyanto of Indonesia.

Prakash won a bronze medal at the first World Games in 1981. However, that very year he also won the Albo World Cup after defeating Hon Gen of China.

During these games Prakash took a number of decisions which influenced his international performance. He decided to become a 'licenced player' and also to shift his base to Denmark from India. His aim here was that he would be playing with the best European players on a regular basis as it would have a positive impact on his game.

However, he was also at a loss because of this decision because being a 'licenced player', he wasn't allowed to play in the Asian Games held at New Delhi. In this year, two major and opposing badminton associations, namely the International Badminton Federation and the World Badminton Federation, decided to merge and become a single association.

In the year 1972 he was given the Arjuna Award. He has won about 15 international titles and was the world number one in 1980 and 1981.

After retiring from active sports, Prakash became the Chairman of the Indian Badminton Association. Then he opened an academy for training young badminton aspirants at Bengaluru. His main aim has been to organise tournament camps and workshops to maintain the high standards of the game and to inspire new players.

Prakash Padukone is a resident of Bengaluru and lives there with his wife Ujjwala and two daughters. His daughter Deepika Padukone is a model and actress.

Achievements

- ☆ *In the year 1972, Prakash Padukone was given the Arjuna Award.*
- ☆ *He has been the national champion for nine continuous years.*
- ☆ *He won a bronze medal at the Asian Games in Teheran in 1974.*
- ☆ *He clinched a gold medal at the Commonwealth Games held at Edmonton in Canada.*
- ☆ *In 1980 he won the Mini Grand Slam in badminton by scoring victories in three major international championships like the Danish Cup, the Swedish Open and the All England Championship.*
- ☆ *He won a bronze medal at the first World Games in America in 1981.*
- ☆ *He won the Albo World Cup in 1981.*
- ☆ *He was world number one in 1980 and 1981.*

Badminton

Saina Nehwal

Date of Birth: 17th March 1990

Saina Nehwal came into news in all major newspapers and news channels at mere 16 years of age, after she won the Grand Prix in 2006, thereby becoming the first woman player to win this title. In September 2008, Saina Nehwal won the World Junior Badminton Championship.

Prior to Saina, another young player from Hyderabad who has been in headlines for sometime now, is Sania Mirza, who is considered the best tennis player of the country in the women's category. Saina created a record by defeating Julia Jiyan Paei Wong of Malaysia in the Philippines Open Badminton Championship in Manila. In this competition Saina secured the seventh place and defeated the world number 66.

Saina's coaching took place at the academy set up by the star badminton player of India, Pullela Gopichand in Hyderabad. She was under the tutelage of none other than the badminton veteran himself. Saina could not believe her win, while her coach Pullela Gopichand was more than happy. Saina gave the complete credit of her victory to her coach and he was only too proud of his student.

Prior to Saina, ex-badminton expert and woman player Aparna Popat had reached the semi-finals of the Swedish Open in 1999. At that time she had defeated the number-four player from Germany, Ju Huvaivan, in the quarter-finals. Saina's ranking at that time was 86, whereas in the previous year she had stood at number 185.

Saina Nehwal was born on 17th March 1990 at Hissar, Haryana. Her father Harvir Singh works as a chief scientist at the Indian Agricultural

Research Centre at Hyderabad. Her family had shifted to Hyderabad in1998. In 1999 her parents realised that their younger daughter Saina had great interest in badminton. Saina's mother Usha too had been a badminton champion at the university level. She inspired Saina to go ahead and then Saina began to get training at the Pullela Gopichand Coaching Academy.

Saina started playing at the age of nine years. Her initial coaches in this game were Nani Prasad, Goverdhan Reddy and S.M. Aarif.

In the Philippines Open Badminton Championship, Saina surpassed the expectations of her coach Gopichand. Before she had left for Manila, it was being said that these young players of 16-17 years should first try their hands at the B-Grade tournaments before moving towards major championships and tournaments. Saina proved them wrong and broke the common myth that only an experienced player can win in international tournaments.

Saina's major titles include the Asian Satellite badminton champion in 2005, Junior Czech Open, national junior and sub-junior, the senior national runner-up (twice) and as member of the team that won seven medals at the Commonwealth Youth Games in 2005.

Her chief characteristics are her attacking shots and half volleys. Saina loves to watch movies and read during her free time.

In September 2006, Saina Nehwal reached the world-ranking of 30 with her jump of 11 points. This has been her career's best ranking so far.

Saina Nehwal ensured a place for herself in the finals of the Junior World Badminton Championship in 2006. She became the first woman badminton player of the country to win a four-star badminton tournament. Saina had won a bronze medal for India in the mixed doubles event in the Commonwealth Games.

Saina's talent came to the forefront in 2006 when she defeated Sarojita Chanceri Sukot of Thailand in the quarter-finals of the Uber Cup at Jaipur to register a victory for India. After that Saina defeated Susan Hallam of England apart from other veteran players in Australia. Saina also defeated Bellingham of New Zealand where she won the bronze medal.

Saina could not achieve much in the Doha Asiad held in December 2006, but she gave a tough fight to the world number 14 — Erico Hirose.

Achievements

- ☆ *Saina became the champion at the Asian Satellite Badminton and the Junior Czech Open in 2005.*
- ☆ *She won the national junior and sub-junior titles.*
- ☆ *She was twice the runner-up of the senior National Championships.*
- ☆ *She was a member of the team that won seven medals at the Commonwealth Youth Games in 2005.*
- ☆ *She created history after she won the Philippines Open Badminton Championship in Manila in 2006.*
- ☆ *In September 2006, she reached the world-ranking number of 30.*
- ☆ *In September 2008, she became Junior World Badminton Champion.*
- ☆ *In 2009, Saina was awarded the Arjuna Award.*

BILLIARDS AND SNOOKER

All cue sports are generally regarded as having evolved into indoor games, probably from golf and more distantly from the stickless bocce and bowling. The word 'billiard' is possibly derived from the French word *billart*, meaning 'mace', an implement similar to a golf club, which was the forerunner to the modern cue. The game was often played with three or sometimes four balls on a table without holes (or obstructions in most cases, five-pins being an exception) in which the goal is generally to strike one object (target) ball with a cue ball, then have the cue ball rebound off one or more of the cushions and strike a second ball. Variations include three-cushions, straight rail, balkline variants, cushion carroms, Italian five-pins and four-ball, among others.

India has produced many billiard players, of world ranking, who have drawn crowds with their artistry and genius in the game. Among the most famous players of this game, Wilson Jones' victory in the World Amateur Billiards Championship in 1964 took India into the world of glory as the country had produced, at last, its first world champion in any sport.

After Jones's retirement, it was Michael Fereira who was able to fill the vacuum created and he went on to win four world billiards titles. Even after he left, he did not leave his attachment to the game and tried to persuade the authorities to give a fair treatment to Indian billiard players who had won glory for the country.

Geet Sethi came and left an indelible mark on the game. He is one of the most famous Indians to win titles in billiard. In his astounding career, Sethi won as many as eight world billiard titles and is regarded as one of the best players in the game the country has ever produced.

The latest addition to the game includes the prodigious Pankaj Advani, who shot into limelight by becoming the first player to win both the point format and the time format titles in the World Billiard Championship held in 2005.

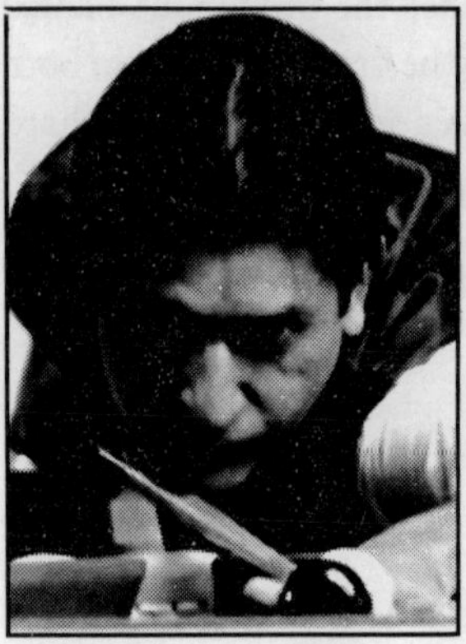

Billiards and Snooker

Geet Sethi

Date of Birth: 17th April 1961

Geet Sethi created a sensation when he won the juniors title in billiards and snooker in 1979. At that time Michael Ferreira and Subhash Agarwal were the two famous billiards players of their time. Geet Sethi entered the senior rank in a matter of time.

Geet Shriram Sethi was born on 17th April 1961 in New Delhi. He developed an avid interest towards both billiards and snooker at a very young age, but because of the age factor he was prohibited entry in the clubs. Then he went to Ahmedabad where his life changed forever. The working committee of the Gujarat Sports Club recognised his interest and talent for the game and as an exception, allowed him to play the game at the members' tables. There he met the ace player of the time, Satish Mohan. Geet continued to learn by observing the senior and famous players of his time.

After completing his schooling at St. Xavier's School and graduation at St. Xavier's College at Ahmedabad, he completed his MBA before joining the Tata Oil Mills as manager. He then made Ahmedabad his permanent residence.

In 1982, Geet Sethi sent the spirits soaring in the sportsworld by defeating Michael Ferreira in the Nationals for the seniors' title. He also won the junior doubles title.

In 1985, Geet Sethi won the International Snooker Championship in England and also the International Billiards Championship at Windsor. He had his moments of fame when he defeated the 74-year old Bob Marshal in the finals of the World Championship in New Delhi. This competition lasted for eight hours. In addition to this, he also won the national senior doubles title in 1985. He won this tournament three more times subsequently.

In the year 1987, Geet Sethi created history in the World Championship at Belfast, Ireland and won the title after defeating Subhash Agarwal and Joe Crech of Malta. The very same year he became the only player in the world to score 147 points (the highest) in snooker.

Achievements

- ☆ *Geet Sethi came into news after winning the World Amateur Billiards Championship in 1985 and 1987.*
- ☆ *In the National Snooker Championship at Guntur, Andhra Pradesh, he made 147 breaks. This was the first time when an amateur (non-professional) made higher breaks than a professional.*
- ☆ *In the 1992 World Professional Billiards Championship, he set a world record with 127 breaks.*
- ☆ *He won the World Professional Billiards Championship in 1992, 1993, 1995, 1998, 2001 and 2006.*
- ☆ *In 1992-1993, he was awarded the highest sports honour of the country — the 'Rajiv Gandhi Khel Ratna' award.*

Billiards and Snooker

Michael Ferreira

Date of Birth: 1st October 1938

Michael Ferreira is the only billiards player of India to be honoured with the Padma Bhushan. He is recipient of the 'Shivaji Chhatrapati Award' from the Maharashtra state government in 1971, the Arjuna Award in 1973 and the 'Fair Play Award' from the International Olympics Committee in 1983.

Michael Ferreira was born on 1st October 1938 in Bombay. The seven-time billiards champion, Michael Joseph Ferreira built an attraction for this three-ball game in the last days of his school. After doing his schooling from St. Joseph's School in Darjeeling, he completed his college education from St. Xavier's College at Bombay and law from the Government Law College, Mumbai. After school, his attachment to snooker kept growing and he continued to play serious billiards for a number of years

Michael Joseph Ferreira was known as Mike or Bombay Tiger among his friends. He set a number of records in billiards. He even outdid the achievements of his trainer and guru, Wilson Jones to set 16 world records. He got his name entered in the *Guinness Book of World Records* for breaks of 1,149 and 995.

Michael Ferreira secured the 13th rank in world rankings. In 1970 and in the 1980's he brought fame and glory to India after he won the amateur world title thrice, the World Open Tournament once and had his name registered among the top 15 professional players of the world.

He started playing at the national level in 1960. In the National Games at Bengaluru in 1963, he secured a break of 300 points even though he lost to Wilson Jones in the finals.

His game was much appreciated in the World Amateur Championship held in New Zealand in 1964 even though he lost by six points in the semi-finals. But this defeat inspired him to perform better and soon he became a famous player at the international level.

In the year 1969, he set a world record with 629 points at the World Amateur Meet in London. In 1970, he won the national title and then continued to win the title seven more times.

After this, in 1970, he won the World Championship title, the World Professional Championship title at Queenschurch in New Zealand. In the year 1970, he won all the major tournaments of the world and became a star after winning this competition.

Achievements

- ☆ *Michael Ferreira was the national champion seven times. He won this title for the first time in 1970.*
- ☆ *He set up the world record 16 times.*
- ☆ *He name was entered in the* Guinness Book of World Records *for breaks of 1,149.*
- ☆ *In the year 1970, he won the World Championship title at Melbourne.*
- ☆ *He was given the 'Shivaji Chhatrapati Award' by the Maharashtra government in 1971.*
- ☆ *He was honoured with the Arjuna Award in 1973.*
- ☆ *Ferreira was given the 'Fair Play Award' by the International Olympics Committee in 1983.*
- ☆ *Michael Ferreira was honoured with the Padma Bhushan.*

Billiards and Snooker

Pankaj Advani

Date of Birth: 24th July 1985

Pankaj Advani has emerged as one of the best billiard and snooker players. He has won three world titles in both billiards and snooker. He is the first player to win both the billiards and snooker titles on the basis of his time scores. He was honoured with the highest sports honour of the country—the 'Rajiv Gandhi Khel Ratna' award for 2005. He was awarded the Padma Shri in 2009.

Pankaj Advani has emerged as one of the best billiards players of India. Prior to him Geet Sethi had already attained international success in the game.

Pankaj Advani was born on 24th July 1985 in Pune (Maharashtra). He created history after he won three world titles at the age of 19 years.

He was attracted towards this game since his childhood and his talent became evident at a very young age. Arvind Savur, who was a snooker champion himself, recognised Pankaj's talent when he was only 10 years of age. At that time Pankaj used to visit the Karnataka State Billiards Association hall with his elder brother.

He became a national champion at the age of 17 years, after which he started displaying his talent in the international sphere. In the year 2003, he won the world snooker title. In 2005, Pankaj Advani became the first player to win the IBSF Billiards Championship on the basis of points and timing.

No one had ever imagined that Advani would defeat his opponent Devendra Joshi 6-2 on the basis of points. At that time he displayed exemplary courage and efficiency. On the basis of the time-based competition, Pankaj defeated the seven-time world champion, Geet Sethi, after a six-hour exciting competition.

It is expected that Pankaj Advani would defeat well-established players in the times to come. He has managed to keep his pride and ego in check despite becoming successful at such a young age. He has been honoured with the highest sports honour of the country, the 'Rajiv Gandhi Khel Ratna' award for 2005.

In September 2009, Pankaj Advani won the World Professional Billiards title at the Northern Snooker Centre in Leeds in England. He defeated his Russion counterpart Mike Russell. With this he became only the second Indian after Geet Sethi to win this title in its 139-years history. Now he enjoys the rare distinction of being both the world IBSF and professional champion. Advani is five-time IBSF World Billiards Champion.

Achievements

- ☆ *Pankaj Advani has emerged successful in both billiards and snooker.*
- ☆ *He won three world titles in both billiards and snooker at the age of 19 years.*
- ☆ *He is the first player of the world to win the IBSF Billiards Championship on the basis of points and time, and win world titles.*
- ☆ *In the year 2003, he won the IBSF World Billiards Championship in Malta.*
- ☆ *Pankaj was honoured with the 'Rajiv Gandhi Khel Ratna' award for 2005.*
- ☆ *He is the only player to have achieved a "grand double" of winning both the points and timed formats at the IBSF World Billiards Championship in both 2005 and 2008.*

Billiards and Snooker

Wilson Jones

Date of Birth: 2nd May 1922

The full name of Wilson Jones is Wilson Lionel Garton Jones. He is the first billiards player of Independent India to win the World Championship twice in 1958 and 1962. He earned the Arjuna Award in 1962, Padma Shri in 1965, the Maharashtra government's 'Gaurav Puraskar' in 1990 and the 'Dronacharya Award' in 1996.

Twice world champion, Wilson Jones, was 12 times the national billiards champion and five times the national snooker champion.

Wilson Jones was born at Pune, Maharashtra on 2nd May 1922. He was quite adept at playing marbles as a child. Besides this passion, he enjoyed peeping through the windows to watch his uncle play billiards. His age did not qualify him to enter the billiard room. He would not have imagined that one day he would be known as 'emperor of the game' that he couldn't even see properly then.

Wilson Jones studied at the local Bishop High School and St. Vincent's High School. Then he joined the war service in 1939. Jones worked as Security Officer with Mazagon Docks in Mumbai from 1947 to 1950. Then he joined the House of Vissanji, from where he retired as personal assistant to the Chairman in 1989. Vissanji himself was an ardent lover of this green baize game. Therefore Jones had free access to the billiards table at Vissanji's large villa at Napean Sea Road.

Jones progressed rapidly and won his first national title in 1950, defeating T.A. Selvaraj. Next year he repeated his victory over his same opponent, T.A. Selvaraj. He trounced Chandra Hirji to win the title in 1953. Afterwards, till 1958, Hirji remained his main rival. Jones remained the amateur billiards champion of India for 12 years, between 1950 and 1966.

Wilson Jones started playing snooker earlier in 1948 and won the Amateur Snooker Championship of India for the first time. The championship crown he wore again four times in 1952, 1954, 1958 and 1960. He won the State Billiards Championship eight times and the State Snooker Championship six times.

Wilson Jones attempted for the first time the world title in World Amateur Billiards Championship at Kolkata in 1951 but ended up coming last. The following year he went to London to participate in the World Championship, but luck did not favour him again. It was tough going for him in London. He got a meagre allowance of one pound a day, and he had to spend money for boarding, lodging and eating from his own pocket. He nevertheless returned to India with the Best Sportsman Award. In 1953, Wilson Jones finished fourth in the round-robin matches in Sydney.

The big moment in Wilson Jones's life came in 1958, when he became the first Indian player to win the coveted World Amateur Billiards Championship, which was held at Great Eastern Hotel in Kolkata. He had to satisfy himself with the third place in the next World Championship held in England as he had earned a masterly break of 598.

Achievements

- ☆ *Wilson Jones remained national billiards champion 12 times. He won his first national title in 1950.*
- ☆ *He was five times the national snooker champion.*
- ☆ *He won the State Billiards Championship of Maharashtra eight times.*
- ☆ *He became the state snooker champion six times.*
- ☆ *He won the World Amateur Billiards Championship in 1958 held at Kolkata.*
- ☆ *He earned the Arjuna Award in 1962.*
- ☆ *He was awarded the Padma Shri in 1965.*
- ☆ *Jones was given the Maharashtra government's 'Gaurav Puraskar' in 1990.*
- ☆ *He received the 'Dronacharya Award' in 1996.*

BOXING

According to archaeological evidence, it was the Berbers and Egyptians who started this sport as early as 3000 BC, and the relief carvings of the 3rd millennium BC from Sumeria depict players boxing with each other. The earliest evidence of boxing in the Mediterrarnean region is found in the Minoan civilisation of 1500 BC.

The ancient Greeks and later the ancient Romans started a sport called 'pugilism', which was very much like boxing. It was different from the ancient Greek wrestling as it was based on the use of fists.

According to a Greek legend, their hero and ruler Theseus, who lived around the 9th century, invented a form of boxing in which two men sat face to face and beat each other with their fists until one of them was killed. Over time the boxers took to fighting while standing and wearing gloves (with spikes) and wrappings on their arms, below the elbows, although otherwise they were completely naked.

The other form of boxing was gladiatorial. The participants in these fights were usually criminals and slaves who hoped to become champions and gain their freedom; however, the men who were free also fought in the encounters. Eventually the fist fights became so popular that even aristocrats started fighting but this practice was ultimately banned by Caesar Augustus. In AD 393, the Olympics were banned by the Christian emperor Theodosius and in AD 500, boxing was banned altogether by the ruler as he considered it an insult to God because it disfigured the face, the image of God. Boxing became popular in Europe throughout the Middle Ages and beyond.

Unlike modern boxing, there were no different weight classes. Fights were not separated into rounds, and the fight had no time limit, and ended in a knockout, or with the fighter abandoning the fight, or fighting till the death of one of the fighters occurred. Instead of gloves, the fighters wrapped their hands in strips of hardened leather, which protected the fist from getting injured. Long fights were decided by an alteration of free punches, with the first to strike a free punch being decided by the toss of a coin.

There have been many informal forms of boxing throughout the centuries, since getting two people to fight with fists is in essence a primitive sport, but boxing is now regulated typically in a series of one to three-minute intervals, called rounds. Victory is achieved if the opponent is knocked down and is unable to get up before the referee counts to 10 (a knockout), or if the opponent is deemed too injured to continue (a technical knockout). If there is no stoppage of the fight before an agreed number of rounds, the winner is declared either by the referee's decision or by the judges' scorecards.

In India, despite the strenuous efforts of the Indian Amateur Boxing Federation, Indian boxers have failed to land the knockout punch at big events. At a time when most sports are trying to reach out to the younger generation banking on the popularity of star players, boxing in India languishes in the sidelines with no world-class talent in the horizon.

In the 2006 Colombo SAF Games, even though the Indian boxers managed to bag four gold medals, Pakistan walked away with the top honours, claiming seven gold medals.

Boxing

Dingko Singh

Date of Birth: January 1978

Dingko Singh is one of the best boxers of India. He was the winner of the King's Cup at Bangkok in 1997. After that he won a gold medal in the Asian Games in Bangkok in 1998.

Dingko Singh is counted among the best boxers of India today. He was born in January 1978 in a far-flung village called Lamlung in Imphal district of Manipur and was brought up in an orphanage. Dingko Singh put his heart and soul into becoming the champion boxer of India. His full name was Nagango Dingko Singh. He was given assistance under the Special Sports Area Scheme of the Indian Sports Authority. He came into news at the age of 11 years when he won the sub-junior title in national boxing at Ambala in 1989.

He won international acclaim after he emerged the winner of the Kings Cup in Bangkok (Thailand) in 1997. At that time he was declared the best boxer of these games. A year after this, Dingko's second success came to him in Bangkok itself. Bangkok proved lucky for Dingko Singh. In the 54-kg category, Dingko defeated the number two player of the world, Timur Tulyakov (from Uzbekistan) and won a gold medal in the Asian Games at Bangkok in 1998. This tournament was also important for him because he had changed his category from 51 kg to 54 kg only a few months earlier. In the semi-final tournament, Dingko defeated the number three player of the world, Wongprates Sontaya (Thailand) and the audience went wild with anger on seeing their player lose.

Achievements

- ☆ *Dingko Singh is one of the best boxers of India.*
- ☆ *He won the Kings Cup at Bangkok in 1997.*
- ☆ *He won a gold medal in the Asian Games at Bangkok in 1998.*

Boxing

Hawa Singh

Date of Birth: 16th December 1937
Died: 14th August 2000

One of the best boxers and heavyweights of the country, Hawa Singh gave a new dimension to this game during his years of service and made the country proud. First as a boxer and later as a coach, he was associated with the sport till the end of his life. He was awarded Arjuna Award in 1966 and honoured with the 'Best Sportsman Trophy' from the Chief of the Army Staff in 1968. The 'Dronacharya Award' for the year 1999 was presented to him.

Hawa Singh was known both in India and in Asia as the man who not only won the Asian Games heavyweight title but was also the man who went on to retain it in the next edition of the Games.

Hawa Singh was born on 16th December 1937 at Umarwas village in Bhiwani district of Haryana. He always had a liking for boxing. Therefore boxing became a family game for Hawa Singh with son Sanjay Kumar also wearing national colours. He claimed a silver medal in the Asian Junior Championship held at Bangkok.

Hawa Singh not only saw many triumphs at the national level, but it is difficult to say how many boxers became victorious because of the perfect training he imparted. He even taught the coaches the secret of winning and achieving success. He updated the knowledge of a number of coaches. Hawa Singh was a master, superior in this field in every respect.

Hawa Singh won gold medals twice at the Asian level and earned fame in the whole of Asia. It appeared as though he was the king of the ring, having no opposition. These two gold medals made him a legend in Indian boxing. No other boxer has achieved such success like him. The two victories in the Asian Games — the first in the Asian Games at Bangkok in 1966 and the second, again in Bangkok in 1970, when he gave Indian boxing the much needed medal.

Although it was expected that India would repeat its feat in the 1974 Asian Games, Teheran, but unfortunately the Indian, despite knocking down his Iranian opponent, was denied a gold medal by the referee. Hawa Singh would have been indeed very happy if the giant boxer Bura had won the gold medal that he deserved.

Apart from the gold medals in the Asian Games, Hawa Singh added many glorious chapters in the history of Indian boxing. He scored a record victory in his category in the Services and the nationals for as long as 11 years, from 1961 to 1972. No other boxer gained such success and figure at the top in the national as well as in the Services, as Hawa Singh did.

Hawa Singh enrolled himself into the 3rd Guards of the Indian Army in 1956. He went through the championship at all levels before winning the Western Command title in 1960. He defeated the Services champion, Mohabbat Singh, in the final round. From then on till 1972, Hawa Singh remained the undisputed king of the heavyweight event in India.

On looking to his success in the Asian Games, the Government of India honoured him with the Arjuna Award in 1966. He was given the 'Best Sportsman Trophy' by the Chief of the Army Staff in 1968. He was declared the winner of the 'Dronacharya Award' posthumously for the year 1999, but he died suddenly at Bhiwani on 14th August 2000. The end came just 15 days before he was to receive the 'Dronacharya Award' on 29th August from the President of India. However, the award was received by his wife Anguri Devi.

Achievements

- ☆ *Hawa Singh was the national champion in boxing for 11 years continuously (from 1961 to 1972).*
- ☆ *He was champion of the Services for 11 years.*
- ☆ *He won a gold medal in 1966 at the Asian Games in Bangkok.*

- ☆ *He again won the gold medal in the next Asian Games in 1970 at Bangkok.*
- ☆ *He won the 'Best Sportsman Trophy' from the Chief of the Army Staff in 1968.*
- ☆ *He was declared the winner of the 'Dronacharya Award' for the year 1999 and was awarded posthumously.*

M.C. Mary Kom

Date of Birth: Ist March 1983

M.C. Mary Kom is a woman boxer who earned a lot of recognition and fame for India in the international arena. She thrice won the world champion title in the 46-kg category. Mary Kom was born in Manipur and to honour her, the road going towards Manipur Sports Village has been named the Mary Kom Road.

M.C. Mary Kom won the World Boxing Championship title through a hat-trick at the age of 24 years in 2006. She was born in a mediocre family in a small town called Kangthei in Manipur state. Mary Kom's full name is Mangte Chungneijang Mary Kom and it had been given to her by her father M.Tonpu Kam and mother Saneikham Kam. The Mangte family is very proud of their daughter's achievements.

Mary Kom went to the Loktak Christian Model School and St. Xavier's School, Moirang in Manipur with a lot of difficulty. She gave her higher secondary examination from Aadimjati High School, Imphal, but she could not manage to pass the exam. As she did not want to reappear for the exam, she decided to quit school and give her examination from the National Open School.

Mary Kom was inclined towards athletics right from the very beginning, but when she entered athletics, she discovered that she was really influenced by boxing. She found no interest in the books meant for studying in Class XII. Her other three sisters and a brother were adequately educated, but they could not secure good jobs even then. Thus Mary Kom was determined to take boxing seriously. Despite the poor financial condition of her family and lack of proper diet, she decided to go ahead and pursue boxing.

She was imparted training in boxing by three different coaches — Imbocha, Narjit and Kishen. Khoibi Salam gave his complete support to Mary Kom so that she could reach her target of becoming a boxer. Her role model was Laila Ali. Mary did not take long to learn all the nuances of boxing and soon became an efficient boxer, but only after successfully completing the most arduous training given by her coach.

Mary won the State Women's Boxing Championship in the year 2000 and never looked back after that. Her killer instinct made her win one medal after another. She always had the instinct of a hunter who never returns home empty-handed. She also won the National Boxing Championship from 2000 to 2005 and the entire state of Manipur is proud of her achievement. The seeds of her victory at the international level were sown at the Second Asian Women's Boxing Championship in Hissar, where she won a gold medal. Then she again won a gold medal at the Third Asian Women's Boxing Championship in Taiwan.

After making a mark at the Asian level, she attained success at the international level as well. She won a silver medal at the First Women's World Boxing Championship in Pennsylvania (America) in 2003 and subsequently won a gold medal at the Women's World Boxing Championship in Antalya (Turkey) in 2000. She won the World Boxing Championships at Norway and Hungary as well.

Mary, who had longed for money to buy a copy of the Holy Bible in her childhood days, was winning gold medals as she grew up.

M.C. Mary Kom has a strong never-say-die spirit which helped her reach this level. Whenever she was in need of money to practice at the national and international competitions, her relatives and her church never let her down. Mary has been offered the job of a Head Constable in the police service because of her achievements.

She has been given the Arjuna Award, while the Manipur government has named the road going towards Manipur Sports Village as Mary Kom Road so as to honour her. The Youth and Sports Department of Manipur has given her a flat worth 13 lakh rupees. The Tata Group has also offered her a job in their prestigious establishment.

Mary Kom has been given the title of the 'Queen of the Ring'. She gave birth to twins in August 2007. Her husband's name is Onler.

Her journey to success continues unabated during subsequent years. In November 2008, Mary Kom won Women's World Boxing Championship.

Achievements

- ☆ *Mary won the National Boxing Championship from 2000 to 2005.*
- ☆ *She won a gold medal at the Second Asian Women's Boxing Championship in Hissar.*
- ☆ *She again won a gold medal at the Third Asian Women's Boxing Championship in Taiwan.*
- ☆ *She was successful in the Women's Boxing Championship at the international level and earned recognition and fame for India. She has thrice won the world champion title.*
- ☆ *She won a silver medal at the first Women's World Boxing Championship in Pennsylvania (America) in 2003.*
- ☆ *She has been given the Arjuna Award by the Government of India.*
- ☆ *She has also been awarded the Padma Shri.*
- ☆ *In the year 2007, she was nominated for the 'Rajiv Gandhi Khel Ratna' award.*
- ☆ *In 2008, she became Women's World Boxing Champion.*
- ☆ *In 2009, Mary Kom was honoured with the 'Rajiv Gandhi Khel Ratna' Award.*

Boxing

Vijender Kumar

Date of Birth : 29th October 1985

When the Indian boxer Vijender Kumar reached the semi-finals of the boxing championship at the 2008 Beijing Olympics, Indians were excited over this news as reaching the semi-finals meant that Vijender Kumar will surely get a medal either bronze or silver. He created history when he got the first Olympic bronze medal in boxing for India. He won his bronze medal in 75 kg. category.

Vijender Kumar was born on 29th October 1985 in Kaluwas village, 15 km. from Bhiwani, Haryana. He is middle weight boxer. His height is 182 cm (6ft.). His father Mahipal Singh is a bus driver (who drove buses overtime to raise funds for Vijender's training). His mother is a housewife. He is fond of modelling too. He was inspired to join boxing by his younger brother Manoj, a former boxer himself.

Vijender did his schooling from Kaluwas Secondary School in Bhiwani and finally a bachelor's degree from Vaish College. He worked overtime to pay for coaching at the Bhiwani Boxing Club.

Before leaving for Beijing Olympics (2008), Vijender Kumar had joined the Haryana Police and resigned from the Railways. He joined as an Inspector, but could not go to office on this post as he had to go to Beijing. But when he reached the semi-final of boxing at the Beijing Olympics, the Haryana Government promoted him to the post of DSP as an award. Haryana Government also gave him a Rs. 50 lakh cash award. He defeated Carlos Gongora of Ecuador 9-4 in the quarter finals on August 20, 2008 which guaranteed him a medal but he lost to Cuba's Emilio Correa in the semi-finals on 22nd August 2008 and got a bronze medal.

On the day of his quarter finals his father prayed for his success at a *Shiva* temple in Haryana. The people of Vijender's home-town Kaluwas like the game of boxing very much. More than 100 people go to Bhiwani to learn boxing tricks. When Vijender entered the semi-finals in the Beijing Olympics, Haryana Government declared a cash prize of Rs. 50 lakh for him. The town of Kaluwas erupted with celebrations on 20th August 2008 when Vijender was assured of an Olympic medal. The celebration was like that of Diwali celebration. Sports-lovers danced to music, fired crackers and beat drums to express their joy.

In September 2009, Vijender won a bronze medal in World Boxing Championships held in Milan. It is a big achievement for India for it is the country's first-ever medal at the World Championships.

Vijender boxed recreationally in his childhood and used to go to Bhiwani Sports Authority Centre for boxing practice, where coach Jagdish Singh spotted his talent. Vijender won a silver in his sub-junior nationals and then finished the 2nd sub-junior in the same position.

On winning a bronze Olympic medal, Spicejet airlines offered him free lifetime travel, Steel Authority of India gave him Rs. 15 lakh as cash award. Maharashtra Government gave him Rs. 5 akh cash award.

Achievements

- ☆ *He won a gold medal at the Sub-junior International at Germany in 2001.*
- ☆ *He won a gold medal at the Junior YMCA International in 2002.*
- ☆ *He won a gold medal at the 2003 Goa Cup International.*
- ☆ *He received a silver medal at the Afro-Asian Championship in 2003 at Hyderabad.*
- ☆ *He won a silver medal at the SAF Games at Islamabad in 2004.*
- ☆ *He won a silver medal in Olympic qualifying at Karachi in 2004.*
- ☆ *He got a silver medal at Commonwealth Boxing, Scotland in 2005.*
- ☆ *He won a silver medal in 2006 Commonwealth Games at Melbourne.*
- ☆ *He won a gold medal at SAF Games, Colombo in 2006.*

☆ *He won a bronze medal in 2006 Doha Asian Games.*

☆ *He won a bronze medal in 2007 Asian Championship.*

☆ *Vijender won a bronze Olympic medal in boxing in Beijing Olympics, 2008 and created history.*

☆ *In 2009, Vijender Kumar received the highest sporting honour—the 'Rajiv Gandhi Khel Ratna' Award.*

☆ *In September 2009, Vijender Kumar won a bronze medal in World Boxing Championships in Milan.*

CHESS

Chess is a checkerboard game for two players, each of whom moves 16 pieces on 64 squares arranged in an eight-by-eight square according to fixed rules across the board and the opponent tries to capture or checkmate the opponent's king. At the start, each player (one controlling the white pieces, the other controlling the black pieces) controls 16 pieces: one king, one queen, two rooks, two knights, two bishops and eight pawns. The object of the game is to checkmate the opponent's king, whereby the king is under immediate attack and there is no way to remove it from attack on the next move.

It is believed to have originated in India around the 6th century, though it continued to evolve as it spread to Europe during the Byzantine times; its rules practiced even today, were first accepted in Europe in the 16th century. Sometimes called 'western chess' or 'international chess' to distinguish it from its predecessors and other chess variants, the current form of the game emerged in Southern Europe during the second half of the 15th or early 16th century after evolving from similar but much older games of Indian and Persian origin.

Today chess is one of the world's most popular indoor games, played by millions of people worldwide in clubs and also, online on the computer.

It is a recreational and competitive game played between two players. The first official world chess champion, Wilhelm Seinitz claimed his title in 1886. In 1997, a match between Gary Kasparov, the world champion and a computer proved for the first time that machines are able to beat even the strongest of human players. India's Vishwanathan Anand is the current world champion. Theoreticians have developed extensive chess strategies and tactics since the game's inception.

India's chess scenario is looking rosy indeed with a bevy of youngsters making it big at the international arena. India is fast emerging as a chess powerhouse thanks to the growing number of international grandmasters. With young talents giving their older counterparts a good run for their money, parents are encouraging their wards to consider chess as a career option. Though Bobby Fischer, Gary Kasparov and Anatoly Karpov are world-renowned figures in the game of chess, our country's Vishwanathan Anand is a young player whose rise in the sport has been a source of inspiration to an entire generation of future Indian chess players.

Dibyendu Barua

Date of Birth: 27th October 1966

Dibyendu Barua is the second grandmaster of chess in India. He has won the national title thrice. He has been a talented player right from his childhood. However, he could not play according to the expectations of the people after growing up.

After Vishwanathan Anand, Dibyendu Barua is the second grandmaster of chess in India. He earned the title of 'International Master' after defeating world's number two Viktor Korchnoi, in London.

Dibyendu Barua was born on 27th October 1966. In 1978, at the age of 12 years, Dibyendu took part in the National Championship and became the youngest player to participate in the tournament. His entry became the topic of discussion in every sphere of chess. People started identifying him as the new talent in chess.

Barua was only 16 years of age when he earned the title of 'International Master' by defeating world's number two, Viktor Korchnoi in London. In 1983 he won the National Championship title for the first time. Despite such a wonderful start, his career could not take up as was being expected of him. Barua could win the grandmaster title in 1991 after a gap of nine years of winning the 'International Master' title.

Due to lack of financial resources and adequate training, Dibyendu could not perform according to the expectations of the people. He could not reach up to the success level of Vishwanathan Anand.

He has won the national title thrice, becoming the national champion for the last time in 2001 when he gave a tough fight to many young players.

Achievements

- ☆ *Dibyendu Barua became the second grandmaster of chess in India.*
- ☆ *In 1978, at the age of 12 years only, he became the youngest player to participate in the National Championship.*
- ☆ *In his childhood, he was being seen as a child prodigy.*
- ☆ *In 1983 he became a national champion.*
- ☆ *Barua won the grandmaster title in 1991.*
- ☆ *He has won the National Championship title thrice.*

Koneru Humpi

Date of Birth: 31st March 1987

Koneru Humpi made an excellent start by winning a gold medal in the National Chess Championship at the age of nine years. She has also won the title of the 'Best Woman Grandmaster' title. She is India's youngest woman grandmaster.

Koneru Humpi's father, Koneru Ashok is Humpi's coach. Humpi won a gold medal in the National Chess Championship in the nine-years category in Mumbai. Later she won a gold medal in the junior category girls' National Chess Championship held in 1997 at Chennai.

Koneru Humpi did her schooling from the Chalapathy Residential School, Guntur. Her mother's name is Koneru Lata and her sister's name is Koneru Chandrahasa. The Bank of Baroda is her sponsor. She was born on 31st March 1987 in a place called Gudivada near Vijayawada, in Andhra Pradesh.

Her father named his daughter Humpi because the word 'Humpi' means 'champion in a foreign language'. His desire behind calling her Humpi was that she would grow up to be a world champion and fulfil all his unfulfilled dreams. Humpi's grandfather, K. Prem Chand Rao is a mathematics lecturer who taught till the age of 73 years. He too was fond of playing chess in the club.

A few years ago, when Koneru's father Ashok and mother Lata purchased a computer instead of a television in their middle-class life, people made a lot of fun. Humpi's mother still remembers the time when people poked fun at them for purchasing a computer. Now that Humpi has become a world champion, her parents laugh at others' attitude at that time.

Koneru Humpi's father Ashok tutored his daughter so well that the government of Andhra Pradesh decided to give him the status of a state coach. In addition to this, the government also decided to give him a cash prize of five lakh rupees for his excellent coaching abilities. Ashok himself has been a state champion twice. He won the South Indian Open Championship in Guntur in 1985. He describes his relationship with Humpi like the relationship of Dronacharya with Arjun. While all parents aim high for their children they do not make proper efforts to promote them. Ashok devoted all his efforts to making Humpi a brilliant player in childhood itself.

She came to recognise the pawns and moves of chess from the age of five years. Once when Ashok was playing chess and was unable to think of a move, Humpi suggested a move to him when she was only six years of age. Ashok was shocked at this move as it was very correct. Whenever he tried to test her capability she astonished him completely. It was then that Ashok decided to start coaching her in chess. He used to coach 10 other students alongwith her. Koneru became a national champion at the young age of nine years.

Ashok was a chemistry lecturer prior to this, but when Humpi secured the fourth position in the junior category, he decided to quit his job and start coaching Humpi full time. Later Ashok started facing the financial crunch due to dearth of sponsors when making attempts to increase the ELO rating on the international front. At this opportune time the Bank of Baroda came ahead to sponsor her and then there was no looking back for her. Humpi gives complete credit for her success to her father.

Humpi has earned fame for India in the field of chess. In the year 1998, Humpi won gold medals in three competitions and has since added many medals to her tally. She participated in the National Rapid Chess Championship in Guntur in the under-12 category in 1998. In 1998 she won a gold medal at the National Chess Championship for girls in Calicut in the under-15 category. Then she won a gold medal at the National Chess Championship in Aurangabad in the under-15 category.

She won a gold medal at the National Chess Championship in Ahmedabad in the under-14 category in the year 2000.

Then, at the age of 16 years, she participated in the World Cup Chess Tournament in 2002 in Hyderabad. After winning in the initial stages, she lost to Ju Yuhua of China with a score 0.5-1. 15. After this particular game, Humpi's father and coach Ashok admitted that she had made some wrong moves during this game. Maybe she wanted to change some of her moves in the beginning, but in the end she had to lose the game because of her mistakes and her irregular moves.

Humpi has achieved so much at such a young age that she still has a lot of scope ahead to show her prowess. She also has the calibre of becoming the world champion through her hard work. In addition to playing chess, Humpi is also fond of watching TV and Telugu and Hindi movies. She also likes reading books. She looks up to Vishwanathan Anand as her role model.

India's youngest woman grandmaster Humpi is number two in the world ranking, yet she is unable to find a good sponsor. Under these circumstances, this player from Vijayawada had to take up the job of a personal administrator in ONGC in August 2006. Koneru contends that chess is an expensive game and that players have to often travel to foreign countries to take part in chess tournaments. Koneru laments that most of the companies only want to sponsor cricketers.

Apart from being the lone chess player of India who has donned the (men's) title of grandmaster, Humpi was deprived of a foreign coach. However her ELO rating as on August 2006 was 2545.

Koneru Humpi gave a very good performance in the Doha Asian Games held in December 2006. She won a gold medal in the Women's Rapid Chess Championship. Then she again won a gold medal at the team event, the Classical Swiss Round. Doha Asian Games again brought her a gold medal in chess and she won a gold medal at the team event along with K. Sasikiran and Hari Krishna. The trio of grandmasters Koneru Humpi, K. Sasikiran and Hari Krishna won eight rounds in a row and reached a score of 21 in the nine-round competition, thereby moving ahead of China by 5 points. In the Women's Championship, Humpi defeated Irene Kharasiyama easily. In this manner India defeated Indonesia with 2.5 points in comparison to 0.5 points and won the gold medal wilth one round still remaining.

Achievements

- ☆ *Humpi is the youngest Indian girl to have won the title of woman grandmaster. Prior to her, the title was won by Judith Polgar of Hungary at the age of 15 years.*
- ☆ *She won the woman grandmaster title at the age of 15 years and it is a world record.*
- ☆ *She is the first Indian girl to have won the title of grandmaster twice.*
- ☆ *She is the first Indian girl to have become the world number one among the top 20 players.*
- ☆ *She is the first Indian girl to have reached the 16th position in the top 50 women's list.*
- ☆ *She is the first Indian girl in the history of chess to achieve such a high ELO rating.*
- ☆ *She is the first Indian girl to win in the World Junior Women Chess Championship.*
- ☆ *She is the first Indian girl to win the world title in chess.*
- ☆ *She has been a continuous winner in the age goups of 10, 12 and 14 years category in the world*
- ☆ *She has been a winner of the Asian Junior Chess Championship.*
- ☆ *In the 61-year old history of chess in Britain, Humpi became the youngest winner of the British Women Chess Championship.*
- ☆ *She is the only girl to have won the Men's Asian Chess Championship in the under-12 category.*
- ☆ *She is the only girl to have won the Men's National Chess Championship in the under-14 category at Ahmedabad.*
- ☆ *She is the youngest international woman master.*
- ☆ *She is the recipient of the 'Young Achiever Award' given by* Sportstar *for the years 1997 and 1998.*
- ☆ *She is winner of the gold medal at the World Junior Girls Chess Championship in Athens (Greece) in 2001.*

☆ *She won a gold medal at the under-14 years category in the World Chess Championship in the Spain in 2000.*

☆ *She won a silver medal at the under-12 years category in the World Chess Championship in Spain in 1999.*

☆ *She won a gold medal in the under-12 years category in the Girls World Chess Championship in Spain in 1998.*

☆ *She won a gold medal in the under-10 years category in the World Chess Championship in Spain in 1997.*

☆ *She scored a victory in the Smith and Williamson British Championship in 2002.*

☆ *She won a gold medal at the Hotel Lipa Grandmasters Chess Tournament in Hungary in 2001.*

☆ *She won a bronze and a gold medal at the Commonwealth Chess Championship in 2000 in Sangli in the woman's and under-16 girls competition respectively*

☆ *She won a gold medal at the British Women Championship in 2000 in Somerset, England.*

☆ *She won a gold medal at the Asian Junior Chess Championship in Mumbai in 2000.*

☆ *She won a gold medal at the Commonwealth Chess Championship (under-16 years category) in Bikaner in 1999 and a bronze medal in the women's category in the same year.*

☆ *She won the woman master title at the National Women's Tournament in Calicut in 1999.*

☆ *She won a gold medal at the Mind's Sports Olympiad in the under-21 years category in London in 1999.*

☆ *She won a gold medal in the under-12 years category in Asian Boys Chess Championship in Ahmedabad in 1999.*

☆ *She was honoured with the Arjuna Award in 2004 for her achievements in chess in the year 2003.*

☆ *The Hero Honda Sports Academy nominated Humpi as the best chess player for the year 2004.*

Chess

Krishnan Sasikiran

Date of Birth: 7th January 1981

Krishnan Sasikiran holds the third rank in the FIDE rating after Vishwanathan Anand and P. Hari Krishna. He became the international chess grandmaster.

Krishnan Sasikiran has earned a lot of fame for winning in a number of international events. He is an extremely talented player.

Sasikiran was born on 7th January1981. Sasikiran made a very late entry into the game of chess — at 12 years of age, which is considered rather late for a chess player and established an identity for himself by winning prestigious competitions

Sasikiran won the international chess grandmaster title at the Commonwealth Championship at Sangli, Maharashtra in 2000. In 2000 itself he won the Pentamedia Category XI GM Tournament in Chennai. Then in 2001 and 2002, he won at the Hastings International Chess Congress in England.

After having tasted many victories, Sasikiran kept climbing up the ladder of success. He won the fourth Asian individual championship in 2003 and also the Politikan Cup at Copenhagen in the same year. In the Sigeman Tournament in Denmark, Copenhagen, he tied for the first position with Jan Timman.

In the Amtel Masters Chess Tournament in May 2007, Sasikiran was defeated in the last round by Walesin Topalov of Bulgaria and so he had to be content with the second position. He was leading till the penultimate round when Topalov moved ahead with his better strategy.

Achievements

- ☆ *Sasikiran won the International Chess Gandmaster title in the year 2000 at the Commonwealth Championship at Sangli, Maharashtra.*
- ☆ *In 2000, he also won the Pentamedia Category XI GM Tournament in Chennai.*
- ☆ *In 2001 and 2002, he won at the Hastings International Chess Congress in England.*
- ☆ *He won the fourth Asian Individual Championship in 2003.*
- ☆ *He also won the Politikan Cup in Copenhagen in 2003.*
- ☆ *In the Sigeman Tournament at Denmark, Copenhagen, there was a tie for the first position between Sasikiran and Jan Timman.*

Chess

Manuel Aaron

Date of Birth: 30th December 1935

Manuel Aaron has won the National Chess Championship nine times. He is the first Indian player to have won the 'International Master' title. Manuel is the first chess player to have been honoured with the Arjuna Award.

It can be said that it was Manuel Aaron, who initiated India into chess, has been the first player to play an important role in making the international sports arena aware of the rising power of chess in India. He has left a great impression among the international chess fraternity with his good game.

Manuel Aaron was born on 30th December 1935. He was the uncrowned prince of Indian chess and was in absolute control of the Indian chess world from the fifties to almost the middle of seventies. He became the first Indian player to have won the 'International Master' title.

Aaron won the National Chess Championship nine times. He was the winner of the national title for five continuous years from 1969-1971. He also won the Chess Championship a whopping 11 number of times in a state like Tamil Nadu, which boasts of its lineage in chess.

In the West Asian zonal final, Manuel defeated C.J.S. Purdy of Australia by 3-0 and Sukien Momo of Mongolia by 3-1 to become the international grandmaster in 1961. This was a great achievement since it was only the beginning for chess in India.

In 1962, Manuel qualified for the Stockholm inter-zonal final where he was pitted against veteran grandmasters like Lajos Portisch and Wolfgang Uhlmann. By the time the game reached its end, Manuel was on the last position. Manuel Aaron was given the Arjuna Award for his achievements. He is the first chess player to have been honoured with the Arjuna Award.

The Indian team participated in a number of tournaments under the leadership of Aaron. Some of these were the Chess Olympiad in Leipzig, Germany in 1960; a tournament at Varna, Bulgaria in 1962 and the Chess Olympiad in Tel Aviv in 1964.

Achievements

- ☆ *Manuel Aaron established an identity for himself and for India in the international sports arena in chess.*
- ☆ *He was the winner of the national title for five continuous years, from 1969-1971.*
- ☆ *He became the first Indian player to have won the 'International Master' title in 1961.*
- ☆ *He defeated Sukien Momo of Mongolia by 3-1 in the West Asian Zonals in 1961.*
- ☆ *In the Asian Australian zonal final, Manuel defeated C.J.S. Purdy of Australia by 3-0. Thereafter he became the international grandmaster in 1961.*
- ☆ *He is the first chess player to have been honoured with the Arjuna Award in 1962.*
- ☆ *He participated in a number of Olympiads on behalf of India and also led the Indian team in the Chess Olympiads.*

Chess

Parimarjan Negi

Date of Birth: 9th February 1993

Parimarjan Negi is the youngest Indian player to have won the grandmaster title. He became the youngest 'International Master' in the year 2005.

Parimarjan Negi is the latest name to be added to the list of extraordinary young chess players. Born on 9th February 1993 in New Delhi, Parimarjan has been a student of Amity International School, New Delhi. He made news when he won the grandmaster title at a very young age and also became the youngest Indian player to have won it.

This chess prodigy, who took his first step in the sphere of chess at the age of four years, did not take very long to make an impression in the international arena. His first international success came in 2002 when he won the Asian Championship in the under-10 category in Teheran.

In the year 2005, Parimarjan Negi became the youngest 'International Master'. He earned his third and final I.M. Norm at the International Open held at Sorte in Spain.

On 1st July 2006, Parimarjan became the second youngest grandmaster. Apart from him, Sergey Karjakin had also become a grandmaster when he was even younger. Parimarjan won the title in the form of third and final I.M. Norm at Chelyabinsk Region Superfinal Championship at Satka in Russia. Subsequently, he also broke the record of P. Harikrishna (of India) who was the youngest grandmaster till then.

In May 2007, Parimarjan played very well and drew with the junior champion Javen Aandriyasan in the fifth round of World Youth Star Tournament. This increased his joint score.

Achievements

- ☆ *Parimarjan Negi is the youngest Indian player to have won the grandmaster title.*
- ☆ *He made his presence felt at the national level at the age of four years.*
- ☆ *His first international success came in 2002 when he won the Asian Championship in the under-10 category in Teheran.*
- ☆ *In July 2005, he became the youngest 'International Master' after he earned his third and final I. M. Norm at the International Open held at Sorte in Spain.*
- ☆ *In July 2006, he became the second youngest grandmaster.*

Chess

Tania Sachdev

Date of Birth: 20th August 1986

The glamour girl of Indian chess, Tania Sachdev became the queen of Asian Women's Chess Championship on 11th September 2007 in Iran. In 2007 itself she had won the National Championship title as well. It is her dream to win the World Chess Championship one day. Her biggest title till date happens to be the Senior Asian Championship. She has also become the grandmaster.

Tania Sachdev is the eighth Indian woman chess player to become a grandmaster. The title of grandmaster had earlier been held by S. Vijayalakshmi, Koneru Hampi, S. Minakshi, Arthie Ramaswamy, Nisha Mohota, Swati Ghate and Dronavalli Harika.

Tania Sachdev was born on 20th August 1986 in New Delhi. She is a student of history. Tania is the best chess player of north India so far. All the other chess champions have hailed from southern India till now.

In the finals of Asian Championship in Teheran, in 2007, Tania defeated the Chinese champion, Ju Wenjun, ending the tournament in a draw with 6.5 points and winning the title. After winning this championship, she not only won a gold medal, but also qualified for the World Women's Chess Championship.

Tania and top seed Lufei Ruan had the same number of points, but owing to a better tie-breaker, Tania took over and the Chinese player had to be satisfied with a second position.

In the final round of this championship, Lufei Ruan had defeated the player of the host country, but had to yield to Tania because of Tania's tie-breaker. Her FIDE rating is 2342 points.

Tania gives complete credit for her performance at the Asian Championship to her coach.

Tania tasted her first international success at the age of eight years when she had won five titles at the British Championship in Norwich in 1994. This was a landmark in the history of chess. She also won the International Master Norm and also the National Championship in the under-12 category in 1997 at the age of 12 years. She won this title in the same category again in 1998. Tania won the National Championship in the under-19 category in 1999 in New Delhi.

Achievements

- ☆ *Tania tasted her first international success at the age of eight years when she won five titles at the British Championship in Norwich in 1994.*
- ☆ *She won the National Championship in the under-12 category in 1997 and again in 1998.*
- ☆ *She won the National Championship in the under-19 category in 1999 in New Delhi.*
- ☆ *In the year 2007, she won the Asian Championship title to become the Asian grandmaster. She also won a gold medal.*
- ☆ *In 2009, Tania was honoured with the Arjuna Award.*

Chess

Vishwanathan Anand

Date of Birth: 11th December 1969

Vishwanathan Anand became the youngest Indian to win the International Master Title at the age of 15 in 1984. In 1987, he became the first Indian to win the World Junior Chess Championship. In 1988, at the age of 18, he became India's first Grandmaster. He became the undisputed World Champion in 2007 and again won this title in 2008. With this win, he became the first player in chess history to have won the World Championship in three different formats: Knockout, Tournament, and Match. He was awarded Padma Shri at the age of 18, and in 2007 he was awarded the Padma Vibhushan. He is also the first recipient of Rajiv Gandhi Khel Ratna Award in 1991-92, India's highest sporting honour.

Grandmaster Vishwanathan Anand became India's first world chess champion by beating Russia-born Spanish rival, Alexei Shirov for the third time in a row and closing the six-game match of the FIDE World Chess Championship in the fourth game on 24th December 2000. This crushing victory which won Anand $660,000 as prize money, is a performance that will be hard to repeat in a world championship.

Anand is the 15th world chess champion in a line starting with Wilhelm Steintz in 1986.

Vishwanathan Anand added a fourth international title to his collection in 2002. He created history as he rebounded strongly from a first-game loss to beat veteran Anatoly Karpov of Russia in the final of the sixth edition of the Corsica Open Chess Tournament held in Bastila,

France. In the year 2002, Anand won the EuroTel title in Prague in May, followed by the Chess Classic-Menz title in July, the World Chess Cup in Hyderabad in October and the Corsica Tournament in November. He was awarded a prize-money of $ 46,000.

Anand, who ironically lost in the FIDE World Championships final to Karpov in the rapid games tie-breaker earlier in 1998, took his revenge by defeating the 52-year-old Russian in their last two finals at EuroTel Championships in Prague and Corsica. It was a very interesting and gripping battle between two of the greatest giants of our times. The clash was witnessed by a large audience that included more than 200 school students and for whom seeing a match between two former world champions was indeed a treat.

Anand fulfilled his dream of being a world chess champion in the year 2002 but it took him about three years to reach the number one position in FIDE rating. Anand, who began his career in the year 1984, completed his record book in 2007. Anand reached the coveted number one position in FIDE rating after winning the Linarez Morelia Chess Championship. After this historic win, Anand's FIDE ELO points reached 2816 and he became the number one chess champion in the world.

Anand's plethora of awards and trophies is just about enough to make even the best players turn green with envy.

The Indian maestro, popularly known as 'Vishy'or the 'Tiger from Madras', was born on 11th December 1969 and is the youngest amongst his three siblings. He is the only one to play chess in his family.

Anand was conferred the prestigious International Chess Oscars for two successive years, in 1997 and 1998, in a poll by chess journalists drawn from 55 countries in the world. The Chess Oscar is given to the star performer of each year and Anand became the first Asian and the only non-Russian apart from American wizard Bobby Fischer to receive the award.

Anand learned chess at the tender age of six from his mother while in the Philippines. His asset is the lightning speed with which he plays his moves.

Anand's success began from the age of 13 years in 1982, when he won the Tamil Nadu Junior Chess title. At the age of 15, he won the National Junior Chess title and became the youngest national champion at the age of 16. In 1987 he became the first Asian to win the World Junior Championship.

In 1985, he was awarded the prestigious 'International Master' title after he won the Asian Junior Chess Competition for the second time. He remained the national champion continuously from 1986 to 1988. He was also awarded the Arjuna Award by the Government of India for his accomplishments and with it also earned the coveted grandmaster title — again a first for an Indian.

His climb to the upper echelons was as dramatic as his popularity around the globe. The chubby-faced Indian became everyone's darling as he went on climbing the ladder of success.

Anand got his first international recognition in 1990 in the series 18 competition in Italy, where he managed to give a tough challenge to international veterans, Anatoli Karpov and Gary Kasparov. Russia had dominated this game played in 159 countries of the world for long. America's Bobby Fischer made a mark for himself for a few years in the 114-year-old chess history. Vishwanathan Anand was the first non-Russian after Fischer to make a name in the history of chess.

Anand carved a special niche on the chess-board by winning the stongest tournament at that time — the Reggio Emillia in Italy in 1991, ahead of Kasparov and Karpov.

Kasparov, the strongest chess player of any era with ELO rating of 2800 plus, had by then rebelled against FIDE and floated his own World Championship and invited Anand to be his challenger.

In the subsequent finals played in Groningen, a tired Anand fought well but the Russian kept his hold on the title.

His best effort before the World Championship was a decisive win at the revived chess World Cup in Shenyang, China, where the field was as strong as that of the world.

Anand's father was on a deputation assignment to Philippines where chess was an extremely popular game. "When I introduced him to the game, he was six years old and I had no idea he would become a world champion one day," said Sushila Viswanathan of her son Anand. "There was nothing unusual about him. He was a normal child," she said. "He took a liking to chess and that's why I persisted." Though her son has been basking in the glory of a world beating performance, she remains as inquisitive as ever and even makes an attempt to suggest a few moves to her world-champion son.

Anand himself has said, "But for the support and encouragement provided by my parents, wife and other members of my family, I could not be where I am today."

Humility is one of Anand's traits. "I know nothing of chess. But I know, he is still the same quiet and unassuming boy, I have known," says a relative.

India'a first international master, Manuel Aaron, echoes the view: "Success has not gone to his head. He is still the humble player I have known since he started playing."

The emotional and psychological support provided by his family and wife Aruna have stood him in good stead. "They have been a source of comfort and strength. Aruna always takes care of things like booking tickets, ensuring that my comfort is by my side in any major championship," Anand says, who became the number two player in 1997 after his ELO rating jumped to 2700.

The win in Teheran and his success in Shenyang World Cup have placed Anand in an enviable position as his ELO rating could reach 2800, to make him the second person after Gary Kasparov to do so.

Anand, who is a commerce graduate, has a photographic memory and calculating mind. Talent can make one reach the top five, but upward progress can be achieved only through sheer hard work. The chess wizard puts in eight to nine hours of practice daily.

However, after a major championship, he likes to unwind by listening to music, swimming or watching movies, but only after thoroughly analysing his bad moves, if any. His future aim is to win the first gold medal in the Olympic Games for India through his game.

Unlike world number one Kasparov, who has reportedly nine GMs to assist him, Anand has a smaller entourage — his second Elizibar Ubilava, who has been with him since 1994, and part-time coach and friend Pablo Sam Segundo. Both are Spaniards and assist Anand at his 'second home' in Spain.

Team Anand had reasons to feel gung-ho. Besides picking up a cheque for $660,000 (Rs. 2.97 crore), Anand is the first Asian to win the championship title. He has won seven of the 11 events and the inaugural FIDE World Cup at Shenyang in China.

Success has not come easy for Anand. He has worked for it. A graduate from Loyola College in Chennai, he was determined and focused on chess.

"He is a role model for every sportsperson and youngster to follow. There is no controversy about him; he is level-headed," said Dr. N. Mahalingam, president of the Tamil Nadu Chess Association.

"Anand used to combine his studies and chess quite well. I never had any worry on that count," says Anand's mother.

Anand has also a word of praise for the efforts of the Indian community at Teheran to make him comfortable. Anand, a strict vegetarian, did not have any problems as the Indian community and embassy took turns to provide the cuisine of his desire. "I had no problems and used to get *thayir sadam* (curd rice)," says the affable champion.

His earlier accomplishments include wins at the Linares Super Torneo in 1998; Melody Amber Tournament in 1994 and 1997; the Credit Suisse Master in 1997; Dos Hermanas in 1997; Wijk Aan Zee in 1987 and 1998; Torneo de Madrid in 1998, Dortmund chess in 1996 and 2000 and Tilburg Chess Tournament in 1998.

Anand also has the unique distinction of winning six out of eight tournaments that he participated in 1998. Besides his accomplishments in the classical tournaments, Anand won the strongest rapid championship in Frankfurt in 1998 and 1999. He also has the distinction of winning at the Fritz in Frankfurt in 1998 and 1999.

Anand has won two editions (1999, 2000) of the prestigious Advanced Chess Tournaments that took place in Leon, Spain.

Having kept his reputation intact, Anand has now set himself a bigger aim — break the 2800 barrier in the ELO ratings. As per FIDE rules, a player with 2600+ ratings is fit to be a super grandmaster, one with 2500+ IM. In that order a player with 2800+ rating will be considered a super super grandmaster. Only two players —Gary Kasparov (2838) and

Vladimir Kramnik (2803) have passed that mark and Anand, rated 2752, needs to get nearly 50 points to cross the mark.

Achievements

- ☆ *In 1983-84, Vishwanathan Anand became a champion with 919 points in the National Sub-junior Championship.*
- ☆ *In 1983-86, he became the champion in National Junior Championship in the 'under-9' age-group.*
- ☆ *He won the LLoyd Bank Junior Championship in the under-19 age-group in 1984 and 1985. He was the proud winner of the International Master at the age of 15. He was the first Asian youth to win this honour at such a young age.*
- ☆ *After being a consistent winner for three years, from 1980-88, in the national 'A' class chess championship, he became the youngest national champion.*
- ☆ *He came second in ELO Rating Tournament in 1987 and also won his second grandmaster title that very year.*
- ☆ *In 1992 he became a champion in the Raggio Emila Chess Tournament. He surpassed Kasparov and Karpov in Raggio Emila and managed a first place in a gruelling competition.*
- ☆ *He was a joint winner with Kramnik at the prestigious Dartmond Tournament. This very year he defeated world champion Gary Kasparov in the Swiss Rapid Chess Grand Prix, Geneva.*
- ☆ *In 1997, he became the champion of Knock-out Championship, Gronizen, which was the final of the World Championship. In this tournament, he defeated three players out of 10 — they were Sherov, Jelfend and Adams.*
- ☆ *In 1998, with the FIDE rating of 2,790 points, Anand became the number two in the world.*
- ☆ *In 1998 Anand won the Oscar award in chess at Moscow.*
- ☆ *He became a champion in* Torneo Magitral Communidad de Madrid *and got the highest ELO rating of 2,895 points of his*

career. Till then Gary Kasparov held the magical number of 2,800. Anand was a mere five points behind.

- ☆ *He won the Oscar for the second time in 1999.*
- ☆ *In 2000, he won the FIDE World Championship in Teheran and became world champion in New Delhi by defeating Alexei Shirov in the finals by 3.5–0.5.*
- ☆ *He became a champion in the Duel of Champions in 2001.*
- ☆ *He won the Eurotel World Chess Trophy in Prague in 2002.*
- ☆ *He led the team against Russia and rest of the world to record a historic win in 2002.*
- ☆ *He won the World Cup in Hyderabad and became the champion of the 6th Corsica Masters Rapid Chess Tournament in 2002, by defeating Anatoly Karpov 4-2.*
- ☆ *In 2003 he won the Corus Chess Tournament* Wizk Aan Zee. *In the very same year he was declared the champion at the 12th Amber Chess Tournament, Monte Carlo.*
- ☆ *In 2003 he won the Rapid Chess Classic match and emerged the winner at the Corsica Masters, Bastila, France.*
- ☆ *In 2004, he was declared the winner of Corus Chess Tournament, Wijk Aan Zee. This was Anand's fourth victory at Wijk Aan Zee, after 1989, 1998 and 2002.*
- ☆ *He managed to retain the little of Menz Chess Classic (Germany) for the fourth consecutive time; which is the most coveted championship for world chess champions. This was a record seventh win for super grandmaster Anand. In 2002 he had won the Dartmond title in Germany.*
- ☆ *In January 2006, super grandmaster Vishwanathan Anand won the Corus Chess Championship title for a record fifth time by defeating grandmaster Borus Golfand of Israel. As world champion, Vaseline Topalor and Anand had the same number of points and hence both shared the award.*
- ☆ *After a 5-3 victory at the Menz Chess Classic Tournament, Anand won the Menz title for the fifth time in August 2005,*

after inflicting a crushing defeat over the Russian champion, Alexander Grishuk in two decisive matches.

- ☆ *In August 2006 Anand won the Menz Chess Championship title for the sixth consecutive time and seventh time in all after he defeated Radjabov of Azerbaijan 5-3. This was Anand's ninth title in World Rapid Chess Championship. In March 2007 Anand became the only player to have won the title in three major world championships (Corsica, Linares and Dartmond).*

Honours and Awards at a Glance

- ☆ *Anand was awarded the Arjuna Award for being an exemplary chess player.*
- ☆ *He was awarded the Soviet Land Nehru Award for promoting peace and amity.*
- ☆ *He was awarded the Padma Shri in 1987 and he became the youngest recipient of this award.*
- ☆ *In 1987 he was given the 'National Citizen Award' for his outstanding contribution to chess.*
- ☆ *He was bestowed with an honorary doctorate degree of* Kala Praveen *by Jawaharlal Technological University, Hyderabad in 1988.*
- ☆ *In 1991-92 he was given the 'Rajiv Gandhi Khel Ratna' award.*
- ☆ *He was awarded the 'K.K. Birla Award' in 1995.*
- ☆ *In 1998, he was given the 'Book of the Year Award' by the British Chess Federation for his book,* Visiting Anand – My Best Games of Chess.
- ☆ *In 1998 the Indian sports magazine* Sportstar *awarded him the 'Best Player of the Millennium' award.*
- ☆ *He was honoured with the Padma Bhushan in the year 2000 for being the first Asian to win the World Championship.*
- ☆ *He was nominated as the 'Best Chess Player' for the year 2004 by the Hero Honda Sports Academy.*

CRICKET

Cricket is the most popular game among the members of the Commonwealth. In the countries of South Asia, including India, Pakistan, Bangladesh and Sri Lanka, cricket is played in every nook and corner.

Cricket's origin is uncertain. It was recorded in England in the late 16th century and the first set of rules was formulated in 1744. During England's colonial history, it was exposed to countries around the world. Cricket matches are divided into innings consisting of one turn at batting (approximately 10 batsmen) for each team. Depending on the pre-game agreement, it may consist of either one or two innings.

Cricket is played with a ball and a bat by two sides, each of 11 players. Played on a large grass field, roughly oval in shape, in the centre of which is a flat strip of ground 22 yards (20.12 metres) long called a pitch, the game is called a cricket match. Wickets, usually made of wood, are placed at each end of the pitch and defended by a batsman each.

A bowler from the fielding team throws the ball (with a straight-arm delivery), attempting to hit the wicket at the other end, which is one of the several ways the batsman may be declared out. The ball usually bounces once before reaching the batsman, who is a player from the opposing team. In defence of the wicket, the batsman plays the ball with the wooden cricket bat. Meanwhile, the other members of the bowler's team stand in different positions around the field as fielders who retrieve the ball in an effort to stop the batsman from scoring runs and if possible, get him out. Runs are scored each time the batsmen exchange positions without being declared out. Runs are also scored if the batsman hits the ball to the boundary or out of the boundary without a bounce. The match is won by the team that scores the maximum number of runs.

The aim of the batting team is to score as many runs as possible. A run is scored when both batsmen successfully move to their respective opposite ends of the pitch. The objective of the bowler's team is to get each batsman out (called 'taking a wicket', or a 'dismissal'). The most direct way to dismiss a batsman is for the bowler to bowl the ball so that the batsman misses it and it hits the stumps, dislodging a bail; or if the batsman attempts a run and the fielders may dismiss either the batsman by using the ball to knock down the bails off the set of stumps to which the batsman is closest before he reaches the wicket or before he places his bat in the crease. Other ways for the fielding side to dismiss a batsman include catching the ball off the bat before it touches the ground, or having the batsman adjudged lbw or 'leg before wicket', or if the ball strikes the batsman's body and goes on to hit the wicket.

The game is divided into overs of six balls and at the end of every over, another bowler from the fielding side bowls from the opposite end of the pitch. The two umpires also change positions between overs and the fielders also usually change positions between the overs. Once one batsman is out, he is replaced with the next batsman in the team's line-up. The innings of the batting team ends when the tenth batsman is given out, leaving one batsman not out, but without a partner. When this happens, the team is declared 'all out'. At the end of an innings, the two teams exchange roles and the side that had fielded now comes to bat.

The team that scores the greater number of runs at the end of the completed match wins the match.

Cricket

Ajit Wadekar

Date of Birth: 1st April 1941

Ajit Wadekar is the only Indian captain to have won three series in a row, two of them abroad. This is perhaps the reason that he has been labelled as a lucky cricketer.

Ajit Wadekar was appointed skipper of the Indian team on its tour of the West Indies in 1971. It was the casting vote of Vijay Merchant, Chairman of the Selection Committee, which earned him the captain's position.

Ajit Wadekar's full name is Ajit Laxman Wadekar. He was born on 1st April 1941 at Mumbai in Maharashtra. Besides being a successful captain, he was a stylish left-handed batsman and a brilliant fielder. His international career spanned eight years. Wadekar played 37 Tests, scoring 2,113 runs at an average of 31.07. He scored only one Test century (143 runs) and it was against New Zealand in 1967-68. He could make runs in 90s four times, but could not make a century. He even made 99 once and then was out.

Ajit Wadekar was a student of two prestigious colleges – Eliphinstone and Ruia. He represented Bombay University from 1957-58 to 1961-62. He was the captain of the combined university team when the team played against MCC in 1961-62. His best score in the university sports was 324 against Delhi in 1958-59. On the basis of this performance, he was inducted into the Bombay Ranji Trophy team till 1974-75.

During his career of 17 years, he scored 4,288 runs in 73 matches at an average of 57.94. He played and scored well in Ranji Trophy matches. His career's score of 323 runs was made against Mysore in 1966-67 in the Ranji Trophy match.

Ajit played 18 Duleep Trophy matches from the West Zone side and captained six of them.

During the Indian team's tour of England, Ajit scored 835 run in 1967 in county matches and 242 runs with a highest total of 91 in the Tests. In 1967-68 he scored his first and only Test century during the New Zealand tour. Here he scored 330 runs at an average of 47.14 runs.

Achievements

- ☆ *Ajit Wadekar is the only Indian cricket captain to have won three series in a row, two of them abroad and one in India.*
- ☆ *He scored 2,113 runs in 37 Tests at an average of 31.07 runs.*
- ☆ *He scored only one century in his Test career that was in New Zealand in 1967-68. He made 143 runs.*
- ☆ *He scored 12 centuries in Ranji Trophy matches.*

Cricket

Anil Kumble

Date of Birth: 17th October 1970

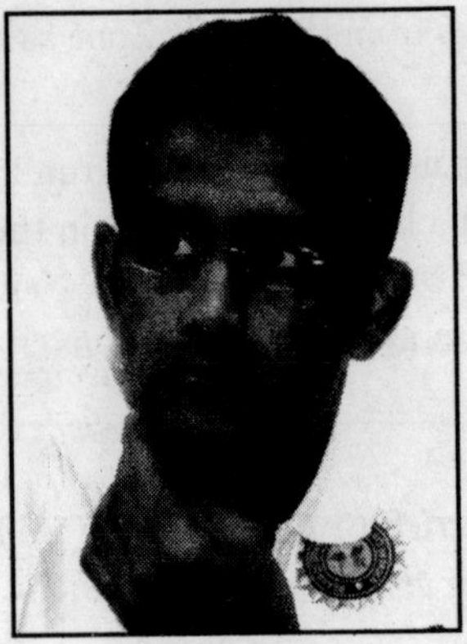

Anil Kumble created cricketing history at the Ferozeshah Kotla Grounds in New Delhi in a Test match against Pakistan when he took 10 wickets in 26.3 overs by giving away a mere 74 runs. Anil became the second cricketer in the world to have taken 10 wickets in a Test match. Prior to this performance, England's offspinner Jim Laker had set a record by taking 10 wickets in an innings. Anil Kumble happens to be India's first spinner and the second cricketer to cross the 200-mark in the limited overs international cricket. In January 2008, in the third Test against Australia at Perth, he became the first Indian bowler and the third in the world to reach the milestone 600 Test wickets by taking Andrew Symonds' wicket.

Anil Kumble's 10-wicket performance not only registered a win for India in the Test match against Pakistan, but also earned him the 'Man of the Match' award. It was due to this record-making performance that Kumble was able to register his name in the cricket's 'Hall of Fame'. The first player who broke the 10-wicket record was Jim Laker on 31st July 1956, made 43 years ago.

Anil Kumble was born on 17th October 1970 in Bengaluru, Karnataka. His initial cricket matches saw him in the capacity of a batsman in the team and therefore he acquired the image of a batsman. In the 1990-match against Pakistan, he made a total of 113 runs in New Delhi. This was also the year in which he started his Test career when in his very first Test match against Graham Gooch's English team, he managed to capture three wickets.

After this Kumble had to wait for a period of one-and-a-quarter years before he could play a Test match. Then he played his first Test against South Africa in 1992-93. In the two-nation tour to South Africa and Zimbabwe, Kumble was one among the successful players. Following this, Kumble always had a very important position in the Indian cricket team. One can say that Kumble has been as successful as his cricketing idol, Chandrashekhar. He made a good identity for himself at the international level and it would not be wrong to say that India has won a number of matches because of his bowling.

Kumble is a non-conventional spinner in the sense that he bowls a googly at one time and a medium-paced ball at other times. He doesn't turn the ball around too much, which is his own characteristic style.

The West Indies team acknowledged his genius in the one-day match at Kolkata. The Sri Lankan team faced his excellent deliveries in the 1994 Lucknow Test match, while Australia had its taste of the genius during 1997-98. The Pakistani team would remember Anil's performance forever when he took 10 wickets at a go in one innings in 1999. Kumble had crossed the five-wicket mark in international cricket a number of times, but it was for the first time that he created history with his 10-wicket performance in 1999.

Kumble completed his 200-wicket mark when playing against Zimbabwe in 1998. He was the first spinner and the second Indian to take these many wickets in international cricket. Kapil Dev had taken 200 wickets too prior to Kumble. It wasn't long before he became the bowler to take his 100 Test wickets in 21 Test matches. This record was made in the year 1995. He was the first bowler to take 100 wickets in a time-span of five years.

Kumble played his first one-day international against Sri Lanka in the Australian Cup at Sharjah. In 1994 he set a record by taking five wickets off 10 overs, giving away only 33 runs.

Kumble was an extremely successful bowler at the Wills World Cup. He was given the captaincy of the Karnataka team in the Ranji Trophy match. He took 13 wickets in the Iranian Cup.

He was given rest from the game after his bad performance during the South African tour in 1997. Then he was again selected to play for India against Sri Lanka. Anil was also part of the Indian team for the World Cup held in 1999.

This soft-spoken spinner was bestowed the Arjuna Award in 1995. Anil Kumble announced his retirement from one-day international cricket in March 2007. At the time of taking his last bow from one-dayers, his words were, "Cricket is merely a game. But when you play and happen to win or lose the game, it appears too much bigger than the game. But when you return home to your family and children, you realise that it is just a game and nothing more."

In January 2008, in the third Test against Australia at Perth, he became the first Indian and the third in the world to reach the milestone 600th Test wicket by taking Andrew Symonds' wicket. His 600 wickets came in 124 matches at an average of 28.68. He is the third cricketer after Muttaiah Muralitharan of Sri Lanka nd Shane Warne of Australia to take 600 wickets in Test matches.

Achievements

- ☆ *Kumble is among the few Indian players to take 100 wickets in a mere 21 Test matches.*
- ☆ *He was the first spinner and the second Indian to cross the 200-wickets mark in international cricket in 1998.*
- ☆ *In a match against Pakistan in 1999 in New Delhi, Anil Kumble performed a miracle by taking 10 wickets off 26.3 overs and 74 runs.*
- ☆ *He was given the Arjuna Award in 1995.*
- ☆ *Till March 2007, Kumble played a total of 113 Test matches in which he took 547 wickets.*
- ☆ *Till his retirement from one-day matches, he played a total of 271 one-day matches in which he took 337 wickets.*
- ☆ *In January 2008, he became the first Indian and the third in the world to reach the milestone 600 Test wicket by taking Australian Andrew Symonds' wicket.*

Cricket

Bhagwat Chandrashekhar

Date of Birth: 17th May 1945

Bhagwat Subramaniam Chandrashekhar is better known as Bhagwat Chandrashekhar. He was one of the four famous spin quartet of Indian cricket and fondly called Chandra by his friends. Chandrashekhar was known as the magician of the Indian cricket team. He had the magical capability of changing a losing match into a winning one and turn the face of the match altogether. It is often remembered that in 1972, in a match at Oval, India registered its first ever victory against England and because of which he was given the Arjuna Award and the Padma Shri by the Government of India. He was declared 'Cricketer of the Year' by Wisden in 1972.

Bhagwat Chandrashekhar was born on 17th May 1945 in Mysore, Karnataka. He was one of the four famous spin quartet of Indian cricket. He had played for Karnataka against Kerala in Ranji Trophy as an undergraduate student at the National College in Bengaluru. This was in 1963-64 and an unforgettable moment for Chandrashekhar as that very year he had played in Duleep Trophy and Iranian Trophy on behalf of his zone and subsequently became a part of the Indian Test team.

At that time, the England team led by Mike Smith was on a tour to India. Chandrashekhar was included in the Indian team under the captaincy of Nawab of Pataudi in the age of 19 years to play in Mumbai. He took five wickets in this match, which marked the beginning of his cricketing career. He played cricket for 17 years. He played his last match in 1979-80 in Pakistan. During these years he played 58 Test matches and took 242 wickets. His average in these matches was 29.74.

Chandrashekhar performed the feat of taking five wickets in an innings close to 16 times. He also performed the astonishing feat of taking more than 10 wickets in a match twice.

Chandrashekhar became a victim of polio in his childhood and it affected his right hand. The effect was more profound on his right wrist because of which his right wrist used to twist a little more while bowling. Thus he was always different from normal bowlers. Actually he was the fastest leg-break bowler because of which even the best of batsmen found it difficult to withstand his bowling.

After joining the Indian team at the age of 19, he played excellently against the West Indies and England. But after that he was forced to remain out of many important series because of a scooter accident. When he was inducted back into the team after a gap of three years, in 1971, during the England tour, the team's decision was questioned.

But he managed to silence all his critics with his excellent performance. He took six wickets for 38 runs at the Oval in 1971 and had the England team all out for a mere 101 runs. Consequently India beat England on its home ground and recorded its first ever win. In 1972, he was selected the 'Cricketer of the Year' by Wisden.

Chandrashekhar was such a talented player that he displayed his skills on not only the Indian pitches but in any type of pitch across the world. During the West Indian tour of India in 1975-76, Chandrashekhar took Vivian Richard's wicket many times and played a key role in the victory of the Indian team against Port of Spain.

In 1978 at Melbourne, Chandrashekhar took 12 wickets for 104 runs and played an important role in India scoring its first ever victory in Australia.

Chandrashekhar was far from being a mere classical leg-spinner; his bowling was rife with many unexpected tricks. He used to bowl a fast googly after a long bouncing run up. His game always appeared to be a mystery because of his amazing skills. While on some days he would appear an extremely easy bowler to the batsmen, on other days he was a terror to them. While playing against the West Indies in India in 1974-75, Chandrashekhar, Bedi and Prasanna put up a memorable performance.

Achievements

- ☆ *Chandrashekhar was one of the four famous spin quartet of Indian cricket.*
- ☆ *He took six wickets for 38 runs at the Oval in 1971 and had the England team all out for just 101 runs. India beat England on its home ground and recorded its first ever win because of Chandrashekhar.*
- ☆ *In 1978 at Melbourne, Chandrashekhar's bowling helped to score the first ever victory for India in Australia.*
- ☆ *He was also awarded the Arjuna Award and the Padma Shri in 1972.*
- ☆ *In 1972 he was selected the 'Cricketer of the Year' by Wisden.*
- ☆ *He remained an extremely talented bowler.*

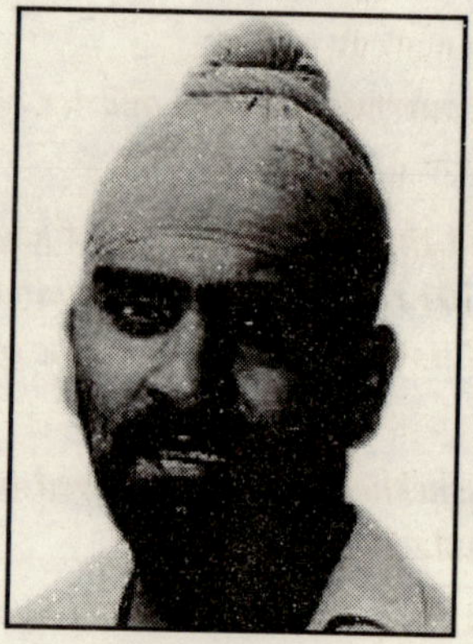

Cricket

Bishen Singh Bedi

Date of Birth: 25th September 1946

Bishen Singh Bedi's name is taken in the same breath as the world's outstanding spin bowlers. He has been an extremely popular player of his time. He was awarded the Arjuna Award in 1969 by the Government of India and in 1970 he was honoured with the Padma Shri.

Bishen Singh Bedi has been an excellent left-handed spinner of his time. He was popular both with the spectators and with the foreign teams.

Bishen Singh Bedi was born on 25th September 1946 at Amritsar in Punjab. He received his education in two famous colleges of Amritsar — Khalsa and Hindu. His father Gyan Singh encouraged him to play cricket. He received coaching from Professor Gyan Prakash and during his college days, Captain Gurupal Singh gave him moral support and cooperation in sports. Therefore, both at school and college, he was a highly successful player. Later on, he played for the Railways and the Punjab team. In 1965, in the North Zone Inter-University final, at Meerut, Bedi performed excellently (playing against Delhi). This was a very commendable performance.

Bishen Singh Bedi was one of the four famous quartet of Indian cricket. Besides him, Prasanna, Venkat and Chandrasekhar were also part of the quartet. Bishan Singh Bedi was different from all these players as he always found a place in the Indian team, while the rest of the three had to be in and out of the team in one or two matches.

Bishen Singh Bedi started his Ranji Trophy career with North Punjab but soon in 1968-69, he was shifted to the Delhi team. Bedi played close to 76 Ranji Trophy matches between 1961-62 and 1980-82. He took 402 wickets and 6,012 runs in Ranji matches.

His best bowling performance was witnessed in 1974-75 in Jammu and Kashmir where he took seven wickets giving away only five runs and taking 13 wickets for 34 runs. Bishen Singh Bedi captained the Indian cricket team in 47 Ranji matches. His best performance was in 1968-69 against Punjab when he scored a hat-trick. Bedi was the captain of the North Zone team for the Duleep Trophy. Apart from this he played three matches in the Iranian Cup and led his team in all the three matches.

His international career took off while playing for the North Zone team against Mike Smith's MCC team. While playing in the Ferozeshah Kotla Grounds in 1966, he put up a very impressive performance on behalf of President's XI against the winning the West Indies team. In fact his performance was so outstanding that it caught the attention of the selection committee and Bedi was immediately selected for the Test match to be played at Kolkata against the West Indies. This match marked the beginning of Bedi's career. At that time no one could have known that for the next 10 years or so, Bedi would exert a powerful influence on cricket and be a formidable force to reckon with.

Bishen Singh Bedi had played in 67 matches till 1979 and taken 266 wickets at an average of 28.71. His prominent success was in the series against Bobby Simpson's Australian team. Even though the Indian team lost 2-3 in the five Test series, it was Bedi's efforts at saving the Test match that would always be commended.

Bedi was given the Arjuna Award in 1969 by the Government of India and in 1970 he was honoured with the Padma Shri. However, Bishen Singh Bedi's biggest achievement was when he was called upon by the United Nations to deliver a lecture on apartheid in sports. He was introduced by the Nigerian chairman of the committee as one of the most outstanding spin bowlers of the world.

Achievements

- ☆ *Bedi played close to 76 Ranji Trophy matches in which he took 402 wickets and scored 6,012 runs.*

- ☆ *In 1968-69 he scored a hat-trick against Punjab.*
- ☆ *He led his team 47 times in the Ranji Trophy.*
- ☆ *He was also the captain of the North Zone team for the Duleep Trophy.*
- ☆ *He had played 67 matches by 1979 and taken 266 wickets in these matches with an average of 28.71.*

Cricket

C.K. Naidu

Date of Birth: 31st October 1895
Died: 14th November 1967

C.K. Naidu's full name was Kottari Kankaiyya Naidu. He was the first Test captain of India in cricket and India's first cricketer to be honoured with the Padma Bhushan. He was chosen the 'Cricketer of the Year' by Wisden in 1933.

Colonel Cottari Kankaiyya Naidu was lovingly called C.K. by one and all. He was the captain of the Indian cricket team in India's first Test match which was played against England in 1932. Despite a strong England team, the Indian cricket team under the captaincy of C.K. Naidu, put up a tough fight.

C.K. Naidu was born on 31st October 1895 in Nagpur (Maharashtra). He played cricket for teams of Andhra Pradesh, Central Provinces and Berar, Holkar United Province and for the team of India.

During the England tour of 1932, C.K. Naidu played in all the 26 'A' level matches in which he scored 1,618 runs with an average of 40.45 and took 65 wickets. The very next year, i.e. in 1933, he was declared 'Cricketer of the Year' by Wisden.

C.K. Naidu was more than 6' tall and he was a left-handed player. He had a tough athlete-like physique. Therefore, with his powerful strokes and hard hitting he was able to easily reduce the pressure of the opposite team. He gained a lot of popularity during 1926-27 after he scored 153 runs in 187 balls in 100 minutes in Mumbai. This score included 11 sixes and 13 fours. He played this match on behalf of the Hindus against A.R. Gilligan's M.C.C.

C.K. Naidu holds the record of hitting the maximum number of sixes by a foreign player in a particular season in England. In 1932, Naidu played an outstanding game and hit 32 sixes.

Nevertheless his international cricket career was short- lived. He played only seven Test matches, but managed to make a name for himself in the Indian cricket world. For his achievement, the Government of India honoured him with a Padma Bhushan, which is the third biggest national award of the country.

He passed away on 14th November 1967 at Indore, Madhya Pradesh.

Achievements

- ☆ *C.K. Naidu was the first cricket Test captain of India.*
- ☆ *He was declared 'Cricketer of the Year' by Wisden in 1933.*
- ☆ *He was India's first cricketer to be honoured with the Padma Bhushan in 1956.*
- ☆ *He participated in 26 'A' level matches and scored 1,618 runs with an average of 40.45 and took 65 wickets.*
- ☆ *In 1926-27, while playing on behalf of the Hindus in Mumbai, he scored 153 runs in 187 balls in 100 minutes which included 11 sixes and 13 fours.*

Cricket

Diana Idulji

Birth: 26th January 1956

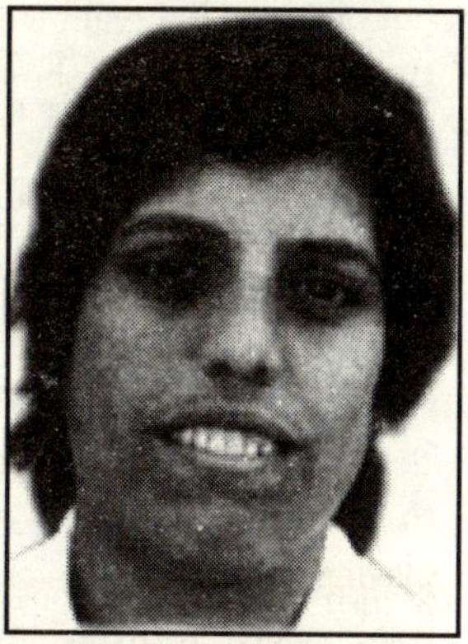

Diana Idulji grew up with Indian women's cricket. The first ever international women's match in India was played against Australia in 1975 and Diana was a member of the Indian women's team. It was her first match in which she took six wickets for a mere 48 runs and scored an unbeaten 48 runs. The beginning of her cricketing career was of great importance and remained so for the next 20 years.

Diana Idulji was born in Mumbai on 26th January 1956. She was extremely fond of sports since her childhood. She grew up playing with the boys in the Railway colony. At the national junior level, she played table-tennis and basketball but later got associated with cricket. For some time she was with the camp, where Lala Amarnath was the coach. Afterwards she joined the Mafatlal Nirlon camp and learnt to play cricket.

Diana is known as an all-rounder. Her left arm spin was excellent and many a times she was declared the best bowler, so much so that she was often called the 'Bishen Singh Bedi' of women's cricket. Her record of taking the maximum number of wickets in women's Test cricket remains unbeaten. She has taken 87 wickets in 23 matches.

Diana has been associated with Indian women's cricket right from its early days and she has seen it evolve from then to its present form. In 1971, Mrs. Aloo Bannerjee started the first women's cricket club called Albees where Diana watched the first ever women's cricket take roots in 1973. Officially the Women's Cricket Association was inaugurated and she became its member. The first championship match was held in 1974 at Pune. The Bombay team was the winner of the competition and Diana was a member of the team.

After this Diana participated in 21 National Championship matches out of which her team won 14 times. She played for the Bombay team six times and 11 times she represented the Railways. She played for 22 continuous years for the Indian team and participated against England, New Zealand, Australia, Holland, West Indies, Denmark and Ireland.

She played thrice in the World Cup matches wherein twice she captained the team. Diana was a member of the Indian team which won the series against West Indies in 1976.

It will not be wrong to say that Indian women's cricket is indebted to Diana. The Indian Women's Cricket Association set an example by playing a benefit match for Diana. This was the first time a woman cricketer was honoured with the 'Shivaji Chhatrapati Award'. In 1983, she was bestowed the Arjuna Award. In 1991, she was awarded the 'Maharashtra Gaurav' award.

Achievements

- ☆ *Diana is a well-known all-rounder in women's cricket.*
- ☆ *She was selected many times for her excellent bowling.*
- ☆ *She holds the record for taking the highest number of wickets in the women's Test cricket.*
- ☆ *She played the first international women's cricket Test match from the Indian side in 1975 against Australia.*
- ☆ *In her first Test match in 1975 she made an unbeaten 48 runs and took six wickets after giving 48 runs.*
- ☆ *She participated in 21 National Championship matches out of which her team won 14 times.*
- ☆ *She played thrice in the World Cup matches wherein twice she also captained the team.*
- ☆ *In 1979 she was honoured with the 'Shivaji Chhatrapati Award' by the Maharashtra government.*
- ☆ *In 1983, Diana was bestowed the Arjuna Award.*
- ☆ *In 1991, she was awarded the 'Maharashtra Gaurav' award.*

Cricket

Irapalli Prasanna

Date of Birth: 22nd May 1940

In the 1970s, Prasanna was an important player in the Indian cricket team. His full name is Irapalli Anatharao Srinivasa Prasanna. He has been a right-handed batsman and was one among the spin quartet. Despite his short height, he was an expert bowler and bowled out batsmen with great ease.

An important member of the spectacular quartet, Irapalli Prasanna was instrumental in taking 25 wickets in four Tests and in recording the first overseas success for India. India won the series against New Zealand in 1967-68.

Prasanna was born on 22nd May 1940 at Bengaluru, Karnataka. Apart from being a member of the Indian cricket team, he was also a member of the Karnataka and Mysore cricket teams. He started his cricketing career against West Indies in 1960-61. After playing in a few Test matches, he took a break of four years to complete his education and get his engineering degree.

Prasanna was re-inducted into the Indian cricket team in 1966 and played against the West Indies in India. In this series, he played, alongwith Chandrashekhar and a newcomer, Bishan Singh Bedi, against a strong West Indian team. Prasanna played cricket under the captaincy of Tiger Pataudi and his best attacking performance was in the international tour against Australia and New Zealand. In the match against New Zealand, India was able to register its first overseas victory because of Prasanna's contribution.

In 1970-71 during the West Indies tour by India, Prasanna played under the captaincy of Ajit Wadekar. However, Prasanna got injured during the tour and Venkataraghavan took his place in the team. Subsequently, Prasanna kept drifting away from the team and Venkataraghavan took over from him. Even though Venkataraghavan and Prasanna had contrasting styles of bowling, it was not possible to accommodate four spinners in the team. So keeping in mind Venkataraghavan's fielding abilities, and his better batting skills, he was given a place in the team instead of Prasanna.

Achievements

- ☆ *Prasanna was one among the famous spectacular quartet.*
- ☆ *He was instrumental in taking 25 wickets in four Tests and in recording the first overseas success for India in the match against New Zealand in 1967-68.*
- ☆ *He displayed a brilliant performance in the eight-Test match international tour against Australia and New Zealand in 1967.*
- ☆ *He bowled the batsmen with ease.*

Cricket

Jhoolan Goswami

Date of Birth: 25th November 1983

The name of Jhoolan Goswami flashed in the headlines of all the major newspapers when she was chosen by ICC as the 'Woman Cricketer of the Year' in September 2007, on account of being the fastest bowler in the world. When Jhoolan's name was announced in the ICC prize ceremony at Johannesburg in South Africa, people could not help being astonished at her reaching a place where no Indian male cricketer had managed to reach so far.

Jhoolan Goswami was born on 25th November 1983 in a suburban township called Chakdah in Nadia district of West Bengal. The 5'11" tall Jhoolan was selected by ICC the 'Woman Cricketer of the Year' at the age of 24 years. Her father Nishit Goswami works in the Indian Airlines. Jhoolan is fondly called Babul at home.

Jhoolan used to play cricket with the boys of the neighbourhood since her childhood days. However, surprisingly at that time, the boys never used to let her bowl as her bowling speed was so slow that they used to hit fours and sixes in a row. The boys often made fun of her bowling and this very fact inspired her to become a bowler. After that she started paying a lot of attention to her bowling style. She was trained at the MRF Academy to polish her skills and took a few tips from Dennis Lilee as well. Her efforts did not go waste and gradually with practice and determination, her bowling speed increased to 120 mph, which incidentally is the speed for many men's teams.

Her bowling is focused and accurate and her run up has acquired finesse. Jhoolan never forgets to acknowledge the important role her coach, Swapan Sandhu, played in her career. After being chosen the 'Woman Cricketer of the Year', Jhoolan said, "My parents were worried about me. At that time my coach Swapan Sandhu made them understand that even women's cricket is becoming popular these days. Women sportspersons used to go to nearby Kolkata to play cricket. I was 13 years of age when I went to play in Kolkata with the permission of my parents. Whatever I am today is due to my coach."

Jhoolan was unable to sit for her Class XII exams four times in a row because of her cricket. She wants to pass this exam in 2008, come what may.

Once Jhoolan was watching the World Cup finals between New Zealand and Australia in the cold winter months of December at Eden Gardens in India. She was so excited by this game that she decided then and there that one day she would definitely play for India. When this fastest woman bowler of the world received the 'Woman Cricketer of the Year' award from the hands of the then captain of the men's Indian team, Mahendra Singh Dhoni, Jhoolan felt as if her dream had been realised not once, but twice.

Jhoolan's journey has not been an easy one. She has reached this position due to hard work and determination. She used to wake up at 4.30 a.m. and travel from Nadia to Vivekananda Park in South Kolkata in a local train, where her coach, Swapan Sandhu used to give training to her. Once when she reached late in the night after playing cricket, her mother made her stand outside the house for many hours. Even her father was not much in favour of her playing cricket.

Today Jhoolan is also known as 'Nadia Express'. This talented bowler, who also won the cricket Oscar, has played very important roles on many occasions to make India win matches. When she won this award, she left the popular favourites like Australian batsperson Liza Sthalaker and English cricketer Claire Taylor behind.

Jhoolan played her first Test match in Lucknow against England on 14-17th January 2002 when she was only 18 years old. She had played in eight Test matches till 2007 and has taken about 33 wickets. She took 96 wickets in 79 one-day international matches.

One of Jhoolan's memorable matches has been the one against England when India won the match. In one of the matches at Taunton, in Leicester, Jhoolan took 10 wickets for 78 runs (33 runs for five wickets and 45 runs for five wickets). The English cricketers had never faced such fast-paced bowling by any Indian bowler; however the British media criticised Jhoolan for her bowling style. Not only did India manage to win the series, but Jhoolan was given the 'Player of the Series' award for her stellar performance.

In Jhoolan's words, "Not many people are aware of the existence of women's cricket. But today thankfully, because of media coverage, people in India are getting to know about women's cricket."

Despite the fact that India lost against Australia in the 2005 World Cup, Jhoolan's performance in the match secured vice-captaincy for her.

In the one-day international matches, Jhoolan secured the second position in Indian women's cricket. Nitu David has more wickets (130 wickets) to her credit than Jhoolan, but she has taken retirement from active cricket. Jhoolan had also played for the Asian team in the Afro-Asian Tournament held in June 2007.

Achievements

- ☆ *Jhoolan Goswami is the only Indian cricketer to receive an individual award from the ICC.*
- ☆ *She bowls at the rate of 120 kmph, which is by far the highest in world women's cricket. Therefore, she has been described as the fastest bowler by ICC.*
- ☆ *She was chosen 'Woman Cricketer of the Year' in September 2007. This award is similar to winning an Oscar in cricket.*
- ☆ *She has played in eight Test matches, taken about 33 wickets and made 540 runs.*

- ☆ *She has taken 96 wickets in 79 one-day international matches and has the honour of reaching the second position in the Indian women's cricket.*
- ☆ *She has made 1994 runs in 79 one-day international matches.*
- ☆ *She was given the 'Special Prize' at the Castrol Awards Ceremony in Mumbai in 2006.*

Cricket

Kapil Dev

Date of Birth: 6th January 1959

In the history of cricket, Kapil Dev is considered a great all-rounder. As the captain of the Indian cricket team, he scored many victories for India. In 1983, India created history by winning the World Cup under the captaincy of Kapil Dev. Three years later, India also won the series against England under his captaincy.

Kapil Dev has been an efficient medium-pace bowler, middle-order hard-hitting batsman, fielder and an excellent captain. He can very well be called a complete cricketer.

Born on 6th January 1959, at Chandigarh, Kapil's full name is Kapil Dev Ramlal Nikhanj. He was a right-handed batsman and a fast right-handed medium-pace bowler.

Kapil Dev is the only Indian cricketer to be awarded three national awards. In 1979-80, he was bestowed the Arjuna Award. He was also given Padma Shri and in 1991 honoured with the Padma Bhushan.

Till the late 1970s there was no good opening bowler in the Indian cricket team. This was the time when Kapil made his entry into Indian cricket. He proved to be an invaluable right-handed medium pacer and the best hitter of his times. He achieved tremendous success as an excellent batsman with the right human sensitivities.

Due to the number of runs he had scored and the record set up, he has been very popular among his admirers. He has been the darling of the media. Many a times, he has completely changed the outcome of a match with his batting and bowling, because of which he is called a 'legendary cricketer'.

Kapil Dev made his entry into cricket when he was just 19 years old, when in 1975, playing his very first match in Ranji Trophy for Haryana, he took six wickets, conceding only 37 runs. His early years in cricket won him great name with his performance of 36 runs and eight wickets against Jammu and Kashmir, and seven wickets for 20 runs against Bengal.

Kapil Dev acquired his initial education at D.A.V. School, and thereafter his higher studies at D.A.V. College, Chandigarh. As captain of the Haryana team, he played in 28 Ranji Trophy matches. His highest score was 193 against Punjab in 1979-80. He represented North Zone in Duleep trophy and in 1982-83 he won all the three matches and created a record. He is one of the four all-rounders of world repute. The rest of the three all-rounders are Hadlee, Botham and Imran.

Kapil Dev gave a new direction to Indian cricket and received appreciation and popularity for himself in the process. In 1983, under his captaincy, the Indian cricket team won the World Cup. These are his eternal achievements.

As a batsman, he touched new heights in cricket. In Tunbridgewales, England, when playing against Zimbabwe, he made an unbeaten 175 runs and got loud accolades for the same. In the 1983 World Cup, he took five wickets for 16 runs in 60 overs, and helped the team amass a total of 266 runs. He made an unbeaten 175 runs. Playing against England in 1990, batting to Eddie Hemmings, he hit four sixes in order to avert a follow-on, and enthralled the audience. He holds a record for taking 434 wickets. Kapil Dev is a cricketer who has not only scored 5,248 runs but also taken 400 wickets. Kapil Dev also has the distinction of playing the maximum number of Test matches. Of late, he served as a coach of the Indian cricket team.

In the year 2002, Kapil Dev was chosen the 'Indian Player of the Century' by Wisden (London). A 35-member selection committee chose Kapil Dev for the award, leaving behind Sunil Gavaskar and Sachin Tendulkar. They were of the view that Kapil Dev had the ability to single-handedly change the result of the match. His immense skills in bowling, batting, fielding and his captaincy could change the fate of any match. No other cricketer can boast of possessing so many positive cricketing qualities.

Kapil Dev played his first Test match against Pakistan in the year 1978-79, when he was just 19-years old. He played in 161 Tests and in 225 one-dayers in his 16-year cricket career. He was given the 'Cricketer of the Year' award by Wisden in 1986.

Kapil Dev's last one-day match between India and West Indies was played in Haryana in 1994-95, after which he took retirement from active cricket.

Achievements

- ☆ *Kapil Dev is the first cricketer to win three national awards. In 1979-80, he was awarded the Arjuna Award, the Padma Shri and in 1991, he was honoured with the title of Padma Bhushan.*
- ☆ *He was the captain of the Indian cricket team which won the World Cup in 1983.*
- ☆ *He has the distinction of taking 434 wickets.*
- ☆ *Playing for the Ranji Trophy at Rohtak, Haryana in 1975, he took six wickets for just 19 runs, when he was just 17-years old. He was playing on behalf of Haryana against Punjab.*
- ☆ *Against Jammu and Kashmir, he took eight wickets for 39 runs and against Bengal he took seven wickets for 20 runs.*
- ☆ *He made his highest score of 193 runs in 1979-80 while playing against Punjab.*
- ☆ *His incredible performance was in 1978 against Pakistan at Karachi where he made 59 runs in 48 balls; the runs consisted of two sixes and eight fours.*
- ☆ *He is ranked as one of the four best all-rounders of cricket.*
- ☆ *He is one Indian cricketer who holds the unique record of taking 400 wickets in first-class matches.*

Cricket

Lala Amarnath

Date of Birth: 11th September 1911

Lala Amarnath is the first Indian cricketer to score a century in a Test match on his debut. He was also the first Test captain of Independent India. His full name is Amarnath Bhardwaj, but he is popularly known as Lala Amarnath to the world.

India won its first Test series under the captaincy of Lala Amarnath. This series was played against Pakistan in 1952.

Lala Amarnath was born on 11th September 1911 in Kapurthala, Punjab. He used to play for Gujarat Hindus, Maharaja Patiala XI, the Railways, Uttar Pradesh and the Indian Test teams.

Lala Amarnath's name came into limelight when he scored a fantastic century in 1933 at Bombay Gymkhana while playing against England. This was his debut Test match. After scoring this Test century, he displayed the attacking phase of an Indian cricketer which was unconventional at that time. In this match when two Indian batsmen were out for 21 runs, Lala Amarnath not only took the situation under his control but guided the team to a comfortable position when he made 100 runs in 117 minutes. He was extremely famous for making the fastest runs in an unexpected scenario.

Lala Amarnath was an extremely independent and outspoken personality. In 1936 he was sent back from the England tour because of his outspoken nature as he had said something against the captain at that time — the captain happened to be the Maharajkumar of Vijyanagaram.

Lala Amarnath lost his most important years because of the Second

World War. Two other cricketers also lost their precious cricketing years due to this war.

Lala Amarnath played his fourth Test match after an interval of 13 years in 1946 in England. He was also the first Test captain of Independent India. In 1947 the Test matches were played in Australia under his captaincy. After this Lala went on to play with the first-grade teams of the world, displaying his ability to play outstanding shots.

During 1951-52, as he did not play well against England, he had to lose his captaincy because of his bad form. In 1952-53 he was appointed captain again for playing the series against Pakistan and rightly so as India won the series.

Lala Amarnath played a total of 24 Test matches in which he made 878 runs with an average of 24.38. He also hit a century in his first Test match which was also his highest score.

Lala Amarnath left for his heavenly abode on 5th August 2000 in New Delhi.

Achievements

- ☆ *Lala Amarnath is the first Indian cricketer to score a century in a Test match.*
- ☆ *He was the first Indian cricketer to score a century in a Test match in his debut.*
- ☆ *He was also the first Test captain of cricket in Independent India.*
- ☆ *India won its first Test series under his captaincy in a match played against Pakistan in 1952.*
- ☆ *He played a total of 24 Test matches in which he scored 878 runs.*

Cricket

Mahendra Singh Dhoni

Date of Birth: 7th July 1981

Mahendra Singh Dhoni scored 183 runs in a one-day international match and created a record for scoring the highest number of runs as a wicket-keeper. The record for the highest number of sixes (10 in all) by a wicket-keeper also goes to the credit of Dhoni. He holds the highest average among the wicket-keepers.

Mahendra Singh Dhoni is perhaps the only wicket-keeper in Indian cricket to carve a place in the hearts of millions of people with his new records and capability to make quick runs.

Mahendra Singh Dhoni was born on 7th July 1981 at Ranchi, Jharkhand (at that time Ranchi was part of the state of Bihar). He has been born and brought up in Ranchi. He is called Dhoni by his friends, whereas his pet name is Mahi.

Mahendra Singh Dhoni started his first-class cricketing career in 1999-2000 and continued for another five years. After that he was selected to play in the international team against Bangladesh on 23rd December 2004. However, Dhoni was declared run-out on the very first ball in this match which was played in Bangladesh.

Luck did not favour him in the first four matches. He played his fifth match against Pakistan in Visakhapatnam in 2005. Dhoni made a whopping 148 runs in 123 balls in this match. At that time it was the highest number of runs made by an Indian wicket-keeper. This score included 15 fours and four sixes. He was given the 'Man of the Match' award for the first time for his performance in this match.

In this very year, Dhoni went on to break his own record and made

183 runs in 145 balls against Sri Lanka in the one-day international match at Jaipur on 31st October 2005. It was the highest number of runs scored by a wicket-keeper in the world. Prior to this, Adam Gilchrist held the record of scoring the highest number of runs — 172 runs.

Dhoni was selected in the Indian Test team because of his exemplary performance in the one-day international matches. He played his first Test match against Sri Lanka in Chennai. Here too Dhoni proved lucky in his fifth match and managed to score 148 runs against Pakistan. His winning streak continued till the end of 2005 and he was given the number one ranking in the ICC (one-day) for 2005-2006.

Mahendra Singh Dhoni was a football goal-keeper before stepping into cricket. It is said that he is extremely fond of milk and consumes close to four litres of milk in a day. However, when asked about the same, though he agreed that he likes milk, he denied having more than one litre of milk per day. He has also acquired a poster-boy status among girls due to his long tresses and good looks.

2006 was not a good year for Dhoni. India had to suffer defeat in the ICC Champions Trophy, DLF Cup, and also in the matches played against the West Indies and South Africa. In the 2007 World Cup too, India could not go beyond the first round. In this Dhoni was out for a duck.

In the one-day international series against Bangladesh after the World Cup, Dhoni was awarded the 'Man of the Series' prize. Dhoni was appointed vice-captain of the Indian team for the one-day international series against England during the tour. During the 2008 tour of Australia, he was again named the captain of the 'Twenty-Twenty' team but he did not prove successful here.

The year 2007 saw the birth of a new format in cricket, which was the 'Twenty-Twenty' series (This constitutes a total of 20 overs bowled by each side and the match gets over in a short time. The younger players too stand a chance to make quick runs.). Many countries of the world took part in this 'Twenty-Twenty' series World Cup which was held at Johannesburg and Durban in South Africa. Mahendra Singh Dhoni was the captain of the Indian team which reached the finals after defeating

Australia. India was pitted against its favourite rival Pakistan in the finals. Dhoni's team defeated Pakistan by five runs and lifted the 'Twenty-Twenty' series World Cup. India won the 2007 World Cup after the 1983 victory almost after a 24-year gap under the leadership of Mahendra Singh Dhoni. In recognition of the same, a number of prizes and rewards were given to Dhoni and his teammates.

However, he continues to enjoy popularity due to his attacking and energetic batting. He loves listening to the songs of Lata Mangeshkar and Kishore Kumar and enjoys cycling. This right-handed batsman also loves to play badminton and computer games in addition to cricket.

Achievements

☆ *Dhoni was given the award of 'Man of the Match' for the first time for his 148-run performance against Pakistan on 5th April 2005.*

☆ *His 148 runs against Pakistan were the highest number of runs ever made by an Indian wicket-keeper.*

☆ *He went on to break his own record and made 183 runs in 145 balls against Sri Lanka in the one-day international match at Jaipur on 31st October 2005. It was the highest number of runs made by a wicket-keeper in the world. He set a world record at this time and was chosen as the 'Man of the Match'.*

☆ *On 13th February 2006, he made an unbeaten 72 runs and was chosen as the 'Man of the Match'.*

☆ *On 16th April 2006, he secured the second position in the ICC ranking.*

☆ *He is the first Indian to hit 10 sixes in a one-day international match.*

☆ *He set a record by hitting 15 fours and 10 sixes, making it a total of 120 runs.*

☆ *He is the first Indian to get the number one ranking from the ICC.*

☆ *He was chosen the 'Youth Icon' by MTV, Pepsi and NDTV in 2006.*

Mansur Ali Khan Pataudi

Date of Birth: 5th January 1941

Mansur Ali Khan Pataudi is a very well-known name in the world of cricket. He happens to be the youngest captain ever to lead his team in Test cricket. He hails from the royal Pataudi lineage and was appointed the captain of the Indian cricket team at the young age of 21 years. At that time all the other members of the team were older to him.

Mansur Ali Khan Pataudi was born on 5th January 1941 in Bhopal, which was the capital of the state of Madhya Pradesh. He is also known to the world as 'Nawab Pataudi Junior' and also as 'Tiger Pataudi'. He was inspired to play cricket by his father, Iftikhar Ali Khan, also known as 'Nawab Pataudi Senior' who happened to be an ardent cricket lover. Iftikhar Ali Khan had learnt the game in England and represented the country in Test matches. Therafter he returned to India and led the Indian team in 1946.

Mansur Ali Khan too started learning cricket in England. He had his schooling and college education in England and captained the team in Oxford University. He is the only Indian to have captained the Oxford University cricket team. Subsequently he joined the Sussex county team and captained it 23 times.

Mansur Ali Khan's cricketing career graph would have shot up much higher had he not injured his one eye severely in a car accident in England in 1961. Even after such a major accident, he didn't lose heart and in the same year played his first Test match between India and England. After that he progressed ahead in his efforts and proved himself to be an extremely outstanding batsman. He was indeed the best batsman of his time.

He played his career's first high-level cricket match for the Ranji Trophy in 1960-61. Then four years later he changed his approach and decided to play for Hyderabad. In 1975-76 he played for Hyderabad. In his 16-year career of Ranji Trophy matches, he made 2,562 runs consisting of eight centuries, nine half-centuries and he was out for a duck seven times. In his farewell match in 1975-76, he made his best 198 runs.

Mansur Ali Khan participated six times in the Irani Cup matches. In the Duleep Trophy matches he represented both the North and South Zones.

He played his first Test match against England in 1961-62. He had played in 46 Test matches till 1974-75 in which he scored a total of 2,793 runs. In the Test matches he hit six centuries and his career's best knock was in 1963-64 against England in which he had made an unbeaten 203 runs.

Tiger Pataudi made his first tour of West Indies in 1962 and for which he was appointed the vice-captain of the team. The team captain at that time was Nari Contractor. But during the match, Nari Contractor fell down when hit by a bouncer and unexpectedly Pataudi was made the captain of the team. At that time Pataudi was only 21 years of age; all the other members of the team were older to him in age. Subsequently Mansur Ali Khan captained the team for many years.

He remained the captain till the tour of West Indies under the leadership of Clive Lloyd in 1974-75. Pataudi led the Indian team in 40 Test matches in which he captained the Indian team in 36 consecutive matches. In these matches, led by Pataudi, India won nine, lost 19 and out of these, 12 matches ended in a draw. Tiger Pataudi started the trend of aggressive batting in the Indian team. He played many fantastic innings that would forever be remembered in the history of Indian cricket.

His wife Sharmila Tagore, his son Saif Ali Khan and daughter Soha Ali Khan are associated with films while his daughter Saba Ali Khan is into designing.

Achievements

- ☆ *Mansur Ali Khan was one of the leading batsmen of his time.*
- ☆ *He became captain of the Indian cricket team at the young age of 21 years. At that time all the other members of the team were older to him in age.*
- ☆ *He captained the Oxford University team and became the only Indian to have done so.*
- ☆ *In his 16-year career of Ranji Trophy matches, he made 2,562 runs.*
- ☆ *He played in 46 Test matches and scored a total of 2,793 runs.*

Cricket

Mithali Raj

Date of Birth: 3rd December 1982

In 1999, when Mithali Raj, a woman cricketer, played her first international one-day match, she was bowled out for a duck. But in her cricketing career, due to sheer hard work, she went on to score the highest of 214 runs in international women's cricket. Mithali created this record in 2002 while playing against England.

Hyderabad's Mithali Raj broke Australia's Karen Bolton's record of 209 runs. In the match at Somerset, Mithali was very nervous as she had not scored well in that series. But her teammates encouraged her to go ahead as they thought that she was the best player of the team.

When Mithali had already scored 208 runs in the cricket ground, she was told that she was on the verge of breaking a record. Then Mithali continued to play with self-confidence and without panicking to score 214 runs. At that time she did not feel that she had done something unique.

Her coach Sampath Kumar made her toil hard so that she could move ahead. He made her practice whether it rained or snowed. When she was in Class XI, he saw her batting, Sampath Kumar had remarked, "Mithali is no ordinary girl. She is capable of becoming an international cricketer like Sachin."

During her childhood days, when her brother was being given cricket coaching, she too used to toss the ball whenever she got an opportunity to do so. At that time she was noticed by cricketer Jyoti Prasad, who also felt that she had the potential to be a good cricketer. Mithali's mother used to hear such things about her daughter right since her childhood.

Mithali feels that it is necessary to encourage women's cricket. Good sponsors have to come ahead for this. However, her parents gave her full-fledged support and encouraged her in every possible way because of which she has attained this position today. Her father Durai Raj was in the Air Force before he joined a bank. He had himself been a cricketer earlier, so he tried to encourage his daughter as best as he coluld. In fact he cut down on his expenses in order to meet her travel expenditure. Similarly, Mithali's mother, Leela Raj, too made a lot of sacrifices for her daughter. She quit her job so that she could be at home to look after her daughter when Mithali came back home, exhausted from her daily cricket practice.

Mithali touched the peak of success at the age of 19 years but she feels that she lost her childhood in playing sports. Being always engrossed in practice, she was unable to enjoy the mundane mischiefs of childhood. Maybe because of this lack in life that even after growing up, she sometimes asks her mother to feed her.

After establishing a record of 214 runs, one significant incident occurred when her mother came to the railway station to receive her. Prior to this her mother had never gone to receive her at the station.

Mithali loves to watch cricket on TV just to see Sachin play his magical shots so that she can also play like him. She loves Sachin's straight drives and square cuts and feels that Sachin's cricketing style is fantastic indeed.

Mithali's desire is that India should win the next women's World Cup and she should be the one to score the maximum number of runs.

The 22-year-old Mithali Raj was honoured with the Arjuna Award on 24th September 2003 for her achievements in cricket in the year 2003. On this occasion she confessed that there was a time when she had to choose between cricket and dance. Mithali used to miss many of her Bharatnatyam classes because of her cricket and so her dance teacher, in exasperation, had advised her to choose between dance and cricket.

After a gap of four years, the women's cricket team toured England again under the captaincy of Mithali Raj in July 2006. All the players had undergone rigorous training to play in the international one-day tournament. This was a step towards the integration of BCCI (Board of

Control for Cricket in India) and Women's Cricket Association of India.

Under the captaincy of Mithali Raj, the Indian team won the two-match series against England in the second Test by inflicting a five-wicket crushing defeat on England. In this way, under her captaincy, the Indian women's cricket team beat India on its own ground. This brought Mithali a lot of appreciation and credit for the victory.

Achievements

☆ *Mithali Raj is the captain of the Indian cricket team for women.*

☆ *In 1999, she, a woman cricketer, played her first international one-day match at Milton Keynes, Ireland and scored 114 runs.*

☆ *She played her first Test match in 2001-2002 against England in Lucknow.*

☆ *She gained fame by making 214 runs in the Test match against England in Tanton and made the highest run record in women's cricket.*

☆ *She was the captain of the Indian women's team in the women's World Cup, 2005.*

☆ *She is also an expert bowler.*

☆ *She was honoured with the Arjuna Award in 2003.*

☆ *She is a trained Bharatnatyam dancer and has given stage shows.*

☆ *She is employed in the Indian Railways.*

Polly Umrigar

Date of Birth: 28th March 1926
Died: 7th November 2006

The actual name of Polly Umrigar (as he is known to the cricketing world) is Pahelam Ratanji Umrigar. He had been an all-rounder with immense cricketing potential. He had the ability of facing any type of ball and made his mark as an extremely capable and good batsman.

Polly Umrigar was a cricketer who could swing the ball far away with ease and with equal ease bowl backwards. As a batsman, he was a very good striker and could handle any type of bowling.

He was born on 28th March 1926 at Sholapur in Maharashtra. He started his Test career at Mumbai in 1948-49. He played his first Test match against the West Indies. He played in 59 matches and scored 3,631 runs, which included two centuries and 14 half centuries. His average run rate was 42.22. His best has been a score of 223 runs, which he scored in November 1948 at Hyderabad against New Zealand. He was a medium-paced bowler. He took 35 wickets with his off-breaks. His best bowling feat was six wickets for 74 runs at an average of 42.08 runs.

Polly Umrigar captained the Indian team eight times — two his team won, two were lost and four were drawn. However, it is still a surprise as to why a talented sportsperson like Umrigar was not given good opportunities for captaincy. He was a wise captain and demonstrated his ability more than once. An example of his leadership quality was seen when he played against Pakistan at Delhi. He brought the match to an extremely interesting position. But, due to Pakistani player Mohammad Hussain's important decisions, the match ended in a draw; otherwise the match was more or less in favour of India. If the match had not been drawn, the credit for the victory in this match would have gone to Polly Umrigar.

Before the entry of Sunil Gavaskar in cricket, Polly Umrigar was the highest run maker. Umrigar performed extremely well in Ranji Trophy matches. He made 4,102 runs and took 138 wickets in the Ranji Trophy matches. He captained the Mumbai team also. In the Ranji Trophy matches, under his leadership, the team won five consecutive matches.

Polly Umrigar always performed well against the West Indies team, whether the match was played in India or outside. Once in a match in the West Indies, his splendid performance was so praised that he came to be called the Palm Tree-hitter. Actually before this in 1952, he had gone to England to play matches and played splendidly.

Polly Umrigar's last farewell match was in 1961-62 at Kingston, where he created history. It can be termed as the climax in his great career. In this match he made 56 and an unbeaten 172 runs. After a first normal over, in the second innings, he just gave away 17 runs in 16 overs, but West Indies won this match by 10 wickets. This match was hailed as Polly Umrigar's match. At that time, it was more than a decade since Polly Umrigar had started playing in Test matches.

In 1962, Polly Umrigar was honoured with the Padma Shri. He had played with almost 10 captains but nobody could ever point a finger to question Polly Umrigar's game. Even after taking retirement from cricket, he kept in touch with Indian cricket. He has been cricket selector and the Indian team's tour manager.

He breathed his last on 7th November 2006, at the age of 80 years.

Achievements

☆ *Polly Umrigar played 59 matches and scored 3,631 runs.*

☆ *In Test cricket, he scored 12 centuries and 14 half centuries with an average of 42.22.*

- ☆ *In 1946, at Hyderabad, while playing against New Zealand he made his highest 223 runs.*
- ☆ *He captained the Indian team eight times.*
- ☆ *He was named the 'Palm Tree-hitter' due to his splendid performance.*
- ☆ *He was awarded the Padma Shri in 1962.*

Cricket

Rahul Dravid

Birth: 11th January 1973

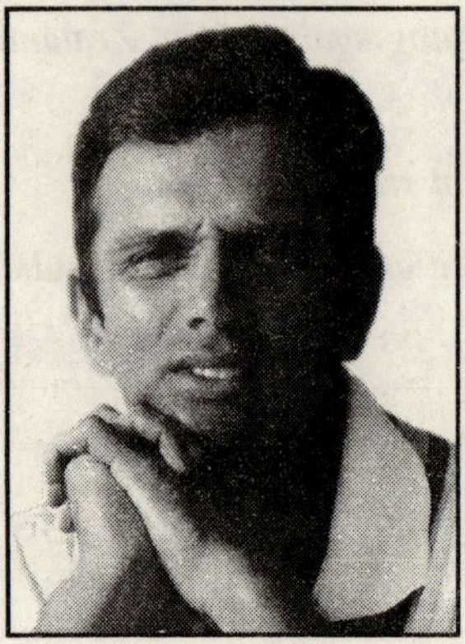

Rahul Dravid is considered an extremely important part of the Indian cricket team. His technique, ability to hold his position on the field for a long time and capability to score runs is widely appreciated. He has saved the Indian team in many difficult situations. He has been honoured with the Arjuna Award and has led the cricket team. His full name is Rahul Sharad Dravid.

Rahul Dravid was born on 11th January 1973 in Indore, Madhya Pradesh. He started playing cricket at the age of 12. He secured a place for himself in the under-15, under-17 and under-18 teams due to his excellent performance in the junior tournaments. Rahul Dravid completed his graduation from the St. Joseph College of Commerce.

Rahul started playing cricket in Ranji Trophy matches in 1990-1991 at Pune against Maharashtra. He was the youngest cricketer from Karnataka to make his first century in a Ranji Trophy match.

In 1995-1996 he secured a place for himself in the international team. He played his first international one-day match in 1996 at Singapore against Sri Lanka. In the 1999 World Cup in England, Dravid was the player to score the maximum number of runs. In the 1999 World Cup, Rahul Dravid along with Saurav Ganguly played the partnership innings with the highest number of runs in a wicket. They made a world record with the partnership of 318 runs.

Rahul Dravid is a player who personifies stability, concentration and efficiency. When the team requires a player to remain on the crease, he stabilises the team situation and when the team is in need of runs, he makes the requisite runs at that time. He has bailed the team out of difficult situations many times.

Rahul's cricketing capabilities are not confined to batting alone. He is also a right-handed off-break bowler and has also been a good wicket keeper. He maintains a calm behaviour in the tensest of situations. He is also known as 'Mr. Reliable' or 'The Wall' for these very reasons. His Test match average is around 50. Rahul Dravid's batting is extremely sound on technical grounds and which has got better with time.

Rahul Dravid was given the Arjuna Award by the Government of India. In the year 2000 he was selected the 'Cricketer of the Year' by Wisden. He is the 12th Indian to be given this honour. He was honoured with this award due to his outstanding performance in the 1999 World Cup in England.

Rahul Dravid is an extremely important player in the Indian team whom the audiences rejoice to watch. He is married to Dr. Vijeta Pendharkar.

Achievements

- ☆ *The Indian team has won a number of matches under the captaincy of Rahul Dravid.*
- ☆ *He made his first century in a Ranji Trophy match. He was the youngest cricketer from Karnataka to achieve this feat.*
- ☆ *In the 1999 World Cup, Rahul Dravid along with Saurav Ganguly played the partnership innings of 318 runs, which is a record as the highest number of runs in a partnership.*
- ☆ *He is a very good wicket-keeper.*
- ☆ *He has been honoured with the Arjuna Award.*
- ☆ *In the year 2000 he was also chosen the 'Cricketer of the Year' by Wisden.*

Cricket

Ranjit Sinhji

Date of Birth: 10th September 1872
Died: 2nd April 1933

Ranjit Sinhji was the first test match player. His full name was Kumar Shri Ranjit Sinhji. He started playing cricket in England. It was to honour him that the first-grade cricket tournament is named Ranji Trophy. The first Ranji Trophy Tournament was inaugurated by Maharaja Bhupinder Singh of Patiala in 1935.

Ranjit Sinhji was one of the best batsmen of India and was an Indian prince who also had the distinction of being the first Indian cricket player.

Ranjit Sinhji was born in western India in a small village called Sarodar in Kathiawad. Born in an affluent family on 10th September 1872 he went to Britain in 1891 to take admission in Trinity College, Cambridge. While studying in the final year, he joined the cricket 'Blue'. There he changed his name (nickname) to Smith and came to be known by this name only.

Later on, he became popular as Colonel, though formally he was addressed as Colonel His Highness Ranjit Sinhji Vibhaji or as Maharaja Jam Saheb of Nawanagar.

After completing his graduation, Ranjit Sinhji started playing county cricket for Sussex. Before this he had never played organised cricket, but in no time he became so good as to play in the final year in summer and won the 'Blue'. He started playing formal cricket at the Lord's in May 1895. Playing for Sussex he made 77 and 150 runs against the MCC.

He played his first Test match for England in 1896, thereby becoming the first Indian to play a cricket Test match.

In 1896, Ranjit Sinhji played this Test match from 16-18 July in

Manchester against Australia. In his first Test match he made 62 runs and 154 runs without being out. Thus, after W.G. Grace, he became the second ever player to make a century in his debut match against England. Ranjit Sinhji was an extremely skilled and fast batsman. He played Test matches between 1895 and 1905.

In 1897-98, on a tour to Australia, he made 1,157 runs, with an average of 60.89. At that time Sussex came to be associated with his name. His name and the name of his dear friend C.B. Fry used to be taken in the same breath most of the time.

Ranjit Sinhji made 1,000 runs in 10 consecutive domestic matches (in Sussex, England). He made more than 3,000 runs (between 1899 and 1900). He was also captain of the Sussex team (between 1899 and 1903).

In 1904, Ranjit Sinhji returned to India to fulfil his domestic responsibilities. Here he continued playing cricket but only for two years, in 1908 and 1912 when he scored more than 1,000 runs both the times. Afterwards he returned to Sussex on somebody's wrong advice. It was 1920 when he tried to play thrice, but by then he was almost 48 years of age and had put on a lot of weight. He had also lost one of his eyes in a shooting accident. Consequently, when he played his last match, he could only make 39 runs.

In March 1907, he assumed the role of Maharaja Jam Saheb of Nawanagar, away from the world of cricket. In this role also he was extremely popular and a generous administrator. His work was extremely noteworthy at the League of Nations and the Chamber of Princes during the World War. Sir Neville Cardus wrote this about Ranjit Sinhji: "After Ranjit Sinhji quit cricket, the game lost its sheen and glamour forever."

In 1897, Ranjit Sinhji wrote a book, *The Jubilee of Cricket*, which was considered as an extremely important book in the world of cricket. Later on, Ranjit Sinhji's nephew, K.S. Duleep Sinhji took to playing cricket for England.

Ranjit Sinhji played a total number of 15 Test matches and all these were on behalf of England. He played against Australia a number of times, scoring a total of 989 runs with an average of 44.95, which included two centuries and six half centuries. He was selected the 'Wisden Cricketer of the Year' in 1897.

Ranjit Sinhji was a genius in the world of cricket as he brought a new dimension in the game. Prior to him, cricketers used to play on front foot alone, but he played brilliant strokes even on back foot, making cuts in a new fashion.

On 2nd April 1933, he breathed his last at the Jamnagar Palace. At the time of his death he was a bit more than 60 years of age.

Achievements

- ☆ *India's premier first-class cricket tournament Ranji Trophy is named after Ranjit Sinhji in his honour.*
- ☆ *He was the first Test cricketer of India. He represented England, Cambridge University, London county and Sussex.*
- ☆ *In 1907, he was conferred the title of His Highness Ranjit Sinhji Vibhaji and Maharaja Jam Saheb of Nawanagar in legacy.*
- ☆ *He was selected the Wisden Cricketer of the Year in 1897.*
- ☆ *After W.G. Grace, he became the second player to make a century in his debut match.*
- ☆ *He introduced a number of techniques and nuances in the game.*
- ☆ *He played a total number of 15 Test matches.*
- ☆ *He wrote a book entitled,* The Jubilee of Cricket *which became a classic in the world of cricket.*

Cricket

Sachin Tendulkar

Date of Birth: 24th April 1973

Sachin Tendulkar has so many records to his credit that it is impossible for any other cricketer to reach his level in the near future. He became the first batsman to make 30,000 runs in international matches while playing against Sri Lanka in Baroda on 20th November 2009. He has an individual record of 12,970 runs in 162 Test matches and 17,178 runs in one-day matches. He is the only cricketer to be awarded the 'Rajiv Gandhi Khel Ratna' award.

"I saw him playing on TV and was struck by his technique. So I asked my wife to come and look at him play. Now I never saw myself play, but I feel this player is playing much the same as I used to play," said Don Bradman, the Australian batsman who is considered the world's greatest batsman.

Sachin Tendulkar has been a hero and role model for the manner in which he continues to play cricket, and conducts himself on and off the field. It seems just like yesterday that Sachin Tendulkar burst on the cricket scene — a callow 15-year old with curly hair, squeaky voice and a world record under his belt — to change the cricket scene forever.

He was almost 15 when he put on 664 runs with Vinod Kambli in a school cricket match in 1988. He was of small built and meek in nature, but he could wield the bat like a genius in cricket. Tendulkar is peerless.

His impact on the Indian psyche, however, goes far beyond his cricketing ability — the thousands of runs he has scored in the game.

Born on 24th April 1973 in Mumbai, Sachin Tendulkar played his debut Test match during 1989-90 at Karachi against Pakistan. He managed to score only 15 runs on the attacking deliveries of Waqar and Wasim Akram.

Like most 11-year olds, he was naughty and somewhat of a problem child for his parents. Then one day, he fell from a tree and his parents had a tough time. His elder brother, Ajit, hit upon the idea of sending him to cricket coaching classes, so all that bubbling energy would find a different outlet. His formal entry into the world of cricket was at the age of 12 when he played club cricket (Kanga League).

It was the beginning of an extraordinary journey. Nearly seventeen years on, that mischievous child became cricket's most feared and respected name in the world. And in a career embellished with awesome feats, Sachin Tendulkar added another century to his name. He became the 17th player in the history of the game to play his 100th Test match.

For a player who is arguably the best batsman of our times and among the finest the world has seen, the first step towards greatness, at the tender age of 16, was the most difficult period as he was very nervous at that time. He had a hard time in his first Test innings but he scored 59 runs in his second Test, which helped him gain confidence.

It won't be wrong to say that Tendulkar has managed to create for himself an image of self-effacing modesty and innocence despite his world-fame status. He is simple, modest and politically correct to a fault. The fame and riches seem to sit easy on him. He delves into his past and says in an emotional tone: "I owe all this to my father. He inculcated in me virtues of simplicity and honesty. He was a teacher of Marathi literature and would always drum into me that life has to be lived with sincerity. When he realised that cricket and not studies would be my life, he did not mind. All he told me was, 'Play the game fairly and give it your best. Don't shirk hard work'."

Sachin does not want to talk about the stand he took by stepping down from captaincy after the return of Mohammed Azharuddin to the team in the year 2000. He reluctantly says, "I don't want to say anything about it. I am going to play my 100th Test and let's talk only about cricket."

Sachin, the superstar, the genial genius, the maestro, whose spectacular stroke- making mesmerises rival captains and cricket contemporaries to drop everything and take notice, is an unassuming person off the field and still relishes the company of close friends like Vinod Kambli and Sanjay Manjrekar, with whom he had started his cricketing career in the Mumbai team. Soon after Sachin secured a place in the Mumbai XI, Sanjay was called to play for the national side. Of course, subsequently, they were to serve India together for years to come.

At the age of 29 years, Sachin played his 100th Test against England. On 5th September 2002, he became the youngest player to play his 100th Test at Oval.

Sachin has been the brand ambassador of many renowned brands like MRF Tyres, Today Ball Pen, Pepsi, Adidas, VISA Master Card and Fiat Palio. He is always in demand to endorse the big brands. In 1995, Sachin signed a seventy-and a-half lakh rupees ($ 7.5 million) contract with World Tel Company for a period of five years, making him the wealthiest cricketer of the world. Prior to this, cricketer Brian Lara had signed the contract for the highest amount of $ 1.2 million with a multinational company.

Sachin set a new record in 2009 when he became the only cricketer to make 30,000 runs in international matches. Apart from 12,970 runs in 162 Test matches, he holds a record of making 17,178 runs in 436 one-day matches.

His full name is Sachin Ramesh Tendulkar and he was christened Sachin by his parents, after their favourite music director Sachin Dev Burman. It is interesting that Sachin's first interview was given by his brother Ajit in an Iranian restaurant in Dadar due to lack of self-confidence in Sachin.

On the cricket field or in the playground of life, Sachin never falters from playing strokes of genius. But he is not averse to talking about his life outside cricket, which is not much, given that when he is not playing, he is honing his skills. He watches movies — his all-time favourite being *Sholay*. He is a great music buff and his favourite group is Dire Straits, yet he says he doesn't miss life outside cricket. Sachin is a devout devotee of Sai Baba and Lord Ganpati.

He aspired to be bowler when he started cricket and also when he joined Dennis Lilee to be coached at the MRF Pace Academy, he was advised to concentrate on batting instead.

Sachin has only added more and more runs to his tally with the passage of time. On 29th June 2007, he completed 15,000 runs while playing against South Africa in Belfast (Ireland). After reaching this total, Sachin became the first player of the world to reach such a high score. During the 2008 tour of Australia, he established a new record with his batting averages. On 20th November 2009 while playing against Sri Lanka at Baroda, Sachin with his individual score of 100 not-out became the first batsman to cross 30,000 runs thereby creating another world record.

Sachin became the first batsman in the history of one-day cricket to score 16,000 runs — a memorable feat which at best appears a distant dream for any other batsman to achieve. He is the only one Indian among the top 10 batsmen of India to get a ranking from the ICC (International Cricket Council). He seems set to stay at the pinnacle for a long time to come as Jayasuriya of Sri Lanka and former Pakistani captain Inzamam-ul Haq, who is third in the list with 11,739 runs, are not anywhere near to surpass the record. Tendulkar, who has scored 11,782 runs in Test cricket is just 172 runs away from displacing the legendary Brian Lara to emerge as the highest run-getter in the longer version of the game as well.

He married Dr. Anjali Mehta on 25th May 1995 and is a proud father of two kids – daughter Sara who means precious and son Arjun. Sachin had met Anjali in 1990.

Achievements

- ☆ *At the age of 12, Sachin made his debut in club cricket (Kanga League).*
- ☆ *After scoring his first hundred in Mumbai schools cricket tournament in 1986, he went on to score over 1,200 runs in school cricket the next year, including two triple centuries.*
- ☆ *He made 100 not out on his Ranji Trophy debut for Mumbai against Gujarat in 1988-89, thus becoming the youngest ever player to represent Mumbai.The next year he made 103 not out on his Irani Trophy debut and was selected for the tour of Pakistan. He later hit 159 in his debut in Duleep Trophy for West Zone against East Zone, thus becoming the only Indian cricketer to have scored centuries in his debut in all the three major domestic tournaments — Ranji, Duleep and Irani Trophies.*
- ☆ *He set a world record in cricket, when he and Vinod Kambli put on 664 runs for Shardashram against St Xavier's in the Harris Shield. He was on 326 not out and was voted the 'Best Cricketer of the Year' by the Bombay Cricket Association.*
- ☆ *At the age of 16, he made 103 not out in his Irani Trophy debut. He went on to become India's youngest player when he was picked for the Pakistan tour.*
- ☆ *In 1991, at the age of 18, Sachin became the first overseas player to represent Yorkshire and was voted 'Cricketer of the Year'.*
- ☆ *He became the youngest cricketer to play his 100th Test match at the age of 29 years.*
- ☆ *His first Test match was played in 1989.*
- ☆ *He was given the 'People's Choice Award' by Wisden, London.*
- ☆ *He is the most successful batsman of the world. On 20th November 2009, with the highest number of centuries to his*

credit, he became the cricketer with the highest – 17,178 runs in one-day cricket.

☆ *He became the vice-captain of the Indian team for the 1993-94 tour of Sri Lanka. He had captained India first against Australia in Delhi in 1996.*

☆ *He was also the first batsman ever to be dismissed by the third umpire on the second day of the first Test against South Africa in 1992.*

☆ *He played 84 consecutive Tests since his debut, before missing the Sri Lanka tour. That too was yet another world record.*

☆ *In 1995, Sachin signed a $ 7.5 million, five-year deal with World Tel. He surpassed Brian Lara's $ 1.2 million deal with a British company to become the world's richest cricketer.*

☆ *He made his maiden Test century when he hit a match saving 119 not out against England at Old Trafford. He was the second youngest player to achieve this feat, after Pakistan's Mushtaq Mohammad.*

☆ *In 1992, at the age of 19, he became the youngest player in the world to make 1,000 runs in Test cricket during the tour of South Africa. He is also the first and only player to score as many as five hundreds in Tests before his 20th birthday.*

☆ *He had an unbelievable season in 1998-99, when he averaged 110.50 against Australia in Tests and one-dayers where he scored 995 runs in 11 innings with one double centuries, five centuries and two fifties. In the same season he bowled his career's best of five wickets for 32 runs against Australia; he completed 7,000 runs in one-dayers and equalled the world record of scoring the most number of centuries of Desmond Haynes by scoring his 17th.*

☆ *On 25th September 1998, Sachin, aged 25 years, set a world record when he scored his 18th one-day century agaist Zimbabwe in Bulawayo in his 191st innings and 198th match.*

- ☆ *In December 1998, he hit a sixer to complete a century in the second Test against New Zealand and equalled Sri Lankan Aravinda de Silva's record of reaching a century thrice with a sixer. He did it twice earlier in Nagpur — once against the West Indies in 1994-95 and second against England at Birmingham in 1996.*
- ☆ *In 2001, he passed another milestone during the third day of the second Test against Zimbabwe in Harare, when he surpassed Dilip Vengsarkar's tally of 6,868 runs to become India's second-highest Test run-getter.*
- ☆ *In August 2004, Sachin made his 69th half-century and came on the same platform as Pakistan's Inzamam-ul Haq of making the largest number of half centuries in one-day international matches. Sachin has 69 half centuries in 339 matches to his credit.*
- ☆ *He holds a world record for 45 centuries in one-day matches and 43 centuries in Test matches.*
- ☆ *With 17,178 runs in 436 matches, he is the player with the largest tally of runs in one-day international matches in the world.*
- ☆ *He broke Azharuddin's record of playing the largest number of matches in India with 339 matches till August 2004. Prior to this Azharuddin had participated in 334 one-day matches.*
- ☆ *He holds the record of winning the 'Man of the Match' award 50 times.*
- ☆ *On 10th December 2005, in Ferozeshah Kotla Ground in New Delhi, Sachin broke Sunil Gavaskar's record of the highest number of Test centuries with (34 centuries), his 35th against Sri Lanka. He also came at par with Gavaskar's record for playing 125 Test matches.*

- ☆ *He is the youngest player to score 10,000 runs in Test matches.*
- ☆ *He was given Wisden's 'People's Choice Award' in July 2002.*
- ☆ *He opened a new chapter in the record books in October 2002 when he became the first batsman to score 20,000 runs in the history of international cricket.*
- ☆ *He is considered an emperor in the advertising world. He broke all records when he signed a rupees 180-crore contract with Iconix in 2006 for a six-year period. A 100-crore rupee contract for five years was signed with him by World Tel prior to this.*
- ☆ *He scored 13,606 runs (till December 2005) in one-day matches.*
- ☆ *By May 2006, he had made 19,469 runs in 132 Tests and 14,146 runs in 362 one-day matches.*
- ☆ *He, at 57.99, has the highest average among those with 100 or more Tests. Miandad (52.57), Gavaskar (51.12) come next.*
- ☆ *He has made 14 centuries at home and 16 abroad but has been unable to score centuries in three countries — Pakistan, Zimbabwe and Bangladesh.*
- ☆ *He is the only cricketer to win the 'Rajiv Gandhi Khel Ratna' Award.*
- ☆ *On 29th June 2007, he completed 15,000 runs while playing against South Africa in Belfast (Ireland). After touching this number, Sachin became the first player of the world to reach such a high score.*

Saurav Ganguly

Date of Birth: 8th July 1972

Saurav Ganguly, who is also fondly known as Dada, has been one of the most successful captains of the Indian cricket team. He is an excellent left-handed batsman with lakhs of fans and followers across the country.

Cricket is the most popular sport of India — the popularity of the game surpasses distinctions and barriers of age, education, caste and gender. During a Test series or a one-day international match, cricket fans love to enjoy their favourite game on radio or television and sometimes even at the cost of their work at home or office.

It would only be appropriate and interesting to learn more about one of the most successful captains of the Indian cricket team. Saurav Ganguly's full name is Saurav Chandidas Ganguly. Born on 8th July 1972 at Kolkata, he is a medium-paced right-handed bowler. He played his first one-day match against the West Indies at Brisbane on 11th January 1992 and his first Test match against England at Lords Stadium in 1996.

His batting shows a complete amalgamation of strength and enthusiasm. He can play excellent shots on the off-side as well. Initially, there was grave criticism at his inclusion in the Test team. It was said that he was given a place in the team because of the quota system. But it was not long before Saurav silenced his critics by scoring a century in his first two Test innings. Also he didn't stop at this alone. He was also given the 'Man of the Series' award for taking the maximum number of wickets.

Initially, Saurav was thought suitable only for Test matches because of his inability to play on-side strokes. But he soon got over this weakness and in the 1997 Sahara Cup in Toronto, he carved a place for himself with his magnificent cricket against the Pakistani team. He performed a feat of making 75 runs in 75 balls and also of taking five wickets for only 16 runs. He also won the 'Man of the Match' award four times in Toronto and was also chosen the 'Man of the Series' for this very reason.

Saurav has played as an opening batsman a number of times alongwith Sachin Tendulkar. Saurav's main problem has always been running between the wickets. He believes in striking a four rather than taking ones and twos.

He was also chosen the 'Man of the Series' against Sri Lanka. He was declared the best batsman of the year in 1997 for making the highest number of runs during the year. India managed to score the highest number of 314 runs against Pakistan because of Saurav's century. His 252-run partnership with Tendulkar is the highest partnership record till date. Saurav and Tendulkar as opening batsman are the fourth most successful openers in the history of international one-day cricket.

Achievements

☆ *He was appointed captain of the Indian cricket team in February 2000.*

☆ *He was chosen the 'Man of the Series' in the five one-day series against New Zealand in November 1999.*

☆ *In the 1999 World Cup, while playing a one-day match against Sri Lanka, he put up a massive score of 183 and broke Kapil Dev's earlier record of 175 runs. This was the highest score made by any Indian player at that time.*

☆ *He was chosen the 'Man of the Series' in the Pepsi Cup in 1999. He made a score of 275 runs and took four wickets.*

☆ *He is among a few players to make a century and take four wickets in one match.*

☆ *He and Tendulkar as opening batsmen are the fourth most successful opening duo in the history of international one-day cricket.*

- ☆ *His 252-run partnership with Tendulkar is the highest partnership record till date.*
- ☆ *He was bestowed the Arjuna Award in 1998.*
- ☆ *He was given the 'Sportsperson of the Year' award in 1998.*
- ☆ *In 1997, he became the only player to make the highest run score in a one-day international match.*
- ☆ *In the Sahara Cup in 1997, he won the 'Man of the Match' award four times in Toronto and was also chosen the 'Man of the Series' for this very reason.*

Cricket

Sunil Gavaskar

Date of Birth: 10th July 1949

Sunil Gavaskar is counted as one of the greatest batsmen of the world. His full name is Sunil Manohar Gavaskar. Till today, Gavaskar is one such player who has made more than 1,000 runs in a calendar year and he performed this miracle not one but four times. Sunil Gavaskar set many world records and in the process broken a number of old records as well. He set a record for making the highest number of centuries (34 centuries) and became the world's first player to make 10,000 runs in Test cricket.

Sunil Gavaskar was born on 10th July 1949 at Mumbai, Maharashtra. His schooling and college education was in St. Xavier's School and St. Xavier's College respectively. He got tutored in cricket while playing for the Giles and Harris Shield Tournament.

He scored well in the Indian school tournaments while playing for the West Zone. He was given the J.C. Mukherji award for his good performance. Thereafter, even while studying in St. Xavier's College, he achieved great success in inter-university cricket. He joined the Dadar Union and played for the Vizzy Trophy. He was then invited to play for the Bombay team, and subsequently for the Irani Trophy and Ranji Trophy.

He set a number of world records and in the process broke a number of old records too. He made a record by making the highest number of centuries (34) and became the world's first ever cricketer to score 10,000 runs in Test cricket. Allan Border broke this record of Sunil Gavaskar later on.

Sunil Gavaskar is one such player even today who has made more than 1,000 runs in a calendar year and he performed this miracle not once, but four times.

He also holds the world record for making 1,984 runs in a year. From 17th October 1978 to 13th October 1979, he set a unique record of hitting two double centuries, six centuries and eight half centuries in his 1,984 runs.

This magnificent batsman who is also known as the 'Little Master', stands at a height of 5'4". He was a successful opener and used to strike at front foot and could play on both left and right side of the wicket.

He scored three consecutive centuries in Ranji Trophy and was selected to represent the country against the West Indies in 1971. He played his first Test match in the month of March at Queen's Park Oval in Trinidad's Port of Spain. The Indian team won against the West Indies for the first time solely due to Gavaskar's unbeaten 65 and 67 runs. He was the first Indian player to have reached such a high score in his first Test match. In this series, he made 116 and 64 unbeaten runs and 117 unbeaten runs in the innings apart from a total of 700 runs. He had made the maximum number of centuries against the West Indies and the highest against any particular team (West Indies).

Gavaskar took retirement from cricket after playing for India from 1970-1987 and making a number of records. Many of his records are unbeaten even till date.

Achievements

- ☆ *Sunil Gavaskar is one of the greatest batsmen of the world.*
- ☆ *He has set a number of records in the world of cricket.*
- ☆ *He set the record for making the highest number of 34 centuries.*
- ☆ *He became the world's first ever cricketer to score 10,000 runs in Test cricket.*
- ☆ *He is the only player to score three consecutive centuries in an innings.*
- ☆ *He remains one player till date to make more than 1,000 runs in a calendar year and he performed this miracle not once, but four times.*

- ☆ *He also holds the world record for making 1,984 runs in a year. He set a unique record from 17th October 1978 to 13th October 1979.*
- ☆ *He played 125 Test matches in which he made 10,122 runs including 34 centuries and 45 half centuries at an average of 51.12.*
- ☆ *He played 108 one-day international matches in which he scored 3,092 runs.*
- ☆ *He made 27 half centuries and one century in one-day international matches.*
- ☆ *He had scored the maximum number of centuries against the West Indies.*
- ☆ *He played a total of 125 Test matches and set a record for the highest 236 runs.*
- ☆ *He made a double century four times and scored 220 runs against the West Indies, 221 against England, 204 and 236 runs against the West Indies to set a world record of that period.*
- ☆ *He made a total of 10,122 runs.*
- ☆ *He scored 97, 91 and 96 runs against Pakistan, 90 against the West Indies and 90 runs against Australia.*
- ☆ *His total average of runs is 51.12.*
- ☆ *He scored a century thrice in both the innings. He is the only player to score 142 and 220 runs against the West Indies, 111 and 137 runs against Pakistan and 107 and 182 runs against the West Indies.*
- ☆ *He has scored 34 centuries in all.*
- ☆ *He has scored 45 half-centuries in all.*
- ☆ *He made 27 half-centuries and one century in one-day international matches and made 3,092 runs.*

Vijay Hazare

Date of Birth: 11th March 1915

Vijay Hazare is considered as India's finest batsman ever. He displayed his potential at the highest level for six years. India won the first Test match against England at Chennai under his .captaincy in 1952.

Vijay Hazare played at the highest level for six years between 1946 and 1952 during which he represented the country in 30 Test matches, scoring 2,192 runs at an impressive average of 47.65 run.

Hazare was born on 11th March 1915 at Sangli district in Maharashtra. He played for Maharashtra, Central India and Baroda teams on the domestic circuit. He batted as well as bowled as an effective right-arm medium pacer. He captured 20 wickets for 61 runs.

His first-class career was fabulous. His average in these matches was 58.38. He played 238 matches and scored 18,740 runs that included 60 centuries. The highlights of Vijay Hazare's first-class career were the two triple centuries he scored. He scored 316 not out and 309 runs — the latter was more memorable as it was out of a total of 387 runs.

Hazare scored seven centuries in Test matches — two of them in the same match against Australia at Adelaide in 1947-48. Two of his other centuries were scored in his first two Test matches as captain against England in 1951.

His had a marvellous wicket-taking ability that helped him take a whopping 595 wickets in first-class matches at an average of 24.61. He was an immensely talented batsman but proved unsuccessful as a captain for he achieved moderate success. He captained in 14 matches. India won just one Test match against England and lost five. The remaining eight matches ended in a draw.

Hazare was appointed chairman of the Indian Cricket Committee (ICC) in 1960. At that time Nari Contractor was the captain of Indian team. The Cricket Club of India honoured him for his good performances with the 'Lifetime Achievement Award' comprising a cash prize of Rs 25,000.

Achievements

- ☆ *Vijay Hazare captained the team that won the first Test match against England in 1952.*
- ☆ *He represented the country in 30 Test matches, scoring 2,192 runs at an average of 47.65 runs.*
- ☆ *He hit seven centuries, out of which two were against Australia in the same match in 1947-48.*
- ☆ *As an effective right-arm medium pacer, he captured 20 wickets for 61 runs a piece.*
- ☆ *In his first-class career, he scored 18,740 runs in 238 mathces.*
- ☆ *He scored 60 centuries in first-class matches at an average of 24.61.*
- ☆ *He captained the Indian cricket team 14 times.*
- ☆ *He was given the 'Lifetime Achievement Award' by the Cricket Club of India comprising a cash prize of Rs 25,000.*

Cricket

Vijay Merchant

Date of Birth: 12th October 1911
Died : 27th October 1987

Vijay Merchant, the veteran cricketer who belonged to the era of Don Bradman, enjoyed the same popularity in his time as Sachin Tendulkar does today. His full name was Vijay Singh Madhavji Merchant. His first-class career's batting average was second only to the incomparable Don Bradman. His average in these matches was 71.64.

The supreme yardstick in cricket for best batsmanship is Bradman and he was known as the 'emperor of cricket'. Ever since the Australian prodigy, since 1948 he had been heralded as the new Bradman. The West Indies player George Headley was known as Black Bradman. Although Sunil Gavaskar has carved many records and made changes in the Test record book, yet he is acknowledged a little lower. But if the figures count, Vijay Merchant with a first class average of 71.64 was next in line to Bradman.

Though Vijay Merchant's Test figures are very different, his Test average was only 47.72. On home pitches he amassed thousands of runs. On his two tours of England, although 10 years apart, he showed batsmanship of a rich class and made over 4,000 runs in the two combined tours.

In India's domestic competition like Ranji Trophy, he fared even better, averaging 98.75 runs in his 47 innings.

Vijay Singh Madhavji was born in a wealthy family on 12th October 1911 in Mumbai, Maharashtra. He became an outstanding college cricketer. When he was only 15-years old, he scored two centuries in a match. Reaching a height of 5" 7', he developed fine footwork and built a stroke repertoire featuring cuts, good drives and later in his career, the brilliant hook stroke.

He represented Hindus in the Bombay tournaments between 1929 and 1946 and Bombay in the Ranji Trophy from 1933 until his retirement in 1952. Among his 44 first-class matches, he scored 11 centuries. (The nine centuries in India were made at Brabourne Stadium.)

Once he scored 359 runs and was not out for nearly 11 hours in an innings against Maharashtra at Bombay in 1943-44. He made 371 runs with Rusi Modi for the sixth wicket and added 210 runs for the eighth wicket.

A year later, he added 373 runs with Modi for the third wicket against Western India. In seven consecutive Ranji Trophy matches Vijay Merchant scored six centuries between 1938-42.

Vijay Merchant played in 10 Test matches and made his highest score of 154 in the last match against England at Delhi in 1951-52. While fielding in this match, he sustained a shoulder injury, which was so serious that he was forced to retire immediately. His previous Test innings — five years earlier at the Oval in August 1946 included a century, i.e. 128 runs.

He often filmed many of his innings to study the results closely to find his mistakes. Although he was not coached in his early days, yet he was much influenced by the stylish batting of L.P. Rai. He played his first Test match in the home series in 1933-34. He made the highest score of 54 at Calcutta in his sixth innings.

In 1936 he toured England and topped the batting with 1,745 at an average of 51.32. In the Test at Manchester, Vijay Merchant scored 114 runs and Mushtaq made 112 runs. They made 203 runs for the first-wicket partnership. In the Lancashire match at Old Trafford, Merchant scored 135 and 77 runs by carrying his bat through both the innings. His success in 1936 earned him the 'Wisden of the Year' award.

He was vice-captain under Nawab of Pataudi (Senior) on the England tour in 1946. He made 2,385 runs, with an average of 74 runs, including seven centuries. He scored these runs against Lancashire and Sussex. In three Tests he scored 245 runs in five innings and in the last at Oval, he scored 128 runs before he was run out.

He missed the tours of Australia and West Indies on account of his poor health. Merchant played his last Test against England in 1951-52 and recorded his third century with his highest Test score of 154 at Delhi. An injury to his shoulder sustained on diving in the field led to his retirement. At that time he had just turned 40.

He played in 10 Tests and all of them against England, spread over 18 years and scored 859 runs. In 47 Ranji Trophy innings, he scored a century on 16 occasions, totalling 3,639 runs at the stupendous average of 98.75. In all first-class cricket matches, Vijay made over 13,000 runs at an average of 71 and took 65 wickets at an average of 31.87 with medium pace offspin bowling.

After retirement from active sports, he became an administrator, writer and broadcaster. As a Test selector, he was responsible for replacing Pataudi Junior with Wadekar as captain of India. He was involved in social work among the handicapped.

He died on 27th October 1987 in Mumbai at the age of 76 years due to heart attack.

Achievements

- ☆ *His first-class cricket career was extraordinary. His batting average of 71.46 runs is second to cricket king, Don Bradman.*
- ☆ *He played only 10 Test matches in which his highest score was 154 which was made in 1951-52 against England at Delhi.*
- ☆ *During his two tours of England, with a gap of 10 years, he made more than 4,000 runs.*
- ☆ *He scored 44 centuries in first-class matches and more than 200 runs 11 times.*
- ☆ *Once he was not out with at 359 runs to his credit.*
- ☆ *He was selected 'Wisden Cricketer of the Year' in 1937.*

Cricket

Vinoo Mankad

Date of Birth: 12th April 1917
Died : 21st August 1978

In his life, Mulvantrai Mankad was affectionately known by his nickname Vinoo. His full name was Mulvantrai Himmatlal Mankad and he set a record by scoring 231 runs with Pankaj Roy to put on 413 runs in the first-wicket partnership. This match was played against New Zealand in 1956. He is one of the only three players to have batted on all 11 positions from one to eleven during his Test career. He was selected 'Wisden Cricketer of the Year' in 1947.

Vinoo Mankad was born on 12th April 1917 in Jamnagar, Gujarat. He played mainly for India, Bengal, Gujarat, Hindus, Maharashtra, Mumbai, Nawanagar, Rajasthan and Western India teams.

He was one of the greatest all-rounders that India has ever produced. He was a right-handed batsman and slow left-arm orthodox bowler. He played 44 Test matches between 1946 and 1959. He scored five centuries with his best score was of 231 runs. He took five wickets eight times and took eight wickets twice in an inning.

His greatest performance was against England at Lords in 1952. In the first innings, he was the top scorer with 72 runs. In the second inning also, he was the top scorer again with 184 runs in an Indian total of 378 and he bowled 31 overs the same day. In this match Mankad bowled 97 overs. He took five wickets for 196 runs. Though England won this match, yet Mankad's all round performance was appreciated very much. He was the first player in more than 30 years to score a 100 (century) and take five wickets in the same Test match and the first Indian to achieve this feat.

His first-class career started in 1935, but he came into prominence when he played against Lord Tennyson's team in India in 1937-38. With a batting average, in the unofficial Tests, of 62.66 and bowling average of 14.53, he headed both the averages. Tennyson said about him that he would certainly get a place in World XI team.

In 1946, he scored 1,120 runs for India in England and took 129 wickets. He remains the only Indian ever to have accomplished this feat. He played his first Test against England at Lords in June 1946.

In 1947, Vinoo Mankad went to England for League cricket and remained available in India to play cricket during the winter. When the Indian team went to England in 1952, he was allowed to play in Test matches only. Indeed the Lords Test was his first first-class match.

In 1952, Vinoo played another memorable match. This was against England and it was played at Chennai. He took eight wickets for 55 runs in England's first inning and four wickets for 53 runs in the second inning, thus helping India defeat England for the first time in a Test match.

In 1956, Vinoo hit 231 runs against New Zealand at Chennai. He established a world record with Pankaj Roy for the opening partnership of 413 runs, which stands till today. His score of 231 runs was a Test record for India at that time and remained so, till it was broken by Sunil Gavaskar in 1983. His average in this series was 105.

He captained the Indian team against Pakistan in 1954-55. In his first-class career, he scored 11,480 runs at an average of 34.78 and took 774 wickets at the average of 24.60. His first-class career ended in 1962.

As a batsman, Mankad had great power of concentration and his defence was strong. His record stand with Pankaj Roy entailed standing on the crease for eight hours. As a bowler, he was a slow left-arm bowler with the old-fashioned orthodox style. His bowling varied from his natural leg-break with a faster one, which earned him a lot of wickets.

He played his last Test match against West Indies at Delhi in February 1959. He left for his heavenly abode on 21th August 1978 at Mumbai, Maharashtra, at the age of 61.

Achievements

- ☆ *Mankad was an outstanding batsman and bowler. He was one of the greatest all-rounders of India.*
- ☆ *He is one of the only three cricketers to have batted in every position from one to eleven, during his Test career.*
- ☆ *In 1946, he scored 1,120 runs and took 129 wickets. He was the first player to have accomplished this feat.*
- ☆ *He scored 231 runs against New Zealand at Chennai in 1955-56. With Pankaj Roy, he made 213 runs to put in a total of 413 runs for the first wicket, a record for the Test.*
- ☆ *In 1952, he scored the highest in both the innings with 72 and 184 runs against England at Lords. He took five wickets also.*
- ☆ *In 1952, he played a memorable game when he took eight wickets for 55 runs in England's first inning and four for 63 runs in the second inning. Thus he played an important role in the victory of India.*
- ☆ *Vinoo took 162 wickets with an average of 31.47 in 44 Tests of his career. He took five wickets eight times.*
- ☆ *He was chosen 'Wisden Cricketer of the Year' in 1947.*

Virender Sehwag

Date of Birth: 20th October 1978

In the year 1999 a new star arose on the horizon of cricket and he caught everybody's attention. He was none other than Virender Sehwag. In his simple and inimitable style he started storming the pitch with his fours and sixes and it was only a matter of time before he had a large fan following on his side. On 4th December 2009 playing against Sri Lanka in Mumbai, Sehwag just missed making history as he got out at 293 runs, just 7 runs short of his third triple century. With two earlier triple centuries to his credit, Sehwag equals the record of Sir Don Bradman and Brian Lara.

Sehwag's full name is Virender Kishen Sehwag and people fondly address him as Veeru. He was born on 20th October 1978 at Najafgarh, near Delhi. His family has their own flourmill.

As he came from a business family, Virender Sehwag did not get cricket as a legacy. There was no one to guide him on how to hold a bat or to tell him how bright his future would be, if he were to succeed in cricket. His success is an example to those young cricket lovers who want to bring name and fame to their motherland by their success in cricket.

Sehwag actually started his career in 1999 against Pakistan by playing in the one-day match at Mohali. In the first Test match of his career against South Africa in 2001, he scored a century. In his initial 11 Test matches, Sehwag made a total of 797 runs, including three centuries and four half centuries.

His parents sought admission for him in the Government Boys Senior Secondary School in Vikaspuri. It can be said that Sehwag was indeed fortunate that his physical training coach, A. N. Sharma was unlike the coaches of other government schools. He recognised Sehwag's talents with his hawk-like eyes and worked very hard with him in order to polish his talent further. A. N. Sharma was a diploma holder from National Institute of Sports and was well versed in the intricacies of the game.

After school, Sehwag took admission in Jamia Millia Islamia for his further studies. There his luck played a positive role again and he got an opportunity to meet Satish Sharma, who was the coach at the Madras Cricket Club. Till that time nobody had heard about Virender Sehwag. When Satish Sharma showed him the way to cricket, Sehwag started playing for the Madras Cricket Club.

Apart from playing cricket, Sehwag is fond of listening to Hindi film songs and loves to play table-tennis. He also likes to swim and spends his leisure time with his family and friends.

Playing alongwith Sachin Tendulkar and Saurav Ganguli was like a dream come true for him. When he started playing first-class cricket, he could never believe that he would be able to play with Dravid, Tendulkar or Ganguly. He had never imagined that such a day would ever come.

He has indeed proved to the world that if a person wants to touch the peak, he can definitely do so with his sincere efforts. On 22nd April 2004, Virender Sehwag got married to Arti.

He touched new heights of success. The fact that he became an urban man from a fairly rural setting is fascinating for all and also made him into a celebrity. Though his Haryanvi accent has mellowed considerably, his style of speaking and manner remains the same.

He has hit many centuries in international one-day matches. When he scored a century in his very first Test match, his father's and brothers' joy knew no bounds. His trainer A.N. Sharma had made him practice his batting in the net for hours for this match.

He has been made the brand ambassador for many companies and he greatly misses the food and delicacies made by his mother when he is out of town. There have been many changes in Sehwag's life over the past few years. He has brought about a change in the playing techniques of the openers. He has a large fan following and his admirers wait to watch him play on the crease and enjoy his stint there. After being ignored from Test cricket for some time in between, he has regained his form as became apparent in the recent Test series against Australia. It must be remembered that it is not possible for his bat to create magic every time.

Achievements

- ☆ *During the March-April matches between India and Pakistan in 2004, Sehwag set quite a few records, which was a matter of pride for the Indians.*
- ☆ *In the match between India and Pakistan played at Multan, Sehwag became the first cricketer to make a triple century with 309 runs. This feat was a major contribution to India's victory over Pakistan.*
- ☆ *He is the first Indian cricketer to hit five sixes in an innings. He managed to do this twice.*
- ☆ *His 228 not out (double century) is the fastest century ever made by any Indian player.*
- ☆ *He scored the highest score against Pakistan with 309 runs in an inning.*
- ☆ *The Hero Honda Sports Academy nominated him as the most outstanding cricketer during the year 2005 for the previous year.*
- ☆ *In January 2006, he made more than 200 runs in an innings for the third time against Pakistan.*
- ☆ *In January 2006, he became the first Indian player to hit the fastest century (63 balls). Prior to him, the record was held by Sunil Gavaskar.*

☆ *He has so far made 18 centuries in Test cricket and 11 centuries in one-day matches.*

☆ *He is the only Indian batsman to have made two triple centuries.*

☆ *He has scored 7 doubles centuries.*

EQUESTRIAN

Equestrian event is a sport that the Turks enjoyed for many centuries. It was an athletic competition in the nomadic Turkish society where the equestrian tradition was very strong. It was said for long that a Turk was born and grew up on horseback. A great many Turks were cavalry officers and their only drink was the horse milk called *kimiz*, which they drank, rode on their horse, played and then perished on horseback. *Cirit* was accepted as a war game by the Ottoman Empire in the 16th century. While its scope has shrunk in the currrent day, *cirit* is still played at weddings and during holidays in Anatolia. *Cirit* entered Anatolia with Alpasian and spread from there to Europe and the Arab lands. It came to be played in German and French-speaking territories in the 17th century.

Today horse riding is a sport in which the riders run their horses at high speed. It includes mainly thoroughbreds with a rider astride or standardbreds with the horse pulling a conveyance with a driver. Though racing is an old sport, the first regularly organised national races were held in England under King Charles II (1600-85) and the first in North America were held at Long Island in 1665. These early races were match events beween two or three horses and were run in heats — a horse had to complete at least two heats to be judged the winner.

By mid-18th century, larger fields of runners and single-race 'dash' events became the norm. Handicap racing emerged in the mid-18th century as well as gambling came to be a standard part of horse racing. Thoroughbred racing, conducted on a flat, elliptical, mile-long track, attracts the largest purses, followed by harness racing and quarter-horse racing.

Equestrian events were included in the Olympic Games for the first time in the 1908 London Olympics and subsequently included during the 1912 Stockholm Olympic Games, in a format very similar to that used at the Athens Olympic Games of 2004. Since 1912, the sport has always been on the Olympic programme, which has been remarkably constant. In 1900, high jump and long jump events for horses were held for the only time, while in 1920, vaulting made a single appearance on the Olympic programme. Otherwise, the programme has rarely varied. Till 1948, in the London Olympics army officers were the only ones who participated in the equestrian event. Up to that time, the growth of modern sport had been rapid, but relatively few competitors were involved in international competitions.

With the inclusion of the sport in the Olympic Games, it became obvious that some internationally recognised rules for the three Olympic disciplines were essential. In May 1921, delegates from 10 national equestrian organisations met in Lausanne to discuss the formation of an international federation.

Prior to 1952, equestrian sport events during the Olympics were contested by men only. In fact, the riders had to be military athletes. More specifically, they had to be commissioned officers. It is said that it was a three-day event usually abbreviated by horse enthusiasts to 'eventing', which began as a test of the cavalry horses. The three-day event was restricted to military officers, while the jumping and dressage competitions were open to civilians, but only a handful of civilian riders competed up to 1948. Military horses were required to travel long distances, negotiate the many natural obstacles, and then perform strict parade manoeuvres. Competitions began in this event in Europe in 1902 and interest in the sport is still concentrated mainly in Europe, North America, Australia and New Zealand. In 1952, these restrictions were lifted, and since then, men and women have competed against each other in the equestrian events.

Equestrian

Major Deep Ahlawat

The horse-riding champion, Major Deep Ahlawat, was given the Arjuna Award for the year 2004. Mirza is the name of his horse and the duo has given an outstanding performance on many occasions. He has also won the bronze medal at the Asian Games.

Major Deep Ahlawat, who hails from Saharanpur, Uttar Pradesh, has won the Best Duo Award alongwith his horse Mirza in the FEI World Challenge Show Jumping at Kolkata. The duo has given many award-winning performances and bagged prizes at various events. In addition to the bronze medal at the Asian Games, Mirza and Major Deep Ahlawat have also won the Asia, Pacific and European horse riding competitions.

Major Deep Ahlawat is an officer at the Raymount Training School and Depot, Saharanpur. He has immense experience in horse riding. He has acquired training in Europe and Australia in horse riding. Major Ahlawat earned name and fame after he won the FEI World Challenge Show Jumping with his horse Mirza at the Williams Ground in Kolkata.

When he was interviewed after winning the Arjuna Award for the year 2004, he said that this award from the Ministry of Sports had given recognition to him and his achievements.

Horse riding is an Olympic Game in which both men and women sportspersons can participate. The average participation age in this event is around 55 years. A rider's performance improves with time and experience and the person also begins to understand the psychology of his or her horse better. It can take several years for the rider and the horse to develop a good rapport.

Deep Ahlawat and Mirza share a relationship of over 12 years. This duo has brought home 70-75 medals.

Accordingly Major Ahlawat was honoured with the Arjuna Award for the year 2004 for his excellent performance in horse riding.

Achievements

- ☆ *Major Ahlawat has won the best duo award alongwith his horse Mirza in the FEI World Challenge Show Jumping at Kolkata.*
- ☆ *Major Ahlawat and his horse Mirza have a number of prizes to their credit. This duo, which shares a rapport for the past 10-12 years, has brought home 70-75 medals.*
- ☆ *Major Deep Ahlawat and his horse Mirze have won the bronze medal at the Asian Games.*
- ☆ *They also won the Asia, Pacific and European horse-riding competitions.*
- ☆ *Major Ahlawat was honoured with the Arjuna Award for the year 2004.*

FOOTBALL

Football is a game in which two 11-member teams try to propel the ball into the opposing team's goal. The goalkeeper within the pernalty area in front of the goal is allowed to stop the ball from entering the goal by using his hands and arms.

The first uniform set of soccer rules was put in place in 1863, when England's Football Association was created. Professional leagues began to appear in the late 1880s, first in England and then in other countries. The Federation Internationale de Football Association was founded in 1904 and it hosts the World Cup every four years since 1930. The English language word 'football' is also applied to grid-iron football (which includes American football and Canadian football), Australian rules football, Gaelic football, Rugby football (Rugby League and Rugby Union), and related games. Each of these games is referred to as 'football'.

Soccer has been included in the Olympic Games since 1908. Now played in all continents in over 150 nations, with over 40 million registered players, it is the world's most popular ball game.

The game involves:

- A large spherical or prolate spheroid ball, which is called a football.
- A team scoring goals and/or points, by moving the ball to an opposing team's end of the field and either into a goal area, or over a line.
- The goal and/or line being defended by the opposing team.
- The players are required to move the ball, depending on the code, by kicking, carrying and/or passing the ball by hand.

- Goals and/or points result from the player putting the ball between two goalposts.

In most codes, there are offside rules restricting the movement of players and players scoring a goal must put the ball either under or over a crossbar between the goalposts. Other features common to several codes include points being mostly scored by players carrying the ball across the goal line and players receiving a free kick after they take a mark/ make a fair catch.

India's football team is controlled by the All India Football Federation, which is a member of the Asian Football Confederation and the FIFA. India qualified by default for the 1950 FIFA World Cup as a result of all their scheduled opponents withdrawing from the competition. However, India did not take up its place in the competition as FIFA insisted on all players wearing the football boots, which the Indian players refused to obey. The Indians have never come close to qualifying for the World Cup but finished fourth in the tounament at the Melbourne Olympics in 1956 and won the 1962 Asian Games gold medal. India reached the semi-finals in the next two Asian Games in what became known as the 'golden era' of Indian football.

Football

Baichung Bhutia

Date of Birth: 15th December 1976

Baichung Bhutia, who was awarded the Arjuna Award in 1998, holds the record of scoring the highest number of goals in international football. Football player Baichung Bhutia is known as the 'torch-bearer' of the Indian football team in the international football sphere among his admirers. He is the most important identity of Indian football for his unique playing style and amazing ability to strike the shots. He can be termed as a player of international calibre and is the first Indian football player to be invited to play for the English Club.

Baichung was born on 15th December 1976 at Tinkitam, near Gangtok in Sikkim. Baichung won the SAI scholarship to take part in the Tashi Namgyal Academy, Gangtok at the age of 11 years. He began to participate in a number of school and club competitions in Sikkim from his childhood. His performance at the Subroto Cup in 1991 brought him into limelight and he got an opportunity to move ahead. He was declared the best player in this game.

His high playing standard was noticed at the Sikkim Governor Gold Cup Tournament in 1991 when he was a member of the Sikkim Blues. He was just 17-years old when he began playing in men's tournaments.

He left school in 1993 to enrol himself in the East India Club for gaining professional training in the game. In the year 1995, he decided to join JCT Phagwara team and his decision proved right as his team won the National Football League match that very year. He was the highest scorer in this match and was thus selected to play in the Nehru Cup.

At the time of Santosh Trophy, he was a member of the Bengal team for a period of five years. In the year 1997, he returned to the Bengal team and was made captain of East Bengal Club from 1998-1999. He represented India in the pre-Olympics for the international qualifying matches, the Nehru Cup, the Asian Games and the SAF Games. He was declared the 'Best Player of the Year' in 1999 and was also chosen the 'Indian Player of the Year'. He received a number of prizes.

Baichung has scored more than 35 goals and has given a new direction to the game at the international level. In the year 1999, he went to Manchester, England to play in the 'Berry Football Cup'. In 2002, he returned to India and joined the Mohun Bagan team for a year, after which he again returned to the East Bengal team and helped the team to win the Asian Club Championship. At that time he got an invitation from FC, the Champion Club of Malaysia and this he accepted. He remained with them from August to October 2003.

In November 2002, Bhutia signed a contract with Adidas India Marketing Private Limited and did the promotion campaigns for the company.

In 2004, Baichung gave an interview to an Indian newspaper where he was asked how he felt on being termed as the Beckham of India. He replied that it indeed gave him a lot of pleasure when he was called the Beckham of India. He was also asked about his temper and if he got angry quickly. He replied that he was normally a very cool-headed person and did not lose his temper easily. He did not remember when he had last lost his temper. Baichung is also referred to as the 'sex symbol' among football lovers. His response to it has been that he does not feel bad when someone calls him so.

Achievements

- ☆ *Baichung was declared the best player of the Subroto Cup.*
- ☆ *In the year 1995, his JCT team won the National Football League match and he was the highest scorer in this match.*
- ☆ *He is the winner of the SAF Games at Nepal in 1999 and the highest scorer.*

- ☆ *In May 1999, he was declared the Asian player of the month.*
- ☆ *He was honoured with the Arjuna Award in 1998.*
- ☆ *In the year 1995, he became the youngest player to score the maximum number of goals in the Nehru Cup Tournament in the match played against Uzbekistan.*
- ☆ *In the year 1995, he was declared the best player of the Calcutta super division as he was the top scorer.*
- ☆ *In 1999, he was declared the best Indian player of the year.*
- ☆ *The same year, he was honoured with the 'Sikkim State Award'.*
- ☆ *He became the first Indian player to play in the Football League in October 1999.*
- ☆ *He became the first Indian player to score in the Football League in April 2000.*

Football

Chuni Goswami

Date of Birth: 15th January 1938

Chuni Goswami was one of the mainstays of the Indian national team for football. He was regarded one of the best players of football and led the Indian team to the first ever gold medal at the 1962 Asian Games at Jakarta. He was given the Arjuna Award in 1963 and the Padma Shri in 1983.

During the golden era of Indian football, Chuni Goswami was declared as one of the most outstanding players in the Indian national team. He played at the striker's position (left inside and right inside). Subimal Goswami was popularly known as Chuni Goswami to the football lovers of India.

Chuni Goswami, the prolific goal-getter of Indian football team, was born on 15th January 1938 at Kishoregunj, Bengal. He received his early education at Thirthopati Institute of Kolkata. His college education was done at Kumar Ashutosh Institution, Kolkata. His school football coach was Sibdas Banerjee. He played his first important match for IFA-XI — an exhibition match at Ranchi before he joined a club of Kolkata League.

He started his professional career with the Mohun Bagan Club in 1954 as a junior-level player. In his debut match, played in 1956, he played for Mohun Bagan against Eastern Railway and scored a goal in the 3-0 win.

In the 1950s and 1960s, the Indian football team played a satisfactory game showing skill and aptitude at the international stage. The credit for the good results at that time goes to Chuni Goswami and a host of capable players. The Indian team was far from being the pushovers they are today.

In 1955, Chuni went on a foreign tour for the first time and played for Mohun Bagan during 1955 and 1956 in Indonesia, Singapore and Hongkong. His first international match was against Indonesia, in which the result was a draw at 4-4.

At the age of 17, Chuni played in the Bengal Santosh Trophy and the Bengal team won by defeating the Mysore team. In 1956, he played for the Indian team against the Chinese Olympic team and won 1-0.

In 1957, he was selected captain of the Bengal team and played in the All India University Football Tournament. His team won against Bombay University 1-0, the solitary goal being scored by him.

The high point of his career was in the 1962 Jakarta Asian Games when India won a gold medal. In the final, the Chuni Goswami-led team defeated South Korea 2-1. These two goals came from P.K. Banerjee and Jarnail Singh.

In 1958 he was given the 'Best Footballer Award' by Calcutta Veterans Sports Club. He was a member of Indian team which played in the Asian Games at Tokyo in 1958 and in the Rome Olympic Games in 1960.

Chuni captained the Mohun Bagan team from 1960 to 1964. During his stint the club did exceedingly well in various national competitions. The game played by the club in the prestigious Durand Cup was considered fantastic at that time.

In 1962 he was given the 'Best Striker of Asia' award. He was the captain of the Indian football team that won a silver medal in the Tel Aviv Asian Cup. In honour of his services to the game, he was bestowed the Arjuna Award in 1963 and the Padma Shri in 1983.

From 1986 to 1989, he was Director at the Tata Football Academy, Jharkhand. He became Sheriff of Kolkata Corporation in 2005. Mohun Bagan honoured him with the 'Mohun Bagan Ratna' award.

He played on the left-inside position, displaying immaculate ball control. His game sense was superb and he knew when the ball had to be released to his co-players. He may be called the greatest football player of India.

Achievements

- ☆ *Goswami played for Mohun Bagan Junior Club from 1946 to 1954.*
- ☆ *He played for Mohun Bagan (Senior) Club from 1954 to 1968. He was the captain of the club for five times.*
- ☆ *He played his big debut match for Mohan Bagan vs Eastern Railway and the team won 3-0, with one goal being scored by Chuni Goswami.*
- ☆ *At the age of 17, he played for the Bengal Santosh Trophy team in 1955. The Bengal team became the champion by beating the Mysore team.*
- ☆ *In 1956, he first played for the Indian team against China in the Olympics. India team won 1-0.*
- ☆ *In 1957, he was captain of the Bengal team and played in the All India University Football Tournament. The Bengal team defeated the Bombay University team and won 1-0.*
- ☆ *In 1958 he was awarded the 'Best Footballer Award' by Calcutta Veterans Sports Club.*
- ☆ *He led the Indian team to win the gold medal at the 1962 Asian Games in Jakarta.*
- ☆ *He was selected the 'Best Striker of Asia' in 1962.*
- ☆ *He was captain of the team that won a silver at the Tel Aviv Asian Games.*
- ☆ *He was awarded the Arjuna Award in 1963.*
- ☆ *He was honoured with the Padma Shri in 1983.*
- ☆ *He remained the Director of the Tata Football Academy, Jharkhand from 1986 to 1989.*
- ☆ *He became the Sheriff of Kolkata Corporation in 2005.*
- ☆ *He was given the 'Mohan Bagan Ratna' award in 2005.*

Football

Jarnail Singh

Date of Birth: 1936
Died: 10th October 2000

Jarnail Singh is regarded as one of the most outstanding football players. He played the role of a defender to guide India to victory. He helped India win a gold medal by his important strike in the 1962 Jakarta Asian Games. He led the Asian All Star Team in 1966. He was honoured with the Arjuna Award in 1964.

Jarnail Singh's full name is Jarnail Singh Dhillon. He has been the most successful football player of India. He was born in 1936 in Hoshiarpur district in Punjab.

Jarnail Singh took the art of defence to new heights, making himself the epitome of strength and stamina.

He played for Khalsa College, Mahipalpur, Punjab from 1952 to 1956. Then he played for Khalsa Sporting Club from 1956 to 1957. He was a member of Rajasthan Club, Kolkata from 1957 to 1958. From 1958 to 1968 he played for Mohun Bagan Athletic Club, Calcutta.

He played a pivotal role in shaping India's football fortunes during the golden era of Indian football and so did his illustrious compatriots. His potential in the game and heroics in the 1962 Jakarta Asian Games cannot be forgotten by football lovers. That is a part of Indian football folklore now. Braving a nasty head-injury that needed six stitches, Jarnail Singh played very well and scored goals in the semi-finals and finals. This fantastic feat of his fetched for India its maiden Asiad gold in football.

In 1964, i.e. two years later, Jarnail Singh was at his best, marshalling the defence and making India the runner-up in the Asia Cup at Tel Aviv.

In 1964, after an outstanding presentation of good players at the Merdeka Tournament in Malaysia, Jarnail Singh took over the reins of the team from Chuni Goswami from 1965 to 1967.

He became the captain of the Indian football team which attained a fair bit of success under him. He captained the All Star Asian Team in 1965-66 and 1966-67.

In the domestic circuit, he was associated with the Mohun Bagan Club for 10 glorious years. Then the green-and-maroon team pocketed all the major titles in football at the national level. He was associated with Mohun Bagan from 1958 to 1968.

After quitting Mohan Bagan in 1969, he went to play for Punjab. He was the coach-cum-player of the team in 1970 when the Indian team won the first Santosh Trophy. He remained the Indian national coach for many years.

He held prestigious administrative posts. He was the district sports officer in 1964. From 1985 to 1990, he became the Deputy Director of Sports, Punjab. He was the Director of Sports, Punjab during 1990 and 1994.

He was honoured with the Arjuna Award in 1964. He breathed his last on 13th October 2000 at Vancouver, Canada.

Achievements

- ☆ *Jarnail Singh is regarded as one of the most outstanding 'defenders' in the Indian football team.*
- ☆ *He played for Khalsa College, Mahipalpur, Punjab from 1952 to 1956.*
- ☆ *He was the member of Khalsa Sporting Club, Punjab from 1956 to 1957.*
- ☆ *He played for Rajasthan Club, Kolkata from 1957 to 1958.*
- ☆ *He was associated with the Mohun Bagan Club for 10 years from 1958 to 1968.*
- ☆ *He was the national coach for India.*
- ☆ *He was the coach-cum-player of the team that won the first Santosh Trophy.*

- ☆ *He was the captain of the Indian football team from 1965 to 1967.*
- ☆ *In 1962 Jakarta Asian Games, he was responsible for taking India into the finals by his stroke play. He scored goals in the final also to fetch India its maiden Asian football gold.*
- ☆ *He played as an able defender in 1964 at Tel Aviv Asia Cup where India became runner-up.*
- ☆ *He was awarded the Arjuna Award in 1964.*
- ☆ *He was District Sports Officer in 1964.*
- ☆ *He became Deputy Director of Sports, Punjab in 1985 and remained in this post till 1990.*
- ☆ *He was Director of Sports, Punjab from 1990 to 1994.*

Football

M. Vijayan

Birth: 25th April 1969

The full name of M. Vijayan, who made the quickest goals in football in the 1999 SAF Games, is Invalappil Mani Vijayan. He made the highest score in the 2003 Afro-Asian Games. He was honoured with the Arjuna Award in 2002.

The life story of I.M. Vijayan, who is one of the best strikers of India, is like the typical story of from rags to riches. He, who became the most important identity of Indian football, used to sell soda water bottles at one point of time in the streets of Thrissur. The place where he stands today is the result of his hard work and dedication.

I.M. Vijayan was born on 25th April 1969, in Thrissur, Kerala. He acquired fame as a football player and played football for A.C., J.C.T.Mills, F.C. Cochin, Kerala police, Mohun Bagan and the Indian teams. He plays at the striker position.

In 1987 he played football at the national level for the first time at the Quilon Naionals at the age of 17 for Kerala police. Vijayan, despite his peculiar and dry personality, left an indelible impression on the minds of his spectators by his game. After working in the police for a period of four years, he left Kerala and moved to Kolkata to join the Calcutta Club as he saw a better future for himself. He spent a few fruitful years here, playing for veterans like Mohun Bagan and East Bengal.

Vijayan continued his excellent performance and started playing international football from 1989. He continued to play attackingly on behalf of the Indian team in various tournaments. He participated in the Nehru Cup, pre-Olympic, pre-World Cup, SAAF Cup and SAF Games. He strengthened the forward line of the Indian team by playing alongside Baichung Bhutia, who is one of the most outstanding football players of our country.

I.M. Vijayan was the first player from Kerala to be honoured with the Arjuna Award in 2002. In addition to this, he was chosen the 'Footballer of the Year' during 1993, 1997 and 1999.

In the SAF Games in 1999, he set a record by scoring the fastest goal in international football. He hit a goal against Nepal after just 12 seconds of coming into the net. When the time for his retirement came, he preferred to retire in style. He retired after playing in the Afro-Asian Games where he hit four goals and set the record for scoring the highest number of goals in these Games. After his retirement, Vijayan starred in an award-winning film called *Santham*, which had been directed by Jayaraj.

Achievements

- ☆ *Vijayan was the most important footballer of India.*
- ☆ *In the SAF Games in 1999, he established a record by making the fastest goal in international football against Nepal after just 12 seconds of coming into the net.*
- ☆ *He retired after playing in the Afro-Asian Games where he scored four goals and emerged as the player to score the highest number of goals in these Games.*
- ☆ *He was honoured with the Arjuna Award in 2002. He was the first player from Kerala to be honoured with this award.*
- ☆ *He acted in an award-winning film called* Santham, *which had been directed by Jayaraj.*

Football

Pradeep Kumar Banerjee

Date of Birth: 15th October 1936

Pradeep Kumar Banerjee, known as P.K. Banerjee, was one of the best players of Indian football. He was a player who scored the first goal in the final of 1962 Asian Games. Later India won a gold medal in that match. P.K. Banerjee led the Indian football team in the 1962 Rome Olympics. He is the first ever footballer to receive the Arjuna Award in 1961.

P.K. Banerjee was one of the stalwarts of Indian football squad that made a name for itself on the international stage. As a dashing forward, P.K. Banerjee made a habit of scoring crucial goals for his team.

Pradeep Kumar Banerjee was born on 15th October 1936 at Jalpaiguri, West Bengal. His father's name was Prabhat Kumar Banerjee. The first club he joined was the Jamshedpur Sports Association, Bihar. He started his professional career also in Jamshedpur. It was in the highly competitive Calcutta League that he excelled when representing the Eastern Railways.

In 1953 he played for the first time in the IFA Shield for the Jamshedpur Sport Association against Hindustan Aircraft Limited. In 1954-1955 he was associated with first class club of Calcutta League — the Aryan Club. From 1955 to 1965 he was associated with the Eastern Railways.

He was a member of the Indian football team that finished fourth in the 1956 Melbourne Olympics. He captained the national team at the 1960 Rome Olympics, where India failed to move from the stage group, though the team played inspirational soccer to hold the mighty France 1-1 through a goal scored by captain Banerjee himself.

In 1961-62 and 1966-67, he was a member of the Railway team that won the Santosh Trophy.

He dazzled in the Asian Games and represented India in three Asian Games from 1958 to 1966. In the 1962 Jakarta Asian Games, India clinched a gold medal with Banerjee scoring goals against all the teams except in the first match against South Korea.

He was honoured with the Arjuna Award and became the first ever footballer to receive this award. Post-retirement, he was associated with football as a coach. He coached the Kolkata giants in football — Mohun Bagan and East Bengal. He was associated with the national team for long and worked as a Technical Director of Tata Football Academy. He was the manager of the Indian football team in 2006.

He was awarded the Padma Shri by the Government of India in 1990. He also received the 'FIFA Fair Play Award' in 1990. In 2005, he was honoured with the 'FIFA Award: India's Footballer of 20th Century'.

Achievements

- ☆ *P.K. Banerjee represented India in three Asiads, from 1958 to 1966.*
- ☆ *He was a member of Indian football team that won the gold medal in the 1962 Jakarta Asian Games.*
- ☆ *He was the member of the Railway team that won the Santosh Trophy in 1961-62 and 1966-67.*
- ☆ *He was the first ever footballer of India to receive the Arjuna Award in 1961.*
- ☆ *He was honoured with the Padma Shri in 1990.*
- ☆ *He was given the 'FIFA Fair Play Award' in 1990.*
- ☆ *In 2005, he was given the 'FIFA Award: Indian Footballer of 20th Century'.*
- ☆ *He has been the coach of East Bengal F.C., Mohan Bagan A.C., and the Indian Team.*
- ☆ *He has been the technical director of Tata Football Academy, Indian team and Mohammedan Sporting Club.*
- ☆ *In 2006 he became the manager of India's national team.*

FORMULA ONE RACE

The Formula One, shortened to FI, is the highest class of auto-racing as defined by the *Federation Internationale de l'Automobile* (FIA), the motor sports' world-governing body. The 'formula' in the name is a set of rules which all the participants and cars must meet.

The Formula One series has its roots in the European Grand Prix motor racing of the 1920s and 1930s. The Formula One World Championship was a new formula agreed after World War II in 1946 with the first non-championship races being held that year. A number of Grand Prix racing organisations laid out the rules for a world championship before the war, but due to the suspension of racing during the conflict, the World Drivers' Championship was not formalised until 1947.

The first World Championship race was held at Silverstone, United Kingdom in 1950 for drivers. A championship for constructors followed in 1958. The National Championship existed in South Africa and the UK in the 1960s and 1970s. Non-championship Formula One races were held for many years but due to the expenditure incurred in organising the competition, the last of these occurred in 1983.

The Formula One race is a massive television event, with millions of people watching each race in 200 countries. The cars race at high speeds, often greater than 320 km/h (200 mph) and the performance of the cars is highly dependent on electronics, aerodynamics, suspension and tyres. Formula One has seen many evolutions and changes through the history of the sport.

Europe is Formula One's traditional centre and remains its leading market. However, Grand Prix events are held all over the world and with new races in Bahrain, China, Malaysia, Turkey and the United States since

1999, its scope continues for further expansion with Singapore scheduled to hold its first night race in 2008. India too is expected to start its schedule in 2010.

Of the 17 races held in 2007, nine are outside Europe. As the world's most expensive sport, its economic effect is significant, and its financial and political battles are widely observed. Its high profile and popularity make it an obvious merchandising environment, leading to high investments from sponsors, translating into extremely high budgets for the constructor teams.

Formula One Race

Naraian Karthikeyan

Date of Birth: 14th January 1977

Naraian Karthikeyan is known as the fastest Formula One driver of India in the world and has been accepted by the British Motoring Press too. His full name is Kumar Ram Naraian Karthikeyan. For the youth of today, he is the symbol of speed and an icon in the form of a car racer.

Naraian was born on 14th January 1977 in Coimbatore, Tamil Nadu. His father G. R. Karthikeyan is a former Indian National rally champion and thus Naraian developed great interest in car games from his childhood itself. It was his dream to become the first Formula One Driver of India and he succeeded to achieve his dream very early in life.

The first race that he participated in was in Sri Perumbatore near Chennai which was called Formula Maruti. Naraian won this race at the tender age of 16 years only. He received his training in the Elf Winfield Racing School in France and became the semi-finalist in the Pilote Elf Competition of Formula Renault car in 1992.

In 1993, Naraian reached India to participate in the Formula Maruti Race. He also participated in the Formula Vauxhall Junior Championship in Britain. After his European racing experience, he took part in the Foundation racing team as Driver No. 2 in the Formula Ford Zetec Series in Britain in 1994. This very year he won the Estoril race and became the first Indian to win the British Formula Ford Zetek Series Championship in Europe. After this Naraian Karthikeyan turned towards the Formula Asia Championship.

In 1995 he participated in four races and proved his mettle at the Shah Alam in Malaysia, leaving a lasting impression by finishing second. He spent the whole of 1996 in Formula One races and participated in all the competitions. He was not only the first Indian, but also the first Asian, to win the Formula Asia International Series.

In 1997 Naraian returned to Britain to participate in the British Formula Opel in the pole position and won at Domington Park. He held the sixth position in the overall scoreboard. In 1998, he participated in the British Formula Three Championship for the first time. Karlin Motor Sport team was also with him. For the next three years he was somewhat successful with this team.

In the two races of the year he secured the third position in the finals. In this race he participitated in only 10 rounds at the Spa Francor Champs and Silver Stone. He secured the 12th position in the overall competition.

In 1997 he won the championship five times and was twice the winner of the Brands Hatch Race. Twice he was able to set records at the pole position, thrice in the fastest lap and two laps. This year he was able to finish sixth among the competitors which included 30 drivers. He reached the sixth position in the Macao Grand Prix.

In 2000, he participated in the British Formula F Championship and stood fourth. At the international Spa Frankor Champs Belgium and Korean Super Prix race, he was able to reach the podium. In the year 2001, Naraian participated in the Formula Nippon F 3000 Championship and found a place for himself among the first 10 drivers. In the same year, he also participated in the Formula One Car Jaguar Race of Silvertone and became the first Indian to test drive in the event. After getting impressed with his performance, Silvertone invited him to take part in the Benson and Hedges Jordan Honda EJ 11.

In 2002, Naraian participated in the Telefonica World Series at the pole position along with Team Tata R.C. Motor Sport. He set a record as the fastest non-Formula One lap-time at Inter Lagos Circuit in Brazil. In 2003, he took part in the Nissan Key World Series and won two races from Minardi Teak and reached an overall fourth position in the championship.

In 2004, Naraian was invited to participate in the race but he could not make it due to the lack of sponsorship funds. Karthikeyan continued to take part in the Nissan Key World Series and won two races from Valencia in Spain and Magni Course in France.

In 2005, Naraian signed a contract with Jordan Formula One team and became the first Formula One ranked driver of India. He performed well at Melbourne but he finished his race with a crash in the Shanghai Grand Prix. Towards the end of 2005, the Jordan team was taken over by Midland. However, Naraian could not become a member of this team because he was unable to pay such a high amount.

In January 2006, Naraian was chosen for the fourth position as test driver at Williams. In 2007 also he continued with Williams and was promoted to the third place. Naraian believes that it is better to take part as a test driver rather than a race driver at the Williams for his Formula One technology.

Apart from car racing, Naraian Karthikeyan is also fond of trap-and-skeet shooting, photography and tennis. He practices yoga and meditation to remain fit. He is married to Pavarna, who is the daughter of an industrialist. Naraian has accomplished his dream of being the first Formula driver of India.

He has opened a motor racing institute in Coimbatore by the name of Speed N.K. Racing where he imparts training to young Indians who are fond of racing like him.

Achievements

- ☆ *Naraian Karthikeyan is the first Formula One driver of India in the world.*
- ☆ *His first victory came at the tender age of 16 years only in Sri Perumbatore, near Chennai in the 'Formula Maruti'.*
- ☆ *He became the semi-finalist in the Pilote Elf Competition of Formula Renault car.*
- ☆ *He came second in the Formula Asia Championship.*
- ☆ *He was not only the first Indian, but the first Asian, to win the Formula Asia International Series in 1996.*

- ☆ *In 1997 he participated in the British Formula Opel Championship in the pole position and won at the Domington Park.*
- ☆ *In 2001, Naraian participated in the Formula Nippon One 3000 Championship and found a place for himself among the first 10 drivers.*
- ☆ *In 2005, he signed a contract with Jordan Formula One team and became the first Formula One ranking driver of India.*
- ☆ *He has opened a motor racing institute in Coimbatore.*

GOLF

Golf is a game in which a player using clubs (limited in number to 14) attempts to sink a small, dimpled ball with as few strokes as possible into each of the nine of 18 successive holes on an outdoor course. Golf is one of the few ball games that does not use a standardised play area; rather, the game is played on a golf course, each with a unique design and typically consisiting of either nine or 18 separate holes. A hole includes a teeing area, a clearing from which the ball is initially driven towards the actual hole or 'cup', a fairway, a long, closely mowed and often angled lane, a putting green, a smooth grassy area containing the hole and often one or more natural or artificial hazards (such as bunkers).

Golf is defined as "playing a ball with a club from the teeing ground into the hole by a stroke or successive strokes in accordance with the rules."

The first game of golf for which records survive was played at Bruntsfield Links, in Edinburgh, Scotland in AD 1456, as recorded in the archives of the Edinburgh Burgess Golfing Society, now called the Royal Burgess Golfing Society. The courses were originally fields of grass that herds of sheep had clipped short in their characteristic grazing style. The oldest playing golf course in the world is the Musselburgh Old Links Golf Course. Evidence shows that golf was played here in 1672 although Mary, Queen of Scots, reputedly played there in 1567.

Golf balls were originally made of wood but it was replaced in the 17th century by boiled feathers in leather, in the 19th century by gutta-percha and in the 20th century by hard rubber.

The principal men's tournaments include the US Open, the Masters, the British Open and PGA Championship. The Ryder Cup is an important international team tournament.

Golf competitions may be played as stroke play, in which the individual with the lowest number of strokes is declared the winner, or as a match with the winner determined by whichever individual or team posts the lowest score on the most individual holes during a complete round. In addition, team events such as four-balls have been introduced, and these can be played using either the stroke or matchplay format.

Alternative ways to play golf have also been devised, such as miniature golf and disc golf.

Golf has increasingly turned into a spectator sport with several different levels of professional and amateur tours in many regions of the world. Players such as Tiger Woods, Jack Nicklaus and Annika Sorenstam are world-renowned golfers today. Sponsorship has become a huge part of the sport and players often earn more from their sponsorship contracts than they do from the sport itself.

Golf

Arjun Atwal

Date of Birth: 20th March 1973

Arjun Atwal is the first Indian golfer who participated in the U.S. PGA tour as a sportsperson. Apart from this, he is one player to have earned more than 10 lakh dollars in the Asian PGA tour. Arjun Atwal also happens to be the first Indian golf player to win the 'Order of Merit' on the European tour. In 2003, he secured the best position in the 'Asian Order of Merit'.

Arjun Atwal is one of the best golfers of India. He was born on 20th March 1973 at Asansol, West Bengal. He achieved an unparalleled success as a professional golf player and is the first Indian golf player to participate in the prestigious U.S. PGA tour.

Arjun learnt the nuances and intricacies of golf while he was still in his teens. He learnt playing golf in the lush green lawns of the Royal Calcutta Golf Club and became a professional player in 1995. His height is 6'1".

After this he kept proving his playing excellence on the Asian tour. He secured the best position as 'Asian Order of Merit'. In 2003, Atwal became the first ever Indian golf player to earn more than 10 lakh U.S. dollars in the Asian PGA tour. He won the game with only one stroke in the Hero Honda Masters game in India and succeeded in winning this huge sum.

He is the second player to get membership of the European Tour after Jeev Milkha Singh. He also is the first Indian to win the 'European Order of Merit'. Atwal won this title in Caltex Singapore Masters in 2002.

In 2003 Atwal was successful on the European tour for the second time. In the Carlsberg Malaysian Open, he registered a four-shot win after defeating the American Open Champion, Retief Goosen.

He participated in the U.S. PGA tour for the first time in 2004 and gave a tremendous performance. The year 2005 was also good for him in terms of his performance, although he had to witness a minor defeat in the Bell South Classic.

Achievements

- ☆ *Arjun Atwal is a top professional golfer of India.*
- ☆ *He is the first Indian golfer to participate in the U.S. PGA tour.*
- ☆ *He is the first ever Indian golfer to earn more than 10 lakh U.S. dollars in his sports career.*
- ☆ *He happens to be the first Indian golfer to win the 'Order of Merit' in the European tour.*
- ☆ *In the year 2003, he won the 'Asian Order of Merit'.*

Jeev Milkha Singh

Date of Birth: 15th December 1971

Jeev Milkha Singh is counted among the topmost Indian golfers in the world. He is the son of the outstanding Indian athlete, Milkha Singh. He is the first Indian golfer to become a member of the European tour. He is also the winner of the Volvo China Open and 'Volvo Masters' of Spain. He was also awarded the 'Asian Player of the Year Award' in the year 2006.

Jeev Milkha Singh won the American Express amateur golf championship for the first time at the age of 13 years in New Delhi. Then he further polished his golfing skills by playing in more amateur tournaments in America.

Jeev Milkha Singh was born on 15th December 1971 in Chandigarh. He is the first Indian golfer to participate in the European tour. He has been participating in the PGA tour from the 1990s and has won many such tournaments and competitions. He stood seventh in the European Tour Qualifying School and became its member the very next year.

Jeev was unable to win a title for six years. It was beginning to appear as if he would not be able to make a name for himself. But it all changed suddenly in the year 2006 which was an extremely successful year for Jeev as it brought a lot of achievements and happiness for him. He began the year by reaching the second position (which was a tie) in the Pakistan Open in January 2006.

He won the Volvo China Open in April 2006, thus becoming the second Indian after Arjun Atwal to win this title. He received a cheque of 6, 66,660 Euro on winning this title and it was the biggest win of his career.

Jeev was down in the dumps after a series of failures. But the Volvo China Open marked a new beginning for him. This is what he had to say, "It was a relief for me. There were times when I was disappointed at how things were not working out for me at all. I wondered why all this was happening despite my being so disciplined. I kept wondering why success was eluding me? But I continued to work hard with an optimistic attitude and finally the day came when I won the Volvo China Open.

After this he got 10 important finishes, which he won during the Asian and European tours. Then he won the Volvo Masters in Spain, which got him an extremely prestigious position. He reached the third position in the U.B.S. Hong Kong Open and it brought him his first prestigious ranking. He is the third Indian after Jyoti Randhawa and Arjun Atwal to achieve this. He then came to be included in the top ranking players of Asia.

Jeev Milkha Singh won the first Casio World Open Golf title in November 2006 in Japan along with a prize money of 2 crore 80 lakh Yen (approximately one crore eight lakh rupees). David Esmile lagged two shots behind and had to be content with the second prize. Jeev secured the world ranking of 63 after this victory.

2006 was a year of achievements for Jeev. He came first in the Asian Tour Order of Merit and won a prize money of $573,442. He has been working very hard towards making a place for himself at the 50th rank. If he is successful in attaining the 50th rank, he will naturally become eligible to play in the Majors.

Jeev's words after the successful performance were, "This has been a perfect year for me. This is indeed like a dream come true for me. First the 'Asian Tour Order of Merit' title, then, the title in the Japan tour. What more could I ask of the Almighty? I have been playing in the Japan circuit for years and this was a title which had been my aspiration for years. I have come very close to winning this title for many years but this is the first time when I have actually won it...I have set a new goal for myself now. After achieving the goals I set earlier, I want to work harder towards my future goals."

After these numerous achievements, Jeev Milkha Singh was chosen for the 'Players' Player of the Year' award by popular vote. In addition to this, he was also given the U.B.S. 'Special Achievement Award'.

After winning four major titles, Jeev Milkha Singh was chosen for another big award at the end of 2006, which was the 'Asian Player of the Year' award. The other two nominations for the award were Prom Misavat of Thailand and Yang Yong Yun of South Korea.

In December 2006, Jeev won the Nippon Series J.T. Golf Cup as his fourth title and thereby qualified for the U.S. Masters. He is the first Indian to qualify for this and it ensures his reaching the 50th rank in the world golf ranking. He was at 55th rank earlier.

Achievements

- ☆ *Jeev Milkha Singh became a member of the European Tour in 1997.*
- ☆ *He stood second (which was a tie) in the Pakistan Open in January 2006.*
- ☆ *He won the Volvo China Open in April 2006.*
- ☆ *He won the first Casio World Open Golf title in Japan in November 2006 with a prize money of $1.2 million.*
- ☆ *He won the Volvo Masters in Spain in 2006.*
- ☆ *He secured the third position in the U.B.S. Hong Kong Open, which also got him the number one ranking.*
- ☆ *In 2006 he won the 'Asian Tour Order of Merit'.*
- ☆ *After winning three major titles, he was chosen for 'Players' Player of the Year' award in the U.B.S. Gala during the Asian tour.*

☆ *He was given the U.B.S. 'Special Achievement Award' in 2006 which was a new award.*

☆ *He was given the title of 'U.B.S. Order of Merit' in 2006.*

☆ *He was chosen for 'Asian Player of the Year' award in 2006.*

☆ *In December 2006, he won the Nippon Series J.T. Golf Cup title in Japan.*

☆ *He is the first Indian to qualify for the U.S. Masters.*

Golf

Jyoti Randhawa

Date of Birth: 4th May 1972

Jyoti Randhawa is one of the best golfers of India. He is the first Indian to win the 'Asian Order of Merit'. He won the 'Players' Player of the Year' award, the 'Indian Open' and the 'Singapore Open' in the year 2000.

Jyoti Randhawa has earned a name for himself in the world of golf. He is the second Indian to have earned the highest world golf ranking in the world.

Jyoti Randhawa was born on 4th May 1972. He stands at a height of 6'5". He is married to actress Chitrangada. He can be called a natural athlete and he excels in other sports, such as swimming and shooting as well. He decided to take to golf after winning the National Sub-Junior title in 1986. After this he won the All India Amateur Championship in 1993, he became a professional golf player.

Jyoti is a regular player in the Asian P.G.A. Tour and has been a continuous winner there. In 1998 and 1999, he registered a win in the 'Hero Honda Masters' and then went on to win the 'Indian Open' in 2000. In the year 2000, he had his first success at the international level. The very same year he won the 'Singapore Open' and became the first Indian to win 'Asian Order of Merit'.

He won great acclaim and popularity after his continuous successes that year because of which he was chosen as the 'Players' Player of the Year' award.

In 2005, he was defeated by Adam Scott in the 'Johnny Walker Classic'and finished second, but due to his excellent performance, he was given a European Tour Card in 2006.

Achievements

- ☆ *Jyoti Randhawa is one of the best golf players of India.*
- ☆ *He holds a high position in world ranking.*
- ☆ *In 1998 and 1999, he registered a win in the 'Hero Honda Masters'.*
- ☆ *He won the 'Indian Open' in 2000.*
- ☆ *In 2000, Jyoti won in the 'Singapore Open', thereby getting international success and winning the 'Asian Order of Merit'.*
- ☆ *In 2000, he was chosen for the 'Players' Player of the Year' award.*
- ☆ *His name is among the 100 best golf players. In world ranking his name ranks second best after Jeev Milkha Singh.*

Golf

Shiv Kapur

Date of Birth: 12th May 1982

In the year 2002 Busan Asian Games, people's attention was drawn to Shiv Kapur after he won a gold medal in golf. Prior to this, his name was fairly unknown among the sports lovers. But subsequently he was seen at a unique platform.

Shiv Kapur is a native of New Delhi and after studying in Modern School, he went to America for further studies. He participated in the Busan Asian Games from there itself. His father Ravi Kapur says, "He started playing golf when he was just eight years of age."

Before the Busan Games, he had already won 12 major world championships when he was just 18 years of age. He is considered the second best amateur golf player. He is the first Indian to win the Malaysian Open Amateur Championship.

After the Busan Games, he came to India to celebrate his first victory with his family. Then he returned to Perdue University, America to pursue his education.

He said at Busan how he had benefitted immensely from his interaction with Laxman Singh, who had won a gold medal at the 1982 Asian Games. This was India's next golden success after all these years. Laxman Singh advised Shiv to play in the Asiad in the same manner as he played in any other tournament so as to keep the pressure away. He continued to encourage Shiv even after his bad score of 75 in the third over in golf. This prompted Shiv to reach his golden destination.

Shiv wants to be an amateur (non-professional) golf player among the top American players. His dream is to play in the U.S. Tour after becoming a professional golfer.

Achievements

- ☆ *In the 2002 Busan Asian Games, Shiv Kapur won a gold medal in golf.*
- ☆ *This was India's next golden success after 1982.*

HOCKEY

Hockey is a game in which two teams compete by trying to manoeuvre a ball, or a hard round disc called a puck, into the opponent's net or goal, using a hockey stick. The dominant version of hockey in a particular region tends to be known simply as hockey, other forms being more fully qualified.

Even though many ancient civilsations played hockey in different variations, the modern game of hockey—field hockey— evolved in the British Isles in the 19th century. Hockey became popular in India when the British regiment played the game in India and introduced it in the British Indian regiments who quickly picked up the game. The first hockey club was formed in Kolkata in 1885-86 followed by Bombay and Punjab.

The hockey playground is rectangular in shape. It is 100'long and 60' wide. The longer boundary lines are called the side lines and the shorter ones are the goal lines. All the lines are 3" wide throughout. Flagposts are placed on each corner of the field at a distance of 1 foot from the centre line.

The game is played between two teams consisting of 11 players each, including the goalkeeper. In the beginning, the captains of both the teams toss for the choice of ends or doing pass. The winner of the toss selects one of the two passes or ends. The captains can change their respective goalkeeper by informing the umpire about the change. The game is divided into two periods of 35 minutes each. At half time the teams change their ends.

The game starts when the umpire blows the whistle. When the ball passes completely and according to the rules over the goal lines between the goal post and under the cross bars, a goal is scored. There are two umpires to control the game and to administer the rules.

Dhyan Chand made the earliest and greatest contribution in raising the prestige of Indian hockey in the world. India made its Olympic debut at the 1928 Amsterdam Games when the team cruised home to its first Olympic gold medal without conceding a single goal. The hallmark of this domination was the wizard of Indian hockey — the legendary Dhyan Chand— who mesmerised the Amsterdam crowd with his dazzling skill.

From 1928 to 1956, the Indian hockey team won six straight Olympic gold medals while winning 24 consecutive matches. This was the golden era of Indian hockey when India dominated the world hockey and produced some of the finest players the game has ever seen. But the Indian stranglehold over the Olympic hockey gold came to an end when Pakistan defeated India in the final of the 1960 Rome Olympics.

Hockey

Ajit Pal Singh

Date of Birth: 15th March 1947

Centre-half Ajit Pal Singh is known as the most outstanding half-back of the Indian Hockey team. He represented India thrice in the Olympics. He captained the team that won the World Cup in 1975. His precise and flawless dispersal of the ball fetched him the Arjuna Award in 1970. He was awarded the Padma Shri in 1992. Besides the national awards, he was also rewarded a petrol pump in Delhi which he appropriately named 'Centre-Half'.

Ajit Pal Singh can be described as the most outstanding half-back of the hockey players. He is named second to E. Pennigar of the Olympic team of 1928 and 1932. He was an expert in hitting the ball in the desired direction.

Ajit Pal was born on 15th March 1947 at Sansarpur village in Jalandhar district of Punjab. He started playing hockey while studying at the Cantonment Board Higher Secondary School, Jalandhar. He played as full-back for the Punjab School team in 1963.

Later he played for Lyallpur Khalsa College, Jalandhar. He captained Punjab University in the Inter-University Tournament in 1966. He played as centre-half for the combined universities team in 1968.

On joining the Border Security Force, he represented his team in all the national hockey tournaments. He made his international debut in 1966 when he was selected for the team that toured Japan.

In 1967, he took part in the pre-Olympic tournament in London. He was selected to play for India in the 1968 Olympic in Mexico. Here India played badly and finished a poor third.

Ajit Pal represented India when he took part in the 1972 Olympics in Munich, winning the bronze medal. He captained the team that played the 1976 Olympics in Montreal.

Besides the Olympics, Ajit Pal represented India at the 1970 Asian Games in Teheran and claimed a silver medal. He was selected for the Asian All Star Team in 1974. Under his captaincy, the team won the Singapore's Post Shuan Tournament in 1971. The same year (1971) he led India in the first World Cup at Barcelona, winning a bronze. He represented the team again in 1972 at the Amsterdam World Cup. The team lost the final to Holland and returned home with a silver medal.

The best of Ajit Pal Singh came in 1975 at Kuala Lumpur when the team led by him won the World Cup, defeating Pakistan. On return to India, the team was given a very warm welcome. Reacting to the jubilation in India, Ajit Pal cheerfully said; "There is nothing sweeter than the World Cup. Hard work was the secret of success."

After leading a World Cup-winning team, he had to face much disappointment because the team coached by him for the 1986 World Cup in London slumped to an all-time low, finishing last among the 12 teams.

Achievements

☆ *Ajit Pal Singh participated thrice in the Olympics (in 1968, 1972 and 1976). In the 1972 Olympics at Munich, the Indian team won a bronze medal.*

☆ *He was member of the team that won a silver medal in the Asian Games in Bangkok in 1970.*

☆ *He was captain of the team that won the Singapore's Post Shuan Tournament in 1971 and won a bronze medal in the First World Cup at Barcelona.*

☆ *He represented the Indian team in 1972 at the Amsterdam World Cup and won a silver medal.*

☆ *He captained the Indian team in the Asian Games, Teheran in 1974 and the team won a silver medal.*

☆ *The team led by Ajit Pal Singh won the World Cup, defeating Pakistan in 1975 at Kuala Lumpur.*

☆ *He was awarded the Arjuna Award in 1970.*

☆ *Ajit Pal Singh was conferred Padma Shri in 1992.*

Hockey

Ashok Kumar

Date of Birth: 1st June 1950

Son of hockey wizard Dhyan Chand, Ashok Kumar got popularity in a short time. But to follow the best performance of his father was a hard task for him. To emulate his father was a challenging task, but he proved his talent to win the Arjuna Award in 1974. In 1975 he scored the winning goal against Pakistan to achieve India's triumph in the World Cup.

At a very early age Ashok Kumar showed his extraordinary ball control and flair for hockey and this prompted the sports experts to draw hasty comparisons between father and son.

He was born on 1st June 1950 at Meerut in Uttar Pradesh. He started playing hockey when he was just six-years old. At first he played for the junior school team. Later he started to play club-level hockey. He represented Uttar Pradesh continuously for four years.

He played for the Rajasthan University in 1966-67 and then in the All India Universities Tournament in 1968-69. Thereafter he shifted to Kolkata and played for the Mohun Bagan Club. He represented Bengal in the National Championship held at Bengaluru in 1971. Later he joined the Indian Airlines as a senior flight purser and represented the Indian Airlines in national tournaments.

Ashok Kumar made his international debut in 1970 in the Bangkok Asian Games, where India lost to Pakistan. He took part in the 1974 Asian Games at Teheran and the 1978 Asian Games at Bangkok and won silver medals in both the Asiads.

He participated twice in the Olympic Games and represented India first in 1972 at the Munich Olympics and then in the 1976, at the Montreal Olympics. On both the occasions the Indian team finished third, settling for a bronze. He played the Pesta Sukha International Tournament in Singapore in 1971 and was selected to play in the All-Asian Star team in 1974. Thereafter he captained the Indian team to the 1979 Esenda Hockey Tournament at Perth. He was selected twice for the World XI team.

He played the match at the first World Cup in Barcelona in 1971 in which India won a bronze medal. He was also a member of the team that won a silver medal at the second World Cup in Amsterdam in 1973. His best performance was seen at 1975 World Cup in Kuala Lumpur, where he scored the most important goal to win the gold medal for India. His fourth and last appearance in the World Cup was in Argentina where India finished sixth.

After retirement from an active sports career, Ashok was appointed manager of the hockey team of Indian Airlines and Air India.

Achievements

- ☆ *Ashok Kumar represented India in the 1974 and 1978 Asian Games at Teheran and Bangkok where India won silver medals.*
- ☆ *He participated in the 1972 Munich and 1976 Montreal Olympic Games and the team won a bronze medal.*
- ☆ *He played for the All, Asian Star team in 1974 and was subsequently selected for the World XI team.*
- ☆ *He played in the 1971 Barcelona and 1973 Amsterdam World Cup tournaments and the team won a bronze and silver medal respectively.*
- ☆ *In 1975 he helped India to win the gold medal in the World Cup at Kuala Lumpur where he scored the last most important goal.*
- ☆ *He was honoured with the Arjuna Award in 1974.*

Hockey

Balbir Singh

Date of Birth: 10th October 1924

Among the living legends, Balbir Singh is one of the topmost players of hockey in India. One of the best marksmen during his playing days, he is admired and adored not only in India but also the world over. Lethal finishing was his forte and goals come from his matchless stick in a magical way. He won the Olympic gold thrice — in 1948, 1952 and 1956. He was the Director of Sports in the Punjab government. An indoor stadium in Moga is named after him. He was awarded the Padma Shri in 1957.

Balbir Singh has remained one of the best strikers in the Indian hockey team. The versatile centre-forward Balbir Singh represented India thrice in the Olympics.

Balbir Singh was born on 10th October 1924 at Haripar village in Jalandhar district of Punjab. He had his early education at Dev Samaj School and D.M. College, Moga. He graduated from Khalsa College, Amritsar.

He captained the Punjab University team that won the Inter-University Championship in 1945. A career in the Punjab police soon followed. He was a member of the Punjab police team that saw a series of victories in many tournaments all over the country from 1948 to 1960. He captained the Punjab state team that won the National Championship in 1949.

Balbir Singh joined the Indian team in 1947 and was selected for the team that toured Sri Lanka in 1947.

He captained India to victory in the matches against Afghanistan in 1950 and against Singapore and Malaysia in 1954. He was selected a member of the team called 'India Wanderers'. This team played matches in New Zealand, Australia, Singapore and Sri Lanka in 1955.

Hockey was introduced in the Asian Games in 1958 at Tokyo. It was Balbir Singh who was selected to lead the country's team. He represented India at the Olympics thrice — in 1948 at London, in 1952 at Helsinki and in 1956 at Melbourne. He captained the team at Helsinki and scored nine of the 13 goals. At Melbourne, the Indian team defeated Pakistan to win the gold medal. The Padma Shri was the most appropriate recognition that came to him the following year, i.e. in 1957.

When his active playing days were over, Balbir Singh was in demand as a coach and manager of the Indian team. He was the team manager when India won a gold at the 1962 International Hockey Tournament in Ahmedabad. He was the team manager at subsequent events too when India won a silver at the 1970 Asian Games at Bangkok, a bronze in the 1982 World Tournament at Amsterdam and a silver at the 1982 Asian Games in Delhi.

He was manager-cum-coach-cum-chief selector for the team that won a gold medal in the Thirld World Cup Tournament at Kuala Lumpur in 1975. Here India won the gold medal in hockey after a gap of 11 years. He was the manager of the team for the Esanda World Cup in Melbourne in 1982.

He was many times honoured for his achievements. He was invited to be the chief guest at the Kennedy Memorial International Hockey Tournament in Washington in 1974. Six years later he was the honoured guest at the 1980 Olympics in Moscow. Balbir Singh lit the sacred flame at the 1982 Asian Games in Delhi.

He was secretary of the Punjab State Sports Council and Director of Sports in the Punjab government till his retirement in 1982. An indoor stadium has been named after him in Moga. Like Dhyan Chand, he has also written a book, *The Golden Hat-trick*.

Achievements

☆ *Balbir Singh represented India thrice in the Olympics. In all the three Olympics (London in 1948, Helsinki in 1952, Melbourne in 1956) India won a gold medal.*

- ☆ *He captained the Punjab state team.*
- ☆ *He captained the Indian team to victory against Afghanistan in 1950 and against Singapore and Malaysia in 1954.*
- ☆ *He was chosen to lead the Indian team in the Asian Games in 1958 in Tokyo.*
- ☆ *He was the team manager when the Indian team won a gold medal in 1982 at Ahmedabad, a silver in the 1970 Asian Games at Bangkok, a bronze in the 1971 World Hockey Tournament at Amsterdam and a silver in the 1982 Asian Games at Delhi.*
- ☆ *He was the manager, coach and chief selector for the team that won a gold medal in the Third World Cup Tournament at Kuala Lumpur in 1975.*
- ☆ *He was secretary of the Punjab State Sports Council.*
- ☆ *He was the Director of Sports in the Punjab government till his retirement in 1982.*
- ☆ *He was awarded the Padma Shri in 1957.*
- ☆ *An indoor stadium has been named after him in Moga.*
- ☆ *He has authored a book,* The Golden Hat-trick.

Hockey

Dhanraj Pillai

Date of Birth: 16th July 1968

Dhanraj Pillai, who played in the centre-forward position, showed striking ability and speed in manoeuvring the ball. He is a proud winner of a number of prizes and awards in his long and spectacular career. In the year 1991, the Maharashtra government bestowed him with the 'Chhatrapati Shivaji Award'. In addition to this, he also won 'Rajiv Gandhi Khel Ratna' award, the Arjuna Award and the Padma Shri.

Dhanraj Pillai's name is taken with great honour in the Indian sports world. This best center-forward hockey player is to Indian hockey what Sachin Tendulkar is to Indian cricket. Just as Indian cricket goes by the power-word Sachin, similarly Indian hockey is incomplete without Dhanraj Pillai. Pillai is the strongest pillar of Indian hockey.

Dhanraj Pillai was born on 16th July 1968 at a place called Khirki in Pune, Maharashtra. His story is the story of a poor boy, who responded to his calling in life after a lot of hard work. Dhanraj spent most of his childhood in the streets of the armament factory in Pune. He received complete moral support from his family comprising of five siblings and that too blessed with moderate finances. He and his brothers were unable to buy new hockey sticks because of their poor financial condition, so they used to tie up old hockey sticks with twine or rope and play with them instead.

Right from his childhood, Dhanraj has been extremely attached to his mother. He says, "It's so hard to imagine that our mother brought up all of us so well despite very stringent resources."

His mother tongue is Tamil, but he can speak Hindi, Marathi and English also. He works as Assistant Manager in the Indian Airlines and is the only Indian player to participate in three Olympics, three World Cups and four Asian Games. Being a senior player, he has been the main ray of hope for the Indian team. In his time he could easily challenge a 15-year old player in his team and also win him over. He loves his game and plays with diligence.

He was chosen for the World XI team in 1994. He led the Indian team in the World Cup in Holland in 1998. He started his career in hockey at the S.V.S. High School in Pune. He was chosen to play for Maharashtra in the Junior National Championship at Imphal in 1985. The very next year he was chosen for the senior level. He regularly played for Maharashtra and Mumbai teams and was part of the Maharashtra team that won the Federation Cup in 1991-92 at Lucknow.

He was chosen the best player twice — the first time was in the series at Belgium, Holland, Spain and England in 1992 and the next time in the Indira Gandhi Gold Cup Tournament in 1994. He had played more than 400 matches till 2003.

Awards

- ☆ *Dhanraj Pillai was given the Arjuna Award in 1994.*
- ☆ *He was given the K.K. Birla Foundation Award for 1998-99.*
- ☆ *In 1999 he was honoured with the 'Rajiv Gandhi Khel Ratna' award.*
- ☆ *He was conferred the Padma Shri in 2001.*

Achievements

- ☆ *Dhanraj Pillai took part in the Alwin Asia Cup in 1989, where the team won a silver medal.*
- ☆ *He was a member of the Olympic team for the Sydney Olympics in September 2000 and the team reached the seventh position.*
- ☆ *In the 1996 Atlanta Olympics the team reached the eighth position and he scored two goals.*

- ☆ *He was a member of the Olympic team for the Barcelona Olympics in 1998.*
- ☆ *He scored two goals in Kuala Lampur in 2002, two goals in Unnechi in 1998, as the captain.*
- ☆ *He was selected for the World XI team.*
- ☆ *He scored two goals at Cologne in 2002 and was declared the 'Player of the Tournament'.*
- ☆ *He won seven medals at the Beijing Asian Games in 1990 and Hiroshima Games in 1994.*
- ☆ *He became the lead flag bearer of the Indian team at the Busan Asian Games in October 2002.*
- ☆ *He won a silver medal for India after scoring three goals.*
- ☆ *He was nominated a member of the 'All Star Asian Games' team.*
- ☆ *The Indian team won a gold medal under his leadership in Bangkok in 1998.*
- ☆ *He has 10 goals to his credit.*
- ☆ *The reached the second position at both the Hiroshima Games in 1994 and at the Beijing Asian Games in 1990.*
- ☆ *The team stood third at Kuala Lampur in 1999 and when he scored three goals.*
- ☆ *He was a member of the team for Hiroshima Games in 1993 and 1989 in New Delhi. His team came second in New Delhi.*
- ☆ *He participated five times in the Indira Gandhi Gold Cup Tournament and won the matches for India in 1990, 1992 and 1994. He was member of the team in 1995 and declared the 'Player of the Tournament' after he scored seven goals in 1999.*
- ☆ *He made India reach the foremost position at Kuala Lampur in 2001 and scored a goal.*
- ☆ *In the Indo-Pak series, he captained the Indian hockey team in 1998.*

- ☆ *In the SAF Games, he led the team to win at Chennai in 1994.*
- ☆ *In the Commonwealth Games, he helped his team reach the fourth position in 1998 and scored five goals.*
- ☆ *His team won the Sultan Shah Cup in 2000 in Malaysia and he scored five goals there.*
- ☆ *He played in Epoh in 1996 and was part of the winning team in the Alps International Hockey Tournament (Austria in 1992) and SAP Sports Hockey Title (Madras in 1994).*
- ☆ *On the Australian tour, the team reached the third position in Sydney in 2000 and he scored a single goal here.*
- ☆ *The Indian team won at Perth in 2000 and he scored two goals.*
- ☆ *He was a member of the team that participated at Amstelvin in 2001, Barcelona in 2000, Belgium in 2000, Hamberg in 1997, Germany in 1995, Vienna in 1993, International Tournament at Pojnan in 1993, BMW Tournament in 1990.*
- ☆ *At the national level, he was member of the hockey team for the Senior Nationals (1997), Junior Nationals (1995), National Games (2002), Jawaharlal Nehru Hockey Tournament (2002) , Lal Bahadur Shastri Hockey Tournament (2002), Gurugappa Gold Cup (2002, 1999 and 1998). He was chosen as the 'Man of the Final' in the Gurugappa Gold Hockey in 1999 and 2002.*
- ☆ *His last participation was in the Athens Olympics.*

Major Dhyan Chand Singh

Date of Birth: 29th July 1905
Died: 3rd December 1979

Major Dhyan Chand Singh was a hockey player and Indian Olympian. He is considered to be the best hockey player till date. People called him the 'Hockey Wizard'. He is said to have mesmerised Adolf Hitler with his excellent playing skills. His birthday on 29th August is celebrated as the National Sports Day in India. The sports stadium at India Gate in New Delhi is named after him. The Indian Government has also introduced an award in the name of Major Dhyan Chand to felicitate sportspersons who continue to be involved in sports despite taking retirement from active sports. The Indian Postal Department has also brought out a stamp in his memory.

Dhyan Chand was born on 29th August 1905 in Prayag (now Allahabad) in a Rajput family. His father was a Subedar in the Army. He too was inducted into the Army in the Punjab regiment after his initial education at the age of 17 years. In the Brahmin regiment, Subedar Major Bhole Tiwari gauged Dhyan Chand's excellent dribbling skills and knack for scoring goals.

At the London Folkstone Festival in 1927, he played extremely well against the English hockey team. In the 10 matches that were played, Dhyan Chand struck 36 goals out of a total of 72 goals.

In 1928, at the Summer Olympics held at Amsterdam in the Netherlands, Dhyan Chand as the member of the Indian hockey team helped India win a gold medal with a score of 3-0, which was only due to Dhyan Chand's magnificent play. He had such control over the ball that it appeared to onlookers that the ball was stuck to his hockey stick. Thus he was known as the 'Hockey Wizard'. Once it so happened that an officer in Tokyo broke his hockey stick to clear his doubt whether Dhyan Chand had hid a magnet inside it. In another instance, a female fan once asked him to play with a walking stick instead of a hockey stick. The fan had more than her fill when Dhyan Chand scored a number of goals with the ordinary stick as well. An artist in Vienna portrayed Dhyan Chand with eight arms in his painting.

In the Summer Olympics at Los Angeles in 1932, the Indian team came back with a gold medal after defeating the American team 24-1, which is a record even now. In this series Dhyan Chand scored eight goals. In this year he had scored 133 goals out of a total of 338 goals at such a speed that spectators often sat shocked in their seats.

The final match at the 1933 Beighton Cup between Jhansi Heroes and Calcutta Customs proved an extremely memorable match for Dhyan Chand. The most surprising aspect of this match was that he had been unable to score even one goal in this match and the Jhansi Heroes had to return back in the third-class unreserved compartment of the train after the match. This is why Dhyan Chand called it a very memorable match.

In the tour of New Zealand and Australia in 1935, 43 matches were played in all and India scored 584 goals. Out of these goals, 201 goals were scored by Dhyan Chand alone. During one of these matches, Dhyan Chand happened to meet Don Bradman in Adelaide, Australia. Bradman could not help exclaiming, "He makes goals like runs in cricket."

An unforgettable incident once occurred in his life in the 1936 Summer Olympics. Dhyan Chand's regiment denied him permission to participate in the event which was due to be held at Berlin. It took repeated requests on Dhyan Chand's regiment to agree to send him there. At last he was given permission. The team reached Berlin under the captaincy of Dhyan Chand to participate in the Summer Olympics. A friendly match was played with Germany before the finals. The Indian team, full of patriotic fervour, hoisted the Indian tricolour in the dressing room and sang the Indian national song, '*Vande Mataram*' there, where it was mandatory to play only the British national anthem.

The Indian team led 1-0 till half time. Then, in the second half-time, India scored seven goals. Immediately after the goals, the Germans started hitting the Indian team. The German goalie struck Dhyan Chand so hard that his teeth came off, but he resumed his game soon.

The Nazi dictator of Germany, Adolf Hitler, had also come to watch the match. He could not bear to see his 'superior team' losing and left the match midway. He also left some of his things behind in the hurry. The authorities suspected foul play on India's part and even directed Dhyan Chand to change his hockey stick during the course of the game. But the goals didn't stop even then. India won the match with a score of 8-1. Three goals were scored by Dhyan Chand in this match. A press reporter gave the following comments on Dhyan Chand's outstanding talent, "A twist of the wrist, a glance of the eye, a rapid turn and then Dhyan Chand's fantastic goal."

The next day after the match, Hitler invited Dhyan Chand to meet him. It is said that Hitler asked Dhyan Chand about the post at which he worked in India. He was shocked to know that this spectacular hockey magician worked at the post of a Naik in the Indian Army. Hitler proposed to Dhyan Chand to come and join the German Army where he would be given the post of a Field Marshall, but Dhyan Chand declined Hitler's offer saying that he had a huge family in India to support and it was not possible for him to leave them behind. Some people conjecture that Hitler had given him an offer to play for Germany and asked him, "What would you charge to play for Germany?" To this Dhyan Chand had said, "Nothing sir, India is my India." He scored a total of 59 goals out of the team's tally of 175 goals in that Olympics.

Dhyan Chand remained associated with hockey even after the Second World War. He played 22 matches against East Africa, in which he scored 61 goals. He retired at the age of 42 years in 1948 from active hockey.

In 1956, he retired from the Indian Army at the post of Major. After retirement from active sports, Dhyan Chand did a diploma course in coaching from the National Sports Institute, Patiala. Dhyan Chand left for his heavenly abode on 3rd December 1979.

Achievements

- ☆ *Dhyan Chand was conferred the Padma Bhushan in 1956 by the Government of India.*
- ☆ *The residents of Vienna (Austria) have installed a statue of Dhyan Chand to honour him. In this statue Dhyan Chand is portrayed with four hands holding hockey sticks in all the four to symbolise his excellent control over his hockey stick and the ball.*
- ☆ *He is the only player to have a statue dedicated to him. His statue stands in the National Stadium at India Gate. In addition to this, his statue was put up in the Medak district of Andhra Pradesh in 2005.*
- ☆ *His birthday on the 29th of August is celebrated as the National Sports Day in India. On this day distinguished sportspersons are given various awards, such as the Arjuna Award and the Major Dhyan Chand Award by the President of India in the Rashtrapati Bhavan.*
- ☆ *The Indian Postal Department has also brought out a stamp in his memory.*
- ☆ *He was known as the 'Hockey Wizard' and the 'Hockey Personality of the Century'.*

MOUNTAINEERING

Mountaineering or mountain climbing is a sport entailing scaling of mountains. It is also known as 'alpinism', particularly in Europe. While it began as an all-out attempt to reach the highest point of unclimbed mountains, it has now branched into different fields of specialisations to address the different aspects of mountains like rock-craft, snow-craft and skiing, depending on whether the route chosen is over rock, snow or ice.

Normally mountaineering is a group activity in which each member supports and is supported by the group's efforts. Its pleasure lies not only in the conquest of the peak but also in the physical and spiritual satisfaction brought about through intense personal effort, proficiency and contact with natural grandeur. The greater rewards do not come without considerable risk and danger.

Mountaineering is even taken up as a hobby or profession involving walking, hiking, trekking and climbing up mountains. All require great athletic and technical ability and experience which are important aspects of the sport.

The first recorded mountain ascent is Roman Emperor Hadrian's ascent of Etna (3,350 metres) to see the sun rise in 121 B.C. Though it is unknown whether his intention was to reach a summit, Otzi ascended at least 3,000 metres in the Alps about 5,300 years ago. His remains were found preserved in a glacier.

The first 'open' peak ascend in modern times was Mont Blanc in 1786. Other Alpine peaks followed, capped by the ascent of Matterhorn in 1865. By 1910, most peaks of the Andes, the Rockies and other Western Hemisphere ranges had been conquered. Beginning in the 1930s, a series of successful ascents of mountains in the Himalayas occurred, culminating in the 1953 ascent of Mount Everest by Edmund Hillary and Tenzing Norgay. Hillary is no longer alive but he has made mountaineering a famous adventure sport.

The 1950s saw the first ascent of the Himalayas starting with Annapoorna peak in 1950 by Maurice Herzog and Louis Lachenal. The world's highest mouintain peak (above sea-level), Mount Everest (8,848 metres), was first climbed on 20th May 1953 by Sir Edmund Hillary and Tenzing Norgay from the south side in Nepal. Just a few months later, Hermann Buhl made the first ascent of Nanga Parbat (8,125 metres) in a siege style expedition, culminating in a remarkable solo push for the summit.

In the 1960s, mountaineering became an increasingly technical sport, emphasising the use of specialised anchoring, tethering and grappling gear in the ascent of vertical rock- or ice-faces.

Mountaineering

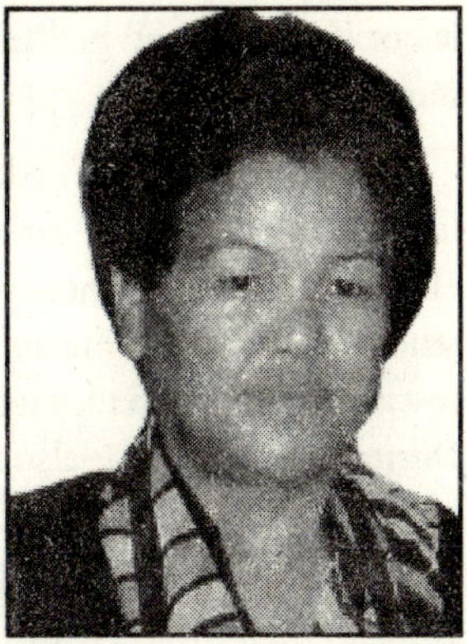

Bachendri Pal

Date of Birth: 24th May 1954

Bachendri Pal is the first woman mountaineer to hoist the Indian flag on Mount Everest in 1984. Years ago it was Tenzing Norgay who had got the honour of being the first Indian mountaineer to conquer the mighty Mt. Everest. Four other women mountaineers of other countries of the world have been successful in their Everest expedition before Bachendri Pal.

Bachendri, who was extremely courageous since her childhood days, found it a great pleasure to wander in the Himalayas in Garhwal. She was a happy-go-lucky and dreamy girl.

Bachendri Pal was born on 24th May 1954 at Nakuri, Uttarakashi (Uttarakhand). Her father's name was Kishen Singh Pal who is no more. He used to transport things of daily needs like rice, pulses, flour on the backs of goats and horses and sell them in Tibet. Thereafter, he gradually settled in Uttarakashi and got married. Bachendri was the third child among his five children.

Being of rebellious nature, she was very different from the other children. She used to entertain her family with her dreams about aeroplanes and other imaginative stories. She used to daydream about the famous personalities that she would get to meet in life. She liked to be independent and bold.

Her first opportunity in mountaineering came at the age of 12 when she set out with her classmates to climb a hill of height 4,000 metres (around 13123.36 ft). She enjoyed this small picnic expedition immensely even though the group could not go down on that particular day because it got dark and she had to spend the night on the hill without proper food and shelter.

As Bachendri turned 13, she was expected to give up her education like all the Garhwali girls of her age and learn home-making skills. However, as determined as she was, she continued with her studies by studying at night. This made her family aware of her strong inclination towards studies and they willingly granted her permission to study further. During this period she also started stitching clothes during her spare time so that she could take care of her increasing expenses.

Seeing Bachendri's dedication and interest towards higher studies, her principal requested her parents to send her to college. On joining college, she took to rifle shooting and defeated her classmates in it and other competitions to emerge a clear winner. Bachendri's parents were extremely proud of their daughter after she completed her graduation as she became the first girl from her village to be a graduate.

Bachendri did not stop at this. After completing her graduation, she did her postgraduation in Sanskrit and also her B.Ed. Despite her good qualifications, she did not get a job anywhere. Wherever she was selected, she was asked to work for a meagre salary at a junior level. Then Bachendri got admission at the Nehru Institute of Mountaineering. Here too, she excelled in the course and was nominated as the best student of the course. It was here that she was told of her capability to scale Mt. Everest and this surprised her greatly.

After this she participated in the advance-level camp at the Nehru Institute of Mountaineering in 1982. There she successfully managed to scale the Gangotri (6,672 metres/21,900 ft) and Rudugera (5819 metres/ 1,9091.207ft). Her trainer was Brig. Gyan Singh who was Director of National Adventure Foundation. He had set up this adventure club to initiate young women into mountaineering. Here Bachendri got a job as a trainer. All this time Bachendri's family was going through a severe financial crisis.

In the year 1984 it was decided to send India's fourth expedition to the Mt. Everest. Four other women mountaineers of the world have been successful in their Everest expedition before Bachendri. In this particular mountaineering group, seven women and 11 men were selected where Bachendri too was one of the members. This was her first actual full-scale mountain climbing expedition. She moved ahead in her task with full courage and determination and dealt with every obstacle with great resolve. There were numerous obstacles, such as slippery mountains, injuries, avalanches, etc., which came in their way, but Bachendri would not let any of these dampen her spirit. The team continued climbing and they reached their mighty destination at last.

On 23rd May 1984 at 1.07 p.m. Bachendri let the Indian tricolour flutter at the peak of Mt.Everest. The peak of Everest is known as Sagar Matha in Nepali. It can be said in other words that Bachendri kissed the *matha* (forehead) of the Sagar Matha and flew the prestigious Indian tricolour on its peak.

Bachendri was honoured and felicitated by the entire nation. She also set up a record of being the first Indian woman who had been successful in climbing the Mt. Everest. After one year, Bachendri again set out on a mountaineering expedition with an all-women team, where she was the leader of the group. Then in the year 1994, she also led an all woman Ganga rafting expedition from Haridwar to Kolkata. She is employed as Deputy Divisional Manager (Adventure Progamme) at the Tata Steel Adventure Foundation.

Achievements

- ☆ *Bachendri Pal is the first Indian woman, who has been successful in climbing the Mt.Everest on 23rd May 1984. She is the fifth woman in the world to be able to do this successfully.*
- ☆ *She set out on a mountaineering expedition to the Everest with an all-women team, where she was the leader of the group.*
- ☆ *In the year 1994, she led an all-women Ganga rafting expedition from Haridwar to Kolkata.*
- ☆ *In 1997, she climbed the Himalaya with an all-women mountaineering team.*
- ☆ *Bachendri Pal's name was included in the* Guinness Book of World Records *in 1990.*
- ☆ *In the year 1985, she was presented with the 'Calcutta Sports Journalists Association Award'.*

- ☆ *This very year, she was honoured with the Padma Shri by the Government of India.*
- ☆ *In the year 1986, she was presented with the 'Calcutta Ladies Study Club'*
- ☆ *She was given a gold medal by the Indian Mountaineering Institute for being the most outstanding mountaineer.*
- ☆ *She was given the Arjuna Award in 1986.*
- ☆ *In 1994, she was presented with the 'National Adventure Award'.*
- ☆ *In 1995, she was honoured with the Yash Bharti Award by the government of Uttar Pradesh.*
- ☆ *Her name was included in the* Limca Book of Records *in 1997.*
- ☆ *In the year 1997, she was presented with an Honorary D.Literature degree by the Garhwal University.*
- ☆ *This very year, she was presented with 'Mahila Shiromani Award'.*
- ☆ *She is the executive member of the organisations like the A.F.M., H.M.I.M. and the Adventure Foundation.*
- ☆ *She is the Vice-Chairman of the Seven Sisters Adventure Club, Uttarakashi and All Indian Women's Judo-Karate Foundation.*
- ☆ *She is the president of the Lion's Club of India.*
- ☆ *She is often invited by countries all over the world to deliver lectures on topics related to mountaineering.*
- ☆ *Bachendri Pal has also authored a book,* Everest — My Journey to the Top.

Mountaineering

Santosh Yadav

Birth: 16th April 1964

Santosh Yadav is an extremely self-confident mountaineer. The fact that she has set up a world record by conquering the Everest peak not once but twice is an example to elucidate this statement. She had never even imagined in her childhood that one day she would grow up to earn fame all over the world and be a mountaineer. She is the only woman in the world to climb the Everest twice. She has been honoured with the Padma Shri by the Government of India for her spectacular achievement.

The Indian society is a male-dominated society. This manifests itself in the belief that most Indian families still consider the birth of a girl child as a bane to their families. The thought of giving birth to a girl child is not encouraged by many families. This had not been the case with Santosh Yadav. The old beliefs had slowly begun to shake prior to her birth. At the time when her mother was pregnant, an ascetic had blessed her with the boon of a son. Her paternal grandmother told him that they wished for the birth of a daughter in the family. It was in such an environment that Santosh was born. She was named 'Santosh' as it meant 'satisfaction' and this is what she brought to her family.

Santosh was born in a village called Joniyawas in Rewari district of Haryana into a family of five brothers. She always aspired to study well and do well in her life since her childhood itself. She loved to dress up in men's attire as a child. Her family was primarily *zamindars*, but is now engaged in business.

Her desire to go to a good school made her parents seek admission for her in a school in Delhi. She moved to Delhi with her mother and brothers for getting education. During her school days, she won a first prize in a handwriting competition. However, her writing speed was relatively slow and this is the reason why she could not complete her question paper despite knowing all the answers. The speed of her thoughts could not match up with her writing speed. Many of her classmates, who used to take advice from Santosh, ended up with better marks in many examinations.

After some time, she returned to Rewari after the Central School was opened. She completed her Standard XII and her family started pressurising her to get married. However, Santosh told them that she would not marry without getting a graduation degree. She said once, "The Almighty listened to my prayers and I got admission in the famous Maharani College of Jaipur. My dream of entering a good college was fulfilled when I got admission here. But I was not aware of the forthcoming turn in my life while pursuing B.A. Economics Honours."

When she was staying at the hostel at Jaipur, Santosh loved to gaze at the Aravali hills from her hostel window. She once said, "I used to leave for Jhalana Dungri hill and watch every morning local people working there."

She loved meeting these people and interacting with them. She started making their sketches. As she was fond of painting since her childhood, she loved to sketch.

After this she developed a fascination for hills and mountains and started enjoying climbing up and down the mountains. In this manner she once reached the mountain peak and was emotionally touched by the scene she saw from the top. It was dawn and from a height it appeared as if the sun arose from the mountains; it was a delightful sight. But after a while, she started feeling afraid and climbed down. On the way, she met a group of boys who were engaged in rock climbing and she felt very happy to see them. She asked one of the boys, "Do you think I can also do this?"

The group replied enthusiastically, "Why not?"

It was then that she understood that what mountaineering was and decided to take to this activity after acquiring proper training. It was extremely difficult for her family to understand and accept Santosh's decision. Initially they were very angry but in the meanwhile Santosh had spent her entire savings on the course organised by Nehru Mountaineering Institute, her father decided to bring her back, but as he was coming down the stairs in a hurry, he slipped and hurt his ankle badly. Santosh's admission at the Nehru Institute of Mountaineering in 1986 was against the wishes of her father.

She said, "The self-confidence I had was because of my father's love. I could take my own decisions after pondering. It was again my self-confidence because of which I topped in my course."

After this, she decided to do the advanced course and her hard work bore fruit. She managed to overcome the cold and height due to her strong will power and physical forbearance. In 1993, she was successful in reaching the Everest peak for the first time. She was the youngest woman mountaineer to conquer the Everest. Again in the year 1994, she was successful in reaching the Everest peak for yet another time. She is the only woman in the world to climb the Everest peak twice. She could attain this phenomenal success because of her physical ability and fitness. Commenting on it, she said, "It was an extremely happy moment for me when I came to India after winning my award. My father gifted me a Maruti car."

Later Santosh Yadav joined the police service. In this job, she could also fulfil her desire of climbing mountains during her holidays. Today Santosh is a good speaker and inspires a lot of people to fulfil their ambitions and move ahead in life. She is working towards the cause of promoting education. She says. "It is very important to have an aim in one's life. Work hard towards your goal. There should be an aim to do something in life; only then can you enjoy your life.

She was awarded the Padma Shri for her achievements. She got married at the age of 25 years. Her parents are happy with her, her achievements and are proud of her celebrity status.

Achievements

- ☆ *Santosh Yadav is the youngest woman mountaineer to conquer the Everest.*
- ☆ *She is the only woman in the world to reach the Everest peak twice.*
- ☆ *She is full of self-confidence and it is because of this that she was able to succeed in her sphere.*
- ☆ *She is recipient of the Padma Shri for her achievements*

Tenzing Norgay

Date of Birth: 29th May 1914
Died: 9th May 1986

Tenzing Norgay, who was popularly known as Sherpa Tenzing, had the honour of being the first Indian to scale Mt. Everest, the highest peak in the world. He, alongwith the famous mountaineer of New Zealand, Edmund Hillary, was successful in reaching the peak for the first time in the world, on 29th March 1953.

Tenzing Norgay was born in a poor peasant family in May 1914 in Kharta valley in Tibet. His exact date of birth is not known, but according to the description of crops and season, it appears that he was born in the month of May. After scaling the Mt. Everest, he started celebrating his birthday on 29th of May every year.

He was known by the name of Namgyal Vagandi in his childhood, but the Lama head changed his name to Nawang Tenzin Norbu, which meant wealthy, fortunate and religious. His father, Ghang La Mingma, was a yak herder. His mother Dokmo Kinzom lived to see the mountaineering feat of her son. He was the 11th child of his 13 siblings, out of whom many did not survive.

Tenzing was also called Khumjung Bhutia and he was a follower of Buddhism. He had taken the citizenship of India in 1933. He visited Kathmandu twice during his childhood and later started living in Darjeeling in West Bengal, amidst the Sherpas.

In the year 1930 when three British officers attempted to climb the Everest from the northern Tibet side, Tenzing accompanied them as their coolie. He got a number of opportunities to do mountaineering, with the most difficult climb being that of the Nanda Devi (east) peak in 1940.

In 1947, he attempted to climb again with three different nationals who were climbing the peak illegally. However, a terrible storm at 22,000 feet foiled their efforts and the three people had to return back.

In the year 1952, a Swiss team tried to climb Mt. Everest once more. Under the leadership of Raymond Lambert, this team tried to scale Mt. Everest from the Nepal side and was successful in climbing up to 8,599 feet.

In 1953, the John Hunt Foundation made the seventh attempt to climb Mt. Everest. Hillary along with Tenzing was successful in this effort for the first time in the world and reached the summit. The two climbers were accorded a warm welcome, on their return, by the people of India and Nepal. In fact, they were even worshipped as incarnations of Lord Buddha and Lord Shiva. The two Everest conquereors were awarded a 'George medal' by the British Government. An interesting fact about this conquest was that in all the photographs that were taken on the peak of Mt. Everest, only Tenzing's face is visible. It was discovered later that since Tenzing did not know how to use a camera, only his photographs could be clicked by Hillary.

Tenzing married thrice. His first wife Dawa Phuti died very young in 1944. The names of his two wives were Ang Lahmu and Dakku and he has four children.

The Government of India honoured him with the Padma Bhushan in 1959. The Himalayan Mountaineering Institute of Darjeeling was set up in West Bengal in 1954 and Tenzing Norgay was made the Director. He was nicknamed 'Tiger of Snows' at the institute. In 1978, Tenzing set up a company by the name of Tenzing Norgay Adventures to undertake trekking trips to the Himalayas. The company is being run by his son, Jamling Tenzing Norgay, who conquered the Everest in 1996.

Tenzing Norgay passed away on 9th May 1986 in Darjeeling.

Achievements

☆ *On 29th May 1953, Tenzing Norgay alongwith Edmund Hillary succeeded in reaching the peak of Mt. Everest for the first time in the world.*

- ☆ *The Government of India honoured him with the Padma Bhushan in 1959.*
- ☆ *He was also honoured with the 'George medal' by the British Government.*
- ☆ *He was apppointed as the Director of the Himalayan Mountaineering Institute at Darjeeling.*
- ☆ *In the year 1978, he set up a company by the name of Tenzing Norgay Adventures for trekking lovers.*

SHOOTING

Shooting is a sport where firing at targets with rifles, handguns (pistols and revolvers) and shotguns involves an exercise done with marksmanship. World championship competitions are held for the small-bore rifle, free rifle, centre-fire pistol, free pistol, rapid-fire pistol, air rifle, air pistol and shotgun. Shooting has been an Olympic sport since the modern games began in 1896; women's events were included in 1984.

Shooting is actually an act or process of firing a gun or other projectile weapons, such as bow or crossbows. The word 'shooting' refers to game hunting which implies the hunting of upland game birds, such as grouse or pheasant, rabbit, deer and other game animals. Shooting can also refer to target shooting and includes shotgun (skeet or trap), all of which use sporting clays. Further, shooting refers to the sport of rifle and handgun precision marksmanship. Here, stationary paper targets or reactive metal targets are used.

There is also a growing sport of cowboy action shooting. Here, competitors wear the attire from the late 1800s and fire period weapons (single-action revolvers, lever-action rifles, and either double-barrel or pump-action shotguns) at a variety of metal and reactive targets. Shooting also encompasses the practical shooting sport of IPSA and IDPA competitions. They strive, with varying degrees of success, to simulate the conditions and requirements of defensive pistol combat. Their goal is to train participants for real-world self-defence using one's personal handgun of choice. There is yet another practical shooting sport — the three-gun competition, in which the contestants use handgun, rifle and shotgun to engage various paper or steel targets during the course of fire.

All these various forms of shooting are fascinating and rewarding activities for people of all ages. The utmost consideration, and one which takes precedence over everything else, is safety. As shooting involves an element of danger, a sober understanding and respect for firearms and specific rules for their safe handling is necessary.

Shooting

Abhinav Bindra

Date of Birth: 28th December 1982

Abhinav Bindra is the youngest recipient of the Arjuna Award and the 'Rajiv Gandhi Khel Ratna' award. He also participated in the Sydney Olympics (2000) and is the youngest Indian player to participate in the Olympic Games. He could only manage to reach the 11th position in the Sydney Olympics. Later, in the 2004 Athens Olympics, he came seventh.

Abhinav, who is also fondly called Abhi by his family and loved ones, was born on 28th September 1982 in Dehradun. He went to witness the Atlanta Olympics with his family in 1999, where he saw a shooting range for the first time and was attracted towards it. Luckily for him, his family too extended complete support to him to move ahead in the sport. After a lot of thought, he chose the air rifle competition for himself and started participating in it. The decision to participate in the shooting competition was taken at the tender age of 15 years.

Abhinav Bindra's name was heard for the first time in the sports circuit after he won a bronze medal with 100.5 points in the 10-m rifle competition in the 2001 Munich World Cup. He astonished everybody after he fired 60 shots within 44 minutes itself, instead of the stipulated time of 45 minutes. He was in the competition along with 105 master shooters from 67 countries. He made a place among the last eight players. Despite being seventh at that time, he reached the third spot with an unbelievable 103.9 points. With this win, he became the first successful Indian player to take part in the men's singles competition at the Olympics.

One important reason for his attraction towards shooting has been the beautiful picture his coach had drawn in his mind about becoming famous in the shooting games. This image was entrenched in his mind so deeply that he only dreamt about being a sportsperson in shooting.

This is what he said about his training, "I practice for about nine hours every day, which includes seven hours of regular shooting practice and about two hours of stretching exercises, like jogging. I am completely exhausted by the time I complete my regime, but it is extremely important for me to do this. The capability of a shooter depends on his ability to focus his attention."

Abhinav has acquired fame and has also won a number of prestigious awards at a very young age. His father has arranged for all the necessary shooting equipments at home so that he could practice at home. He says, "I have an air-conditioned range which is based on the international standards of computer based 'target transport system'. I have seven guns, bullets, jackets and all other essentials of shooting. Therefore, I am completely satisfied with the facilities and equipments I have."

Abhinav is greatly influenced by his parents. His national coaches are Gaby Blueman and Sunny Thomas.

Abhinav's score of 1,161 in the I.S.S.F. World Cup Rifle 3 Position Competition and Fort Bening U.S. Competition made him equal the six-year old record of Subedar Subhaya (in 1999). Abhinav had started practicing for the rifle competition only two months back and this is his first world-class competition in this category. Abhinav's coach for this event was Steneslav Lapidus (Kazhakistan), who had earlier been the coach of the Indian Army. Lapidus said, "I am yet to see a shooter of Bindra's capability even after my coaching experience of 25 years. He has given such a performance after practicing just for two months. I feel that Abhinav Bindra will be an Indian national champion in the coming times."

Awards and Honours

☆ *Abhinav became the first shooter of the world to win four gold medals after he won these medals at the Munich Leg in the 2001 European Rifle Circuit Championship. His medal-winning streak at this competition continued as he also won six gold, four silver and two bronze medals in all the events. In this manner, he managed to win many medals at the 2001 European rifle circuit, which no other shooter had been able to do so far.*

- ☆ *In 2000, he was awarded the 'Diploma of Honour' by the International Sports Shooting Federation.*
- ☆ *In 2002 at the Commonwealth Games in Manchester, Abhinav created a Commonwealth Games record by scoring 1,184 points in six rounds.*
- ☆ *In July 2002, he was given a scholarship under the 'Olympic Solidarity Programme'.*
- ☆ *In 2002 he was bestowed the 'Rajiv Gandhi Khel Ratna' award for his spectacular achievements during 2001 at his performance in Munich.*
- ☆ *In the Commonwealth Games held at Melbourne in March 2006, Abhinav was successful yet again. He broke his own record of Manchester by five points in the 10-m rifle Pears Competition. His 1,189 points also won him a gold medal. In addition to this, he also won a silver medal in the Melbourne Games in the 50-m rifle throw position.*
- ☆ *In July 2006, in the World Shooting Championship (at Zagreb in Croatia), he won a gold medal in the 10-m air rifle competition. He is the first shooter of the country to win a gold medal in the World Shooting Championship. The Punjab government declared a prize of 21 lakh rupees after he won this medal. He feels that shooting should be given prime status among the sports of India as this game has got India the maximum number of medals. He claims that no other game can equal the laurels Indian shooters have earned in this game.*
- ☆ *In 2008 Beijing Olympics, he created history by being the first Indian shooter to win gold medal in 10 meter air rifle.*

Shooting

Anjali Bhagwat

Date of Birth: 5th December 1969

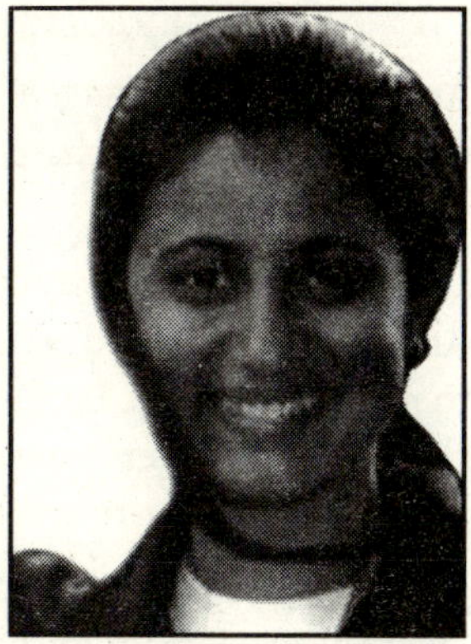

Anjali Bhagwat emerged victorious in the singles as well as doubles event at the air rifle and small bore rifle events in the 2002 Commonwealth Games. A recipient of several awards, Bhagwat was also the proud recipient of the Arjuna Award in the year 2000 and the 'Rajiv Gandhi Khel Ratna' award for the period spanning 2002-03. Some of the other distinguished and noteworthy awards that have been awarded to Anjali Bhagwat include the 'Maharashtra Pratishtha', the 'Chhatrapati Shivaji Award' and the 'Maharashtra Gaurav'.

Anjali Bhagwat or Anjali Vedpathak-Bhagwat, formerly known by the maiden name Anjali Vedpathak, is one of the luminaries from the world of shooting. She was born in a Marathi Deshastha family in Mumbai. A professional rifle shooter, Bhagwat soared to the zenith of fame and success when she won four coveted gold medals for her country in the 2002 Commonwealth Games at Manchester.

The Vedpathaks' younger daughter Anjali was always different. The second of two daughters and one son, this one never wove dreams around Barbie dolls. At a relatively young age, she knew she didn't want a regular 9-5 job. Trekking and learning judo and karate were the hours best spent by her. And her sense of adventure was her best friend. The girl, whose father worked with New India Assurance while her mother was a classical singer, was very sure that she wanted to do something that others wouldn't think about. With single-minded devotion, she chose to join Mumbai's Kirti College, only because the college gave due importance to its National Cadet Corps (NCC) wing. And the world became her playground.

In a sport like shooting, traditionally considered the fiefdom of men, Anjali Bhagwat's emergence as an ace shooter was like a whiff of fresh air. Her achievements have inspired a horde of young women to take up the sport of shooting.

At the 2000 Sydney Olympics, competing as a last-minute wildcard, Anjali put up a spirited performance to become the second Indian woman to reach an Olympic final and reached a creditable seventh position. At the 2002 Manchester Commonwealth Games, she grabbed four gold medals at the 10-metre air rifle and 50-metre rifle 3-position events.

Before her entry into the realm of shooting, the sport was considered an exclusive domain for men. Anjali Bhagwat happens to be the first Indian woman to inspire talented youngsters to follow her footsteps and enter the sphere of this previously male-dominated sport.

Her first stint with shooting occurred during her years as a National Cadet Corps (NCC) cadet. Having realised her talent, Anjali trained under the able tutelage of Sanjay Chakravarthy, won her maiden national title in the year 1990. Her commendable performance in the 2000 Sydney Olympics where she finished seventh earned her several points from the sports critics.

Awards

- ☆ *The 'Shri Chattrapati Shivaji Award' in 1992.*
- ☆ *The 'Maharashtra Gaurav Puraskar' in 1993.*
- ☆ *The 'Vasantrav Naik Pratishthan Puraskar' in 1993.*
- ☆ *The Arjuna Award in 2000.*
- ☆ *The 'Indo-American Society of Young Achievers Award' in 2000.*
- ☆ *The 'Rajiv Gandhi Khel Ratna' award in 2003.*
- ☆ *The 'HISA Sportswoman of the Year' in 2003.*
- ☆ *The 'Times Group Maharashtra Shaan' in 2003.*
- ☆ *The 'HISA Shooter of the -Year' iln 2004.*
- ☆ *The 'Gen-8 Women Achiever's Award' in 2005.*
- ☆ *The 'Teacher's Achievement Award' in 2005.*
- ☆ *The 'FIE Foundation National Award' in 2006.*

Achievements

- ☆ *Anjali is the first Indian shooter to be ranked world's number one in the 10-m air rifle event (women) as per ISSF rating on 3 June 2002.*
- ☆ *She is the first Indian shooter to win.*
- ☆ *She is the first Indian shooter to reach the Olympic finals at the first attempt in the Sydney Olympics, 2000.*
- ☆ *She won a silver medal in the World Cup, Munich, 2002.*
- ☆ *She won the ISSF Champion's Trophy in air rifle (men and women's mixed event), Munich, 2002.*
- ☆ *She earned a silver medal in the World Cup, Sydney, 2002.*
- ☆ *She won a silver medal in the World Cup, Atlanta (USA), 2002.*
- ☆ *She won four gold, seven silver and a bronze medal at the European Circuit 2002, equalling the world record in Den Hague Air Weapon Championship at Hague (Holland), January 2002.*
- ☆ *She won a gold medal in the World Cup, Milan, 2003.*
- ☆ *She won a gold medal in the World Cup, Atlanta (USA), 2003.*
- ☆ *She secured the third consecutive Olympic quota for Beijing Olympics 2008, at Brazil World Cup, 2006.*
- ☆ *Till date, she has won 28 gold, 21 silver and six bronze medals, thus establishing a new record 13 times in international competitions.*
- ☆ *She has won 54 gold, 35 silver and 14 bronze medals setting new records eight times in the national competitions.*
- ☆ *She is a Commonwealth record holder in the 10-m air rifle and sports rifle-3 position till date.*

Shooting

Jaspal Rana

Date of Birth: 28th June 1976

The shining star of shooting, Jaspal Rana has had a scintillating career as he is the proud recipient of the Arjuna Award and has set many records in the national, the world, the Asiad and the the Commonwealth Games.

Jaspal Rana is referred to as the 'torch bearer' of the Indian shooting team. He has made the country proud by winning a number of medals in international competitions. To name a few of them, he won eight gold medals at the SAF Games held in Chennai in 1995 and eight gold medals at the SAF Games held in Melbourne in 1999.

He is counted among the lead shooters of India. He was born on 28th June 1976 at Uttarkashi in Uttarakhand and had his education in Delhi. He did his schooling from the K.V. Air Force School and his university education at St. Stephen's College and Aurobindo College.

He polished his inborn shooting skills to perfection with hard work and efficiency. In no time he became popular in pistol shooting. His father, Narayan Singh Rana made him an expert shooter by giving him proper training. He was sponsored by Samir Thapar of JCT. His coaches, Sunny Thomas and Tibor Ganazol, honed his shooting skills to the highest level under their expert guidance and training.

Jaspal Rana has won over 600 medals in national and international competitions. He was awarded thc Arjuna Award in 1995. Even though he has won the majority of his medals in centre fire pistol competitons, he has been successful in air pistol, standard pistol, freestyle and rapid fire pistol competitions. In fact, he first became famous after he won the gold medal in the junior category at the 46th World Shooting Championship in Milan, Italy. At that time he set a world record score of 569/600.

He has also been successful in the rapid fire pistol competitions, where five targets are hit at the same time in a time interval of eight, six and four seconds. This event relies heavily on muscle coordination and memory, alongwith targeting and shooting. Rana won a gold medal in this event at the 41st National Shooting Championship in 1998 at New Delhi after defeating the famous shooter, Kanwar Lal Dhaka.

Jaspal Rana began his shooting career in the three-week coaching camp held in June 1987 in Delhi. He won a gold medal and a bronze medal in the Delhi State Shooting Championship organised after four months of this camp. He had a taste of glory at the young age of 12 on winning a silver medal at the 31st National Shooting Championship in 1988 at Ahmedabad. He also set a record by winning a record number of medals at Munger in 1992 and at Kanpur in 1994. He won eight gold, one silver and a bronze medal at Munger and 11 medals at Kanpur which included seven in the individual and four team-event medals. Rana set another national record in Ahmedabad in 1993. He scored 590 points in 'centre fire pistol' competition and was able to equal the world record twice. The first event was the National Shooting Championship in 1995 at Coimbatore and the second was the national sports event held at Bengaluru in 1997 when he made record-breaking scores. He was declared the best player in the national sports event in 1997.

For many years Rana's career had been on a low phase. He proved himself worthy of recognition in 1994 and then 12 years later, as a shooter he was almost fading into oblivion when at the Doha Asiad, he performed a spectacular feat by hitting the target with such expertise that he won three gold and one silver medal in 2006 to the delight and pride of all Indians present. He set a new world record with a score of 590 points in the 25 m 'centre fire pistol' competition. In addition to this, he also won the 25-m men's 'standard fire pistol' competition. Rana not only won three gold medals at the Doha Asiad in 2006, but also a silver medal in the 25-m team event in the 'standard fire pistol' competition. He was a member of the team which included Samresh Jung and Raunaq. He surpassed expectations after winning many medals and proving his mettle to the world yet again.

Jaspal revealed in an interview that he greatly believes in spiritualism, but not in religion. His father believes in the teachings of the *Bhagwat Gita* and he tries to emulate the principles laid down in the *Gita*. He is extremely short-tempered and so makes it a point to meditate whenever he loses his cool.

He gives credit for his success to the National Rifle Union. Even his coach-cum-father Narayan Singh Rana admitted that he had not expected Jaspal to do so well.

Achievements

- ☆ *Rana won a gold and a silver medal in the International Shooting Championship at Pyongyong in South Korea in 1993.*
- ☆ *He won a gold medal at the 46th World Shooting Championship in Milan, Italy, thus setting a world record score of 569/600.*
- ☆ *He won two gold, a silver and a bronze medal at the 19th Commonwealth Games in Victoria, in Canada, in 1994 which was a Commonwealth record.*
- ☆ *He won a gold, and a bronze medal at the 12th Asian Games in Hiroshima, in 1994 and created a new Asian Games record with his score of 588/600.*
- ☆ *He won a gold medal at the Asian Shooting Championship in Jakarta in Indonesia in 1995 and created a new Asian Games record with one gold and three silver medals.*
- ☆ *In the first Commonwealth Games held in New Delhi in 1995, he set many new records and received eight gold medals.*

- ☆ *In the 1996 Atlanta Olympic Games, he scored 574/600 points in pistol and 535/600 points in freestyle events.*
- ☆ *In the Second Commonwealth Games in Langkawi, in Malaysia, Rana won four gold and a silver medal in 1997.*
- ☆ *In the Commonwealth Games in Malaysia, he won two gold and two silver medals in 1997.*
- ☆ *In 2006 Doha Asian Games Rana won three gold and a silver medal.*

Shooting

Maharaja Karni Singh

Date of Birth: 21st April 1924

Maharaja Karni Singh is considered a pioneer in competitive shooting in India. Major General His Highness Maharaja Karni Singh was the erstwhile ruler of the state of Bikaner. He had a number of hobbies and many accomplishments to his credit. He had a royal personality and style. He was the first shooter to be awarded the Arjuna Award in 1961.

Maharaja Karni Singh was 23rd in the hierarchy of the valiant Rajput dynasty and thus it was not unusual for him to hold and use weapons. Firing a pistol or using a weapon came as naturally to him as walking or any other routine work.

Born on 21st April 1924 in Bikaner, Rajasthan, he started learning shooting under the guidance and supervision of his father, Maharaja Sadul Singh. It was his father who imparted complete knowledge of guns to him.

Maharaja Karni Singh had his education at St. Stephen's College, New Delhi and St. Xaviers College, Mumbai. He completed his doctorate (Ph.D.) from Bombay University. The topic of his thesis was *The Relation of House of Bikaner with Central Powers from 1465 to 1949*. He also described his memorable moments in shooting in his book, *From Rome to Moscow*.

Karni Singh had his first experience with the pistol at an age of 13 years when he shot down a flying sparrow with precision. This incident gave immense satisfaction to his innate shooter instinct but hurt him emotionally as well. After this incident he decided not to shoot an innocent being for pleasure and make shooting a distinct characteristic of his personality.

Maharaja Karni Singh practiced shooting by shooting down dummy pigeons. Apart from shooting, he was also fond of other sports and this included golf. He was also an artist and a pilot. He was very fond of photography too. He was a Member of Parliament for 25 years from 1952 to1977. He won the National Championship for 17 years in 'clay pigeon trap'category and in skit shooting. He represented India in many international tournaments and won a silver medal in the World Championship.

He was the first shooter to be awarded the Arjuna Award by the Indian government in 1961. His daughter, Rajyashree Kumari, the second born among his three children, also shared her father's interest and won many awards. She too was given the Arjuna Award in 1968.

The House of Bikaner has been associated with royal sports and was a popular haunt for polo during Maharaja Ganga Singh and Maharaja Sadul Singh's times. The royal family reared and bred horses for playing polo. This royal family also had an incredible collection of expensive pistols, rifles and guns. Karni Singh also had a huge collection of cars.

He travelled extensively to various war fronts in the Middle East during the Second World War with his grandfather Maharaja Ganga Singh. He received a number of military awards as well.

Achievements

☆ *Maharaja Karni Singh is considered a pioneer in competitive shooting in India.*

☆ *He was a Member of Parliament for 25 years, from 1952 to 1977.*

☆ *He was also an artist, a pilot, a photographer and a golfer besides being a shooter.*

☆ *He obtained his Ph.D. degree from Bombay University.*

- ☆ *He won a silver medal in the World Shooting Championship.*
- ☆ *He won the National Championship for 17 years in the 'clay pigeon trap' event.*
- ☆ *Maharaja Karni Singh was the first shooter to be awarded the Arjuna Award by the Government of India in 1961.*
- ☆ *His daughter, Rajyashree Kumari, was also an excellent shooter and was the recipient of the Arjuna Award in 1968.*

Manavjit Singh Sandhu

Date of Birth: 3rd November 1976

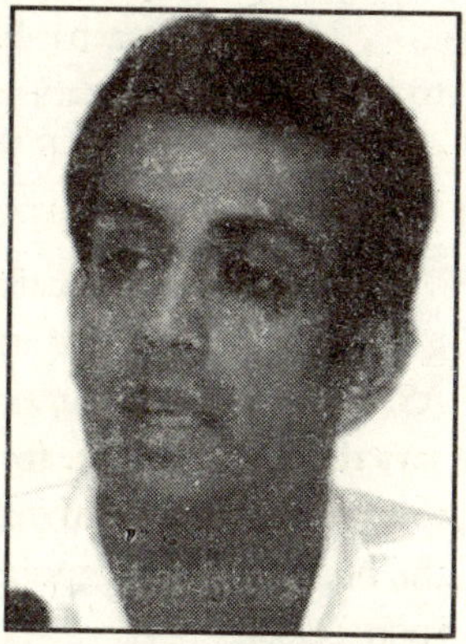

Manavjit Singh Sandhu won a gold medal at the trap-shooting event in the World Championship at Zagreb in 2006. He became the second Indian to win a gold medal at a World Championship. This victory took Manavjit to number one position in world ranking. He was presented the 'Rajiv Gandhi Khel Ratna' award for his outstanding performance on 29th August 2007 by the President of India.

Manavjit Singh Sandhu won a bronze medal at the Commonwealth Games in Melbourne, Australia. In addition to this, he also won an individual medal and a silver medal in the team event in trap shooting.

Manavjit Singh Sandhu was born on 3rd November 1976 in Amritsar, Punjab. Now his permanent residence is at New Delhi. His height is 6'2" and he is a right-handed shooter. Over the past few years, Indian shooters have won a lot of laurels for India at the international level and Manavjit is one of them to win a gold medal at the trap-shooting event in the 49th World Championship organised by the International Shooting Sports Federation (ISSF) in Croatia in Zagreb in July 2006. It was largely because of the efforts of 29-year-old Manavjit that the Indian team could win a silver medal at the ISSF competition with a score of 362 points. Russia came second with 360 while America was third with 359 points.

Manavjit won a gold and a silver medal at Zagreb. Ace shooter Abhinav Bindra had also won a gold medal prior to Manavjit in the World Championship. Thus Manavjit became the second Indian to win a gold medal at a World Championship.

Manavjit's coach is Marcelo Dradi and Manavjit did complete justice to his coach's expectations by winning the gold medal. He also won a silver medal at the ISSF World Cup Competition earlier in America in May 2006. Here Manavjit missed a gold medal narrowly.

Manavjit is gradually improving with time as his game is showing great improvement. He attributes his success to his sponsors, like JCT, ASAI, BILT and the support he gets from the Government of India. He says that there is scope for him to do better in future and has a long way to go yet. He aspires to be a role model for many newcomers and expresses the hope that big corporate houses would come ahead to sponsor the sportspersons.

He was felicitated by JCT on his victory and given a prize of 21 lakh rupees by the Punjab government. He was also given the 'Rajiv Gandhi Khel Ratna' award for his achievement in the year 2006.

Achievements

- ☆ *Manavjit Singh Sandhu has brought laurels to India after his victory at the international forum.*
- ☆ *At the Commonwealth Games in Kuala Lumpur in 1998, he scored 192 points along with Mansher Singh, thus establishing a Commonwealth Games record.*
- ☆ *He won a bronze medal at the Commonwealth Games in Melbourne in 2006.*
- ☆ *He also won an individual medal and a silver medal at the team event in the trap competition.*
- ☆ *He won a gold medal at the trap-shooting event at the 49th World Championship of the International Shooting Sports Federation (ISSF) in Croatia in Zagreb in July 2006.*
- ☆ *He was given the 'Rajiv Gandhi Khel Ratna' award for his achievement in the year 2006.*

Shooting

Rajyavardhan Singh Rathore

Date of Birth: 29th January 1970

In the year 2004, Rajyavardhan Singh Rathore became the first Olympic silver medal winner of India. Lieutenant Colonel Rajyavardhan Singh Rathore of the Indian Army was honoured with the Arjuna Award for 2003-2004 and the highest sports honour of the country — the 'Rajiv Gandhi Khel Ratna' award for the year 2004-2005.

The most 'low profile' shooter of the country succeeded in making India high profile in the low-profile shooter sportsworld. Major Rajyavardhan Singh Rathore proved to the world that the bullet fired from his rifle can never miss the target. He brought a new identity to India, which was known as the nation that always missed the target. It was the same even when he was fighting terrorists in Baramula and Kupwara districts of Jammu and Kashmir between 1994 and 1996. His bullets did not miss their target on 17th August 2004, in the double trap competition too.

India received its first medal in shooting in the Athens Olympics in 2004. However, it is another matter that this medal eluded those shooters who were being considered for the medal.

This was India's fourth individual medal and the first individual silver medal in Olympic history. Prior to Major Rajyavardhan Singh Rathore, wrestler K.D. Jadhav had won a bronze at Helsinki in 1942, tennis ace Leander Paes had won a bronze at Atlanta Olympics in 1996 and weightlifter Karnam Malleswari had won a bronze at the Sydney Olympics in 2000.

After winning the silver medal at the Athens Olympics, 34-year-old Major Rajyavardhan Singh Rathore became the first Indian shooter to win an Olympic medal. He secured the fifth position in the qualifying round with a score of 135 (46, 43, and 46), but he raised his level at the finals by shooting 44 out of 50 targets. He earned a score of 179 points, which earned for him the silver medal. Ahmed al-Makhtoom of United Arab Emirates won a gold medal after scoring 144 points in the qualifying round and 144 points in the finals, which earned him a total of 189 points.

The Indian Army is extremely proud of Major Rajyavardhan Singh Rathore's achievement and released the following statement, "The duty of an Army officer is to bring honour to this country." Rathore draped himself in the tricolour Indian flag when he went to receive his medal.

Rajyavardhan Singh was born on 29th January 1970 and is fondly known as 'Chilly' at home. His wife's name is Dr Gayatri and he is the proud father of two children — son Manav Aditya and daughter Bhagyashri. He lives with his parents in Delhi. After Rajyavardhan Singh won the medal, his wife said, "This silver medal does not only belong to Chilly and the family, but to the entire country. I am happier at this achievement as the entire nation is with us in this moment of joy."

Lt. Colonel Rajyavardhan Singh started shooting in 1998 and soon he was considered among the best trap shooters of the country. In 2003, he won a bronze medal at the World Championship at Nicosia in Cyprus. Before the Olympics, Rathore had said, "It is much easier to shoot on the war front than win an Olympic medal. In a competitive environment, the inner fear resurfaces." He exhibited his prowess in the sportsfield as he has done on the battlefield. After winning, he remarked, "Cricket is extremely important game in our country. I like this game too. But my achievement will attract more people to other games, like shooting."

This Army man could perform this spectacular feat after merely six years of practice and sheer hard work. He also excels in games like basketball, volleyball, cricket, hockey, *kabaddi* and athletics right from his school days. He has participated in the National Cricket Tournament organised by the School Games Federation of India and his fabulous six won him a gold medal.

Rajyavardhan had been given a scholarship by the School Games Federation when he was a student of Class X. After this he performed very well in the basketball team of National Defence Academy (NDA) and won a number of individual medals because of which he was honoured with the NDA blazer, which is the highest sports honour of NDA.

He won gold medals in basketball, volleyball, cricket, boxing and water polo at the Indian Military Academy (IMA). He was captain of the volleyball team and was honoured with the 'Blazer of IMA' award. Being the outstanding player, he was also given the gold medal of the Sikh Regiment. During this course he was declared the best cadet and also given the 'Sword of Honour'.

In 1996, Rajyavardhan did his shooting training at the Army Marxman Infantry School at Mhow. Then he continued with his shooting practice at the Dr. Karni Singh Shooting Range, Tughlaqabad in New Delhi.

Murad Ali Khan, who was also Rajyavardhan's partner in the game, said, "His discipline, hard work, self-confidence and financial status helped him win the medal. Rathore had sketched a very scientific practice plan after his selection. His biggest asset is that this diligent shooter immediately plunges into action without wasting time."

His hobbies include listening to music, playing golf, hunting, and boxing. His highest score has been 191/200. He is influenced greatly by his father and mother.

A number of awards and grants were declared for Rathore after he won the silver medal at Athens. However, these were less in comparison to the annual financial benefits bestowed on a superstar of Indian cricket.

- ☆ Ministry of Sports declared a prize of 50 lakh rupees for Rathore.
- ☆ Indian Olympic Union declared a prize of 11 lakh rupees.
- ☆ The Rajasthan government gave him a cash award of 10 lakh rupees and a flat worth eight lakhs.
- ☆ The Army gave Rathore a cash award of 10 lakh rupees.
- ☆ He was given 10 lakh rupees by AFMC Major.
- ☆ Rathore was felicitated in a ceremony organised by Ghaziabad District Administration. On this occasion various social and industrial organisations presented him with a prize of 10,41,000 rupees.

Lt. Colonel Rajyavardhan Singh Rathore was honoured with the Arjuna Award in September 2004. He received the maximum applause among all the prize recipients when he went ahead to accept his award from the President. This was in a way symbolic of his acceptance as a national hero.

When Rathore was asked to give his reaction on receiving this prestigious award, he said, "I don't think that the Arjuna Award provides encouragement to a player. True encouragement comes only on the field. This kind of help should be given and a player should also be encouraged if he is performing well, as is happening in cricket now. This is a very good thing and it should happen in other games as well."

He said, "It is a matter of great honour for any player to receive an award from the hands of the Hon'ble President of India. When I went to the dais, Ashok Hall was reverberating with the sounds of clapping. It was a matter of great honour for me to meet the President of India in person. This award gives recognition to your achievements."

In the year 2005 the Hero Honda Sports Academy nominated Rajyavardhan Singh Rathore as the best shooter of 2004. He was honoured with the highest sports honour of the country, the 'Rajiv Gandhi Khel Ratna' award in 2005.

In the 18th Commonwealth Games organised at Melbourne, Rajyavardhan Singh Rathore was being considered as the claimant for the gold medal in the 'pairs competition', but he missed his aim. He came second and had to be satisfied with a silver medal only.

In May 2006, Rathore was successful in winning the gold medal at the ISSF World Cup at Cairo (Egypt), which was his greatest achievement so far. He also qualified for the Olympic to be held in 2008 in Beijing.

In the Doha Asiad held in December 2006, he won a bronze medal in the double trap competition and a silver medal in the men's double trap team competition with his teammates, Vikram Bhatnagar and Ranjan Sethi.

Achievements

☆ *He won two gold medals at the Commonwealth Games organised at Manchester (England) in 2002.*

- ☆ *He won a bronze medal at the ISSF World Shotgun Cup in New Delhi in 2003.*
- ☆ *He won a bronze medal at the World Championship at Nicosia in Cyprus.*
- ☆ *He won a gold medal at the Sydney World Cup in 2004.*
- ☆ *In 2004, Rathore won a gold medal at the Czech Masters Cup (Czech Republic).*
- ☆ *He won a silver medal at the Athens Olympics in Greece on 17th August 2004.*
- ☆ *On winning the silver medal at the Athens Olympics, the Chief Minister of Rajasthan gave him a cash award of 10 lakh rupees and was presented a flat in the Rajasthan Housing Board worth 8 lakh.*
- ☆ *He won a gold medal at the Asian Clay Vision Competition at Bangkok (Thailand).*

Shooting

Samresh Jung

Date of Birth: 19th May 1970

Samresh Jung, the Indian shooter who won five gold, two silver and one bronze medal at the 18th Commonwealth Games in Melbourne in 2006, was chosen as the best player of these Games. It was the first time when an Indian player had been selected as the best player of the Commonwealth Games. He created history by winning all these medals. He won two gold medals at the Second South Asian Federation Shooting Championship in 1997. In the 2002 Commonwealth Games, he emerged successful with two gold medals.

Samresh Jung was born on 19th May 1970 in New Delhi. His name is synonymous with one of the best shooters of India. He hails from a family where the members have a natural inclination for shooting. Thus he took to shooting as a duck takes to water in a pond.

Samresh Jung resides in Delhi as an Inspector in the Central Industrial Security Force (CISF). He made his grand entry on ths sports scene when he won two gold medals, one silver and a bronze at the Second South Asian Federation (SAF) Shooting Championship in 1997. After this he was also successful at the 'pairs competition'. He won two gold medals at the Commonwealth Games organised at Manchester (England) in 2002. Out of these, he won one medal with Jaspal Rana in the men's freestyle pairs and another medal in the 25-m standard pistol 'pairs open event'. This was also a 'pairs competition' and his partner in this competition was Jaspal Rana again.

Samresh continued to perform as an average player in international sports events. But the most memorable moment of his life was when he reached the Commonwealth Games at Melbourne in 2006, hoping to win eight gold medals. However, he could only win a silver medal in the first competition. He was greatly disappointed, but soon he overcame his disappointment and captured five medals at the Games. He won these medals in the men's 50-m freestyle pistol (individual event), 10-m air pistol (individual and 'pairs event'), the 25-m 'centre fire pistol pairs' and 25-m 'standard pistol pairs event'.

But the 25-m centre fire pistol (individual competition) and 25-m standard pistol events brought an end to Samresh's hope of winning the maximum number of gold medals. His pistol ditched him at the last moment in the 25-m standard pistol event. His pistol got jammed during the course of the competition. Had Samresh been able to win this last competition, he would have come at par with the records of winning the maximum number of gold medals (six) by two swimmers, Ian Thorpe and Susi O'Neil. Samresh was plagued by the same problem during his practice sessions but they were rectified at that time.

Samresh took it all in his stride and said, "It is all in the game. You cannot expect to win. I regret that I could not end my exercise in these Games in an exciting manner as I had expected."

At the closing ceremony of the Commonwealth Games, Samresh was presented with the 'David Dixon Award', whereby he was declared the best athlete of the 18th Commonwealth Games.

Achievements

- ☆ *Samresh Jung won two gold medals, one silver and a bronze at the (SAF) Games Shooting Championship in 1997 in New Delhi.*
- ☆ *He won two gold and one silver medal at the Commonwealth Games held at Manchester (England) in 2002.*
- ☆ *He was presented the Arjuna Award in 2002.*
- ☆ *In the 2004 SAF Games, he won a silver medal in the 25-m standard pistol event.*
- ☆ *He won two gold medals, two silver and one bronze medal at the 5th Commonwealth Games Shooting Championship in 2005.*

- ☆ *He won a gold medal in the men's 10-m air pistol competition at the National Games in 2005.*
- ☆ *He won five gold medals in the Commonwealth Games in Melbourne in 2006.*
- ☆ *At the closing ceremony of the Commonwealth Games, he was presented the 'David Dixon Award'(best athlete) for his excellent performance.*
- ☆ *In addition to five gold medals in the Commonwealth Games in Melbourne in 2006, he also won two silver medals in the 50-m 'pistol pairs' and 25-m 'centre fire pistol' competition.*

SQUASH

Squash is a singles and doubles racquet game played in a four-walled court with a long-handled racquet and a rubber ball that can be hit off any number of walls (as long as it hits the front wall). It probably originated in the mid-19th century at England's Harrow School. The standard international game uses a relatively soft, slow ball. Hard ball squash, in the US is, however, played on a court with a harder, faster ball. The object of squash racquets is to bounce, or rebound the ball off the front wall in such a way as to defeat the opponent's attempt to reach and return it.

Squash is an indoor racquet sport that was formerly called 'Squash Racquets', a reference to the 'squashable' soft ball used in the game when compared to the hard ball used in the parent game called Racquets. The game is played by two players (or four players in doubles) with 'standard' rackets and is characterised as a 'high-impact' exercise that can place strain on the joints, notably the knees. It can be played at any age and is an easy game to learn. In the modified game, equipment to suit every size and skill level is available.

The court size is codified as 32' long and 21' wide. The squash balls are made with two pieces of rubber compound, glued together to form a hollow sphere and buffed to a matte finish. Different balls are provided for varying temperature and atmospheric conditions and standards of play: more experienced players use slow balls that are smaller and have less bounce than those used by less experienced players (slower balls tend to die in court corners, rather than standing up to allow easier shots).

The players usually spin a racquet to decide who commences serving first and this player starts the first rally by electing to serve from either the left or right service box. For a right serve, one of the server's feet must be in the box and after being struck by the racquet, the ball must strike the front wall above the service line and below the out line and land in the opposite quarter court, unless volleyed by the receiver. The players then take turns hitting the ball against the front wall. The ball may be volleyed (hit while still in the air) or after its first bounce and before the second. Highly skilled players soften attempts to finish the rally by hitting the ball at an angle on to the front wall and into an area known as the 'nick' (the junction between the side wall and floor), which, if done properly, will cause the ball to roll out along the floor and be unretrievable.

The British Squash Rackets Asssociation conducted its first British Open Championship for men in December 1930, using a 'challenge' system: Charles Read was designated the champion, but was beaten in home and away matches by Don Butcher who was awarded the name of champion for 1931. The championship continues to this day, but has been conducted with a 'knockout' format since 1947. The women's championship started in 1921 and it was Heather McKay who remained undefeated for 18 years during the 1960s and 1970s to become the greatest woman player of all time. Among the men, most modern commentators consider Jehangir Khan (1980s) and Jansher Khan (1990s) of Pakistan as the greatest male players in the world.

Squash is an ideal sport for people of all abilities because it can be played either as an enjoyable leisure-time activity or a competitive sport; an individual, team or mixed sport, regardless of weather conditions and with little risk of injury.

Squash

Ritwik Bhattacharya

Date of Birth: 14th October 1979

Ritwik Bhattacharya won a bronze medal for India at the Asian Junior Squash Championship in February 1997. He has been a national champion four times in India. In 1997 he was awarded the certificate for 'Excellence in Squash' and the 'Outstanding All-round Player Award' by the President of India.

Ritwik Bhattacharya is considered to be the best player of India. He is the only Indian player who has played for the PCA tour.

Ritwik Bhattacharya was born on 14th October 1979 in a small seaside town called Puerto Ordaz near Venezuela. He spent his childhood till about eight years of age in sheer frolic in this setting. He used to enjoy swimming and playing baseball. His life underwent a sudden change and he shifted to India. As a child, Ritwik used to complain about small things in India. This included his anguish at not getting Pepsi in India. But soon he outgrew this phase and gradually adapted himself to the Indian scenario. Then he comfortably settled down into a life without Pepsi and such other things.

He kept moving from one place to the other alongwith his father. He reached Chennai at the age of 12 years after spending six months at Allahabad, one year at Bengaluru and one year at Delhi. By this time Ritwik had already studied at eight different schools and learnt four different languages.

With adolescence came a number of changes in Ritwik's life. Pepsi had come to India by this time and also Ritwik had a girl friend at this time.

He has earned a lot of success by playing squash. Ritwik has acquired training and knowledge in squash in America. He is doing his Ph.D. from the School of Computing of Utah University. He was doing his research on the formal ways of identifying hardware and software components. He desired to have his main residence at London so that he could benefit in his game by being coached by Neil Harvey.

In 1996-97 he was given the 'Outstanding All-round Player Award' by the President of India. In the same year (1997) he was given the 'Most Promising Sportsperson' award by the Delhi Press Reporters' Union.

In the year 1997 Ritwik was the national junior champion. After that he became the national squash champion at the age of 19 years in 1998. He again won the National Championships in 2000, 2002 and 2003.

Ritwik participated in the PCA Tour for the first time in 1998. His best ranking so far was in November 2006 when he was 38th in world ranking. He has also been on 51, 60 and 122 ranks at different times. In January 2005, Ritwik won the US$ 6000 ICL Chennai Open Squash Tournament and defeated Siddharth Sude in this game.

Achievements

- ☆ *Ritwik Bhattacharya reached the number one ranking in the Men's Squash National Championship.*
- ☆ *He has won the National Championships in 2000, 2002 and 2003.*
- ☆ *He was ranked 122nd in the international PCA Tour in November 2000.*
- ☆ *In the Tenth Junior Men's Squash Championship in Princeton (USA) held in August 1998, he was the captain of the Indian junior team.*
- ☆ *He was the captain of the Indian squash team in the Tenth Asian Squash Championship held in Hong Kong in July 2000.*
- ☆ *He was the runner-up at the IBA Hong Kong Junior Squash Open in 1997.*

- ☆ *He was the winner of the Indian Junior Open in Mumbai in 1998.*
- ☆ *He was the winner in the Asian Grand Final at New Delhi in 1998.*
- ☆ *He was the winner of the 'Otter Indian Open' at Mumbai in 2000.*
- ☆ *He won in the 'Jaipur Open' held at Jaipur in 2000.*
- ☆ *He is considered the best squash player of India and has participated in six PCA Tours so far.*

SWIMMING

Swimming can be a recreation or sport in which the propulsion of the body through water by combined action of arms and legs is brought about. In other words, swimming is a movement in water, usually without artificial assistance. It is an activity that is both useful and recreational. Its primary uses are bathing, cooling, travelling, fishing and escaping. An individual's ability to swim can be judged by the swimmer's speed and stamina.

Swimming is popular as an all-round body developer and as a competitive sport. It has been included in modern Olympic Games, since their inception in 1896. Events include freestyle (crawl stroke) races at distances of 50, 100, 200, 400, 800 and 1,500 metres; backstroke, breaststroke and butterfly races at 100 and 200 metres; individual medley races at 200 and 400 metres; freestyle and relays at 4 x 100 metres and 4 x 200 metres and the medley relay 4 x 100 metres long-distance swimming competition. Usually of 15-37 miles the races are generally held on lakes and inland waters.

Drawings from the Stone Age were found in 'the cave of swimmers' near Sura, dating back to 2000 BC. There is evidence that swimming was also a very popular sport in Greece and Italy in the original Olympic Games. Athletes would compete in competitions that involved participating in water sports in order to win a prize. In 1538, Nicolas Wynman, a German professor of languages, wrote the first on book swimming.

Competitive swimming in Europe began around 1800, mostly using the breaststroke. The front crawl, then called the *trudgen* (now known predominantly as the 'front crawl' or 'freestyle') was introduced in 1873 by John Arthur Trudgen, who copied the style from the native Americans.

Swimming was a part of the first modern Summer Olympic Games in Athens in 1896. In 1900, the backstroke was included as an Olympic event. In 1908, the world's swimming association, *the Federation Internationale de Natation*, was formed. Butterfly stroke was at first a variant of breaststroke, until it was accepted as a separate style in the 1952 Olympics.

Swimming

Bula Chowdhury

Date of Birth : 2 January 1970

Bula Chowdhury is a long distance swimmer. She is the first ever woman of the world to swim across seven oceans of five continents successfully. She was bestowed the Arjuna Award by the Government of India. She has also received the title of 'Water Fairy' by her admirers. She is recipient of the 'Dhyanchand Lifetime Achievement Award' in 2003. Her full name is Bula Chowdhury Chakravarty.

Bula Chowdhury is an extremely efficient swimmer who has earned name and fame not only in long distance swimming but in competitive swimming as well. Her name first hit the headlines after she won at the national competition at the age of nine years itself. At that time she won six gold medals in all the swimming competitions for her age group.

In her career of 24 years, Bula Chowdhury became the first ever woman in the world to swim across seven oceans and straits of five continents successfully. She accomplished this on 24th August 2004 when she covered a distance of 40 km of Palk Strait between Talaimannar in Sri Lanka to Dhanushkodi in Tamil Nadu in a record time of 13 hours 54 minutes. She was 34-years old at that time. The sea was very tumultuous and she had to swim with against strong winds and rainfall for about a kilometre.

Bula said after meeting the Prime Minister, "I happened to meet the Prime Minister once. He had told me, 'You are a role model for Indian women.' I always remember this statement and am ready to help young swimmers whenever I can."

Bula crossed the English Channel in 1989, and then repeated this magnificent performance and crossed the English Channel yet again in 1999. She became the first Asian to cross the English Channel twice. Then she prepared herself completely for long-distance swimming. She decided that she would break all records in long-distance swimming. She crossed the Strait of Gibraltar (Spain) in August 2000. At this time, her coach and husband, Sanjeev Chakravarty and her 10-year old son, Sarvoojee also accompanied her till Colombo. According to Bula Chowdhury, "This part was the most difficult to swim among all the seven seas. I could manage to swim across this distance and find a place in the *Guinness Book of World Records* with the best wishes of all my fellow Indians." Her swim was sponsored by the Sahara India Group.

Bula crossed the Strait of Gibraltar (Spain) in a record time of 3 hours 35 minutes, which is a world record till date. The Strait of Gibraltar extends from Spain till Morocco over a distance of 20 kms.

In July 2002, she crossed the Toroneus Gulf in Greece stretching over 26 kms. She took 8 hours 11 minutes to cover the distance from a small town called Nikiti Chakidiko near Macedonia, Greece to Cassandra. This was the fourth swim in her dream of crossing the seven seas. She was seventh among the other 29 swimmers who were with her at that time. She braved the vagaries of the unruly weather and other climatic conditions while covering this distance.

Bula Chowdhury became the first Indian woman to swim across the seas of five continents after she successfully crossed over from Three Anchors Bay, near Cape Town, South Africa to Robin Island. She also created a record after she covered a 30-km distance in chilling Antarctica in mere 3 hours 26 minutes. She was not only the first Asian to swim this distance, but also the first woman to achieve this phenomenal record in this shortest time. She started at 10 a.m. to swim across the South African sea at 1.26 p.m. She had already practiced hard to be able to swim amidst sharks in the waters of Antarctica, which is why she was able to accomplish this difficult journey successfully.

In the year 2001, Bula crossed the Tyrrhenian Sea of Italy from Zonnonel San to Felice Cicero. In 2002 she crossed the international Toronoz Gulf in Greece and subsequently she covered the distance between

Catalina Island to San Pedro by swimming across the Catalina Channel of America in 2002.

When she crossed athe Palk Strait between Tamil Nadu and Sri Lanka in August 2004, her happiness knew no bounds and she commented, "I have accomplished my dream with this record. Till almost half the distance, from the coast of Sri Lanka, the winds and tide were high, so it was quite a challenge for me. Up to 5 kilometres from Dhanushkodi, the winds and waves were so strong that it took me more than two hours to cover this distance.

"But my happiness knew no bounds when I touched the Indian shore, my motherland. I felt like I had touched the horizon. But I have to give full credit to my coach and husband, Sanjeev Chakravarty and my son, Sarvoojee for their undeterred support throughout. My husband who has also been an international swimmer attributes my success to the fact that I started swimming at 2 a.m. instead of 6 a.m. in the morning."

She was bestowed the Arjuna Award in 1990. She is popularly known as the 'Water-baby of Bengal'.

Achievements

- ☆ *Bula Chowdhury won the National Swimming Competition at the age of nine years.*
- ☆ *She won six gold medals in all the swimming competitions in her age group at the age of nine years.*
- ☆ *She holds the record of being the first woman in the world to swim across the seven oceans and the straits of five continents successfully.*
- ☆ *She has also been given the title of 'Water Fairy'.*
- ☆ *She crossed the Strait of Gibraltar (Spain) in a record time of 3 hours 35 minutes, which is a world record.*
- ☆ *She has been honoured with the Arjuna Award.*
- ☆ *She was given the 'Dhyanchand Lifetime Achievement Award' in 2003.*

Swimming

Khazan Singh

Date of Birth: 6th May 1964

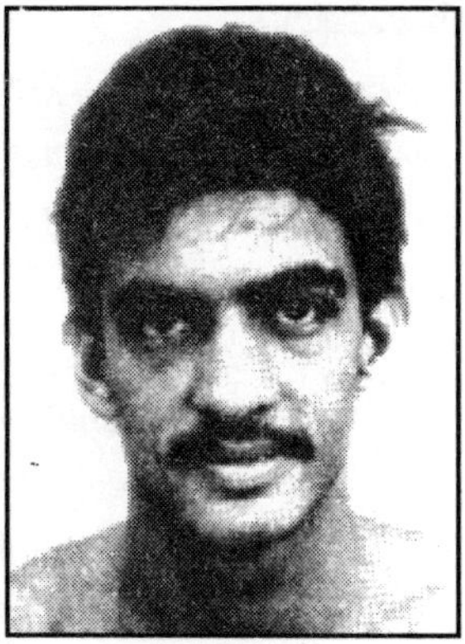

Khazan Singh is one of the most outstanding swimmers of India. He set a national record by winning a gold medal in the 1985 South Asian Federation (SAF) Games held in Kathmandu. Khazan Singh was honoured with the Arjuna Award in 1984.

Khazan Singh's name features on top of the list of extraordinary swimmers of today. Generally speaking, no Indian swimmer has been able to perform to international standards. However, Khazan Singh's performance can be termed as close to international standards.

Khazan Singh was born on 6th May 1964 in Delhi. He performed so well at his debut swimming tournament that his name came into limelight. He won five gold medals at the National School Championship in 1981-82.

Khazan Singh participated in the National Water Sports Championship. Here too he registered his strong presence by winning five gold, two silver and one bronze medal. He also earned fame in the international arena after his success in the national-level tournaments. He won a silver medal in the Asian Games held at Seoul in 1986. As of date, no Indian swimmer has been able to perform this feat in the Asian Games.

In the 1985 South Asian Federation (SAF) Games held in Kathmandu, Khazan Singh won a gold medal in the 100-metre freestyle swimming competition and also set a new national record of 55.34 seconds. He won a bronze medal in the Asian Swimming Championship held at Beijing in 1988. He was honoured with the Arjuna Award in 1984.

Achievements

- ☆ *Khazan Singh had acquired success at the international level in swimming, which no other Indian swimmer has been able to do so far.*
- ☆ *He won five gold medals at the National School Championship in 1981-82.*
- ☆ *At the National Championship in 1982, he won five gold, two silver and one bronze medal.*
- ☆ *In the 1985 South Asian Federation (SAF) Games held in Kathmandu, he won a gold medal. This no Indian swimmer has been able to do so far.*
- ☆ *In the 1985 SAF Games, he won a gold medal in the 100-metre freestyle swimming competition and also set a new national record of 55.34 seconds.*
- ☆ *He won a bronze medal in the Asian Swimming Championship held at Beijing in 1988.*
- ☆ *He was honoured with the Arjuna Award in 1984.*

Swimming

Mihir Sen

Dat of Birth : 16th November 1930
Died: 11th June 1997

Mihir Sen was not only the first Indian, but also the first Asian to cross the English Channel in 1958. He acquired an incredible efficiency in salt-water swimming and also set five important records. He was honoured with the Padma Shri in 1959 and the Padma Bhushan in 1967.

Mihir Sen was a barrister at the Calcutta High Court. However, he was popularly known as the record-making swimmer.

Mihir Sen was born on 16th November 1930 at Purulia in West Bengal. His father was a doctor in Cuttack. He went to England to prepare for law practice, but was attracted towards swimming in the English Channel. After his initial unsuccessful attempts at crossing the English Channel, Mihir finally managed to swim across the Channel on 27th September 1958. He was not only the first Indian, but also the first Asian to cross the English Channel. It took him 14 hours and 45 minutes to cross the Channel. His starting point was Dover and he reached Calais on the other side. With courage and swimming talent, he opened doors for forthcoming Indian swimmers to acquire more efficiency in long-distance swimming and try better and new avenues.

Mihir's next adventurous performance was in swimming from Thalaimannar in Sri Lanka to Dhanushkodi in India on 6th April 1966 in a record time of 25 hours and 44 minutes. The Palk Strait is known to abound in poisonous snakes and sharks. He was assisted by the Indian Navy in performing this dangerous feat.

His next achievement was to cross the Gibraltar Strait (which is between Spain and Morocco) on 24th August 1966 in a record timing of

8 hours and 1 minute. Mihir Sen was the first Asian to cross the Strait of Gibraltar. It appeared as if he had taken a pledge to cross all the seven seas. Indeed he covered a number of oceans and set five new records.

On 12th September 1966, he swam across the Strait of Dardanelles and became the first in the world to accomplish this feat. After a gap of nine days, i.e. on 21st September in the same year, he crossed the Strait of Bosphorus.

On 29th October 1966 he started to swim across the length of the Panama Canal, but could cover it in two stages as he was swimming across the length of the canal. He started his endeavour on 29th October and reached his destination on 31st October 1966. He took a time of 34 hours and 15 minutes to swim across the Panama Canal.

Mihir Sen has swum a total of 600 kms in his career. He set a new record in swimming six long distances in one calendar year. He was the first in the world to swim across seven seas of the five continents. In recognition of his achievements, the Government of India honoured Mihir Sen with the Padma Shri in 1959 and the Padma Bhushan in 1967.

He was an incomparable swimmer, who took quite a risk in long-distance swimming endeavours. He was the Chairman of the Explorers Club of India. However, in the last days of his life, he lost his memory and spent his days in a lot of pain.

Mihir Sen left for his heavenly abode on 11th June 1997 in Kolkata.

Achievements

- ☆ *Mihir Sen was not only the first Indian, but also the first Asian to cross the English Channel in 1958.*
- ☆ *He was honoured with the Padma Shri in 1959.*
- ☆ *He was the first in the world to swim across the seven seas of the five continents in 1966.*
- ☆ *He was awarded the Padma Bhushan in 1967.*

TABLE TENNIS

Table tennis, popularly known as Ping-Pong, is based on tennis but is played with wooden paddles and a small hollow, light-weight, plastic ball. It is known as *Takkyu* in Japan and as *Tak-gu* in Korea. The object is to hit the ball so that it goes over the net and bounces in the opponent's half of the table in such a way as to defeat the opponent's attempt to reach and return it. Table tennis is a sport in which two or four players hit the ball back and forth to each other.

A match consists of a best of three or five games, each game being won by the player or team that first reaches 21 points. The game has its origins in England as an after-dinner amusement of upper-class Victorians in the 1880s. Though started in England in the early 20th century, it soon spread elsewhere since the mid-1950s. East Asian countries now dominate the sport. It was introduced in the Olympics for both men and women in 1988.

Mimicking the game of tennis in an indoor environment, everyday objects were originally utilised to act as the equipment. A line of books would be the net, a rounded top of a champagne cork or knot of string as the ball, and a cigar-box lid as the racket. The popularity of the game led the game manufacturers to sell the equipment commercially. The early rackets or paddles were often pieces of parchment stretched upon a frame, and the sound generated in play gave the game its first nickname of Whiff-whaff and Ping-Pong too.

A number of sources indicate that the game was first brought to the attention of Hamleys of Regent Street under the name *Gossia*. The name

Ping-Pong was in wide use before the English manufacturer J. Jacques & Son Ltd trademarked it in 1901. The name Ping-Pong then came to be used for the game played by the rather expensive Jacques equipment, with other manufacturers calling theirs 'table tennis'. A similar situation existed in the United States where Jacques sold the rights of the Ping-Pong to Parker Brothers.

The next innovation was by James Gibb, an English enthusiast of the game, who discovered novelty celluloid balls during a trip to the US in 1901 and found them to be the ideal balls for the game. E.C. Goode invented the modern version of the racket by fixing a sheet of pimpled or stippled rubber to the wooden blade. During the early 20th century the game was banned in Russia due to the belief by the Russian rulers that playing the game had an adverse effect on players' eyesight.

In 1921, the Table Tennis Association was founded in England, and the International Table Tennis Federation (ITTF) followed in 1926. London hosted the first official World Championship in 1927. It soon spread elsewhere since the mid-fifties. Table tennis was introduced as an Olympic sport in 1988.

The game takes place on a hard table divided by a net. Players must allow a ball played towards them only one bounce on their side of the table and must return it so that it bounces on the opponent's side. If the ball does not land on the opponent's side, it is a dead ball, unless the receiving player hits the ball before it passes the end line of the table. The play is fast and it demands quick reflexes. A skilled player can impart spin to the ball, which makes its bounce and the opponent has difficulty in knowing if it will come straight or spin.

Towards the end of 2000, the ITTF instituted several rule changes aimed at making table tennis more viable as a televised and spectator sport. Firstly, the older 38-mm balls were replaced with 40-mm balls. This increased the ball's air resistance and effectively slowed down the game. Secondly, the ITTF changed the scoring system from 21- to a 11-point system. This was intended to make the game more fast-paced and exciting.

The ITTF also changed the rules of service to prevent a player from hiding the ball during service, in order to increase the average length of the rallies and reduce the server's advantage. Both single and double games are played.

Table Tennis

Achant Sharat Kamal

Date of Birth: 12th July 1982

Achant Sharat Kamal is the first Indian player to win a gold medal in table tennis in the 2006 Commonwealth Games. Before that he won the individual gold medal in the 2004 Commonwealth Table Tennis Championship at Kuala Lumpur. The same year he was conferred the Arjuna Award.

Achant Sharat came into the news after he won the first individual gold medal for India in the 2006 Commonwealth Games at Melbourne. Besides winning an individual gold medal, he was instrumental in India's victory in table tennis against Singapore.

Achant Sharat began proving his capability when he captured the senior category title in the state of Tamil Nadu. He won the National Table Tennis Championship in 2003.

After this, he won an individual gold medal in the 16th Commonwealth Table Tennis Championship at Kuala Lampur in 2004. Three Indian players had made it to the finals before Achant but no one had managed to succeed. By winning this medal, he acquired the honour of being the first Indian player to have done so. After this success, the Government of India bestowed the Arjuna Award on him for 2004.

He works in the Indian Oil Corporation.

Achievements

- ☆ *Sharat Kamal won the National Table Tennis Championship in 2003.*

- ☆ *At the 16th Commonwealth Table Tennis Championship at Kuala Lampur in 2004, he won a gold medal in men's singles category. Thus he became the first Indian player to win a gold medal in table tennis in the Commonwealth Games.*
- ☆ *He was conferred the Arjuna Award in 2004.*
- ☆ *He won a gold medal at the Melbourne Commonwealth Games in 2006.*

TENNIS

Tennis is a game played with rackets and a light rubber ball by two players or pairs of players on a rectangular court divided by a low net. Today players use a stringed racket to strike a hollow rubber ball covered with felt (most of the time yellow, but can be any colour or even two-tone) over a net into the opponent's court. The sport is played indoors and outdoors, on hard surface, clay or green grass-court. The game involves hitting the ball over the net into the other half of the court in such a way as to defeat the opponent's attempt to reach and return the ball.

Each player serves for an entire game. Points are scored as 15, 30, 40 and game (the term 'love' is used for zero). A tied score (deuce) requires continued play until a two-point margin is achieved by the winner. Except for the adoption of the tie-breaker in the 1970s, its rules have remained remarkably unchanged since the 1890s.

Originating in Europe in the late 19th century as lawn tennis, with its roots going back to the ancient game of real tennis, the modern game of tennis spread first throughout the English-speaking world, especially among the upper classes. Tennis is now an Olympic sport and is played at all levels of the society, by all ages, and in many countries of the world.

Tennis as a modern sport can be traced to two separate roots. Between 1859 and 1865, Major Harry Gem and his friend Augurio Pereira developed a game that combined elements of rackets and Spanish ball game *pelota*, which they played on Pereira's croquet lawn in Birmingham, England. In 1872, along with two local doctors, they founded the world's first tennis club in Leamington Spa. The *Courier* of 23rd July 1884 recorded one of its first tennis tournaments, held in the grounds of Shrubland Hall. In December 1873, Major Walter Clopton Wingfield designed a similar game, which he called *sphairistike* skill at playing and was soon known as 'sticky' for the amusement of his guests at a garden party on his estate in Llanelidan, Wales. He based the game on the older sport of indoor tennis or real tennis. The first championship at Wimbledon, in London was played in 1877.

Along with its of players, millions of people worldwide enjoy tennis as a spectator sport, especially the four Grand Slam tournaments: Australian Open, French Open, Wimbledon and the US Open. The growth of tennis in Eastern Europe and the Far East has been especially stupendous in recent years.

A recent addition to tennis has been the adoption of 'instant replay' technology coupled with a point challenge system, which allows a player to challenge the official call of a point.

In 1926, promoter C.C. Pyle established the first professinal tennis tour with a group of American and French tennis players playing exhibition matches to the paying audience. In 1968, commercial pressures of some amateurs taking money under the table led to the abandonment of this distinction and inaugurated the open era in which all players can compete in all tournaments and top players are now able to make their living from tennis.

In 1954, James Van Allen founded the International Tennis Hall of Fame, a non-profit museum in Newport, Rhode Island. The building contains a large collection of tennis memorabilia as well as a Hall of Fame honouring prominent members and tennis players from all over the world. Each year, a grass-court tournament is hosted on its grounds, as well as an induction ceremony is held to honour the new Hall of Fame members.

Tennis

Leander Paes

Date of Birth: 17th June 1973

In the 1996 Atlanta Olympics, Leander Paes won a bronze medal, making way for more Olympic medals for India in the times to come. At that time Leander ended the drought of 44 years for medals in individual sports. Leander's performance is a milestone performance as far as the Olympics go. It will not be wrong to say that Leander Paes is one of the greatest players of India.

Leander Paes was born on 17th June 1973 and is an extremely successful tennis player in men's doubles and mixed doubles category. He was born in Goa and brought up in Kolkata. His mother Jennifer Paes was the captain of the Indian basketball team. His father Dr. V.A. Paes was a mid-fielder in the hockey team that won a bronze medal in the 1972 Munich Olympics. Dr. Paes is a doctor by profession.

Leander had his schooling in the Madras Christian College Higher Secondary School. He has his residence at Kolkata and at Orlando, in Florida, USA. He is a right-handed player. He started learning tennis at the age of seven years and acquired his basic knowledge of the game at South Club, Kolkata. In 1985, he received training at the Madras Britannia Tennis Academy and had his coaching from Dabe-o-Meira. Paes attained international recognition in 1990, when he won the junior Wimbledon title and became the number one player in junior world ranking.

Before this he won in the below-14 year category at the Rice Bowl Championship at Hong Kong in 1987. Two years after this, he also won in the below-16 years competition. He also won the senior and the junior National Champion title. At a time when all the ace players of the world display a demeaning attitude towards the Davis Cup, Leander Paes has shown what a proud moment it is for one to play for his motherland. Paes is known as a doubles player in his circuit.

Player Duo: Mahesh Bhupathi and Leander Paes

Leander along with Mahesh Bhupathi achieved the number one ranking as a team in the tennis doubles. Leander became a professional player in 1991.

The story of Mahesh Bhupathi and Leander Paes is almost like a roller-coaster ride with all its ups and downs. This duo has split and come together a number of times. Even though the Indian media and the spectators prefer to be connected with the game of cricket and show comparatively less interest towards other games, the only sports news that is given importance is the game of Leander Paes and Mahesh Bhupathi.

Both these players came together for the first time in October 1994 in the Jakarta Challenger. This pair was defeated in the second round of Atlanta Olympics in 1996. In the same year, the duo made its presence felt in the Davis Cup and in 1997, they touched the pinnacle of success in the game. Leander won a bronze in the 1996 Olympics and earned for India its first individual medal in tennis. When these two players came together as a team, Leander was already a senior due to the Davis Cup and the Olympic medal. However, seniority, game, etc. are factors that do not have much significance when two players come together as a team.

Between 1997-2002, this duo won as many as 22 titles including three Grand Slams for men's doubles. They also won the Wimbledon and the French Open Tournaments. In the year 2002 in April they split and mutually decided not to play together as a team again. Though they split from professional tennis, the two played as a team again in the Busan Asian Games and won a gold medal too.

In 2003, Leander tried to pair up with other players, but could not succeed much. He came together with Mahesh Bhupathi once again for the Davis Cup. This way Leander has been in the news and has won a number of championships every now and then. Mahesh Bhupathi and Leander Paes have won a prize money of around one crore and forty-one lakhs by winning the French Open. However, they were honoured more than this after they won the Wimbledon.

Leander also likes to play golf in addition to tennis. In an interview in 2002, Leander said, "I met the Australian tennis coach, Bob Carmichael, who is also a great golf player. He introduced me to tennis six years ago."

He feels that there are many similarities between tennis and golf. He remarks that golf has taught him to be brave. He says, "As I belong to a family of players, I play all the games with equal interest. The course of DLF is my favourite golf course."

Leander won the second and last reverse singles in February 2004 against host New Zealand with a score of 3-2 in the Davis Cup Asia Oshiana Group. This was an important victory for India.

In 1996, Leander Paes was awarded the 'Rajiv Gandhi Khel Ratna' award for his outstanding performance in tennis. Leander Paes' highest doubles ranking has been number one, which was given on 24th August 1998. His highest singles ranking has been 73 which was on 21st June 1999. Leander has often been called as braggart.

He was awarded the Padma Shri along with Mahesh Bhupathi on 26th January 2001.

The evergreen Leander Paes created history on the tennis court in the year 2006. He won the US Open doubles title for the first time, playing with Martin Dam and also found a place in the finals of the Australian Open. In the Doha Asiad in December 2006, he won the men's doubles title with Mahesh Bhupathi amidst all kinds of speculation and ended the year by winning the mixed doubles title with Sania Mirza.

In Septemeber 2009, Leander Paes won the U.S. doubles title with Lukas Dlouhy of the Czech Republic. Paes now has 10 Grand Slam titles to his credit.

Achievements

- ☆ *In 1990, Leander Paes won the junior Wimbledon title.*
- ☆ *In 1996, he won the individual bronze medal at the Atlanta Olympics.*

- ☆ *In 1999, he reached the finals in the doubles match in all the four Grand Slams, winning the Wimbledon and the French Open. He also won the mixed doubles title in the Wimbledon.*
- ☆ *In 2001, he won the doubles title in the French Open.*
- ☆ *In 2003, he won the mixed doubles title with Martina Navratilova of Wimbledon and Australian Open.*
- ☆ *In 2004, he won the Davis Cup against Japan in Osaka playing excellently. With this victory, Paes became the only Indian player to win the maximum number of singles titles. Prior to this, this record was held by Ramanathan Krishnan. Paes had equalled Ramanathan Krishnan's record of 69 matches in New Zealand. After winning the Davis Cup against Japan in Osaka, he had won 70 matches and lost 39. He also became the only Indian player to have won the maximum number of Davis Cup matches.*

Tennis

Mahesh Bhupathi

Date of Birth: 7th June 1974

The Karnataka-born Mahesh Bhupathi has achieved tremendous success as part of the tennis duo with Leander Paes. This right-handed player was born on 7th June 1974. He stands at a height of 6'2". He has his residences in Muscat, Oman and in Bengaluru. His family is not new to the game of tennis. His father C.G.K. Bhupathi was a tennis player himself and was also a member of the Davis Cup team.

It will not be wrong to say that the combination of Leander Paes and Mahesh Bhupathi took the world of tennis by storm as they provided tough competition to all the other tennis duos in 1999.

In 1997, when Leander had predicted that his pairing with Bhupathi would make them win the Grand Slam doubles title, people laughed at him. They had seen this as too ambitious a talk as the team was ranked number 80 in the world. Both of them didn't lose courage and went on climbing the ladder of success. The Leander-Bhupathi duo reached the semi-finals in seven out of eight Grand Slam Tournaments they participated in. Paes was proved right after they won both the Wimbledon and French titles in 1999. Even in the first tournament of the Grand Slam series, i.e. the Australian Open the duo put up a tough fight.

It is often said that Mahesh Bhupathi is more sensitive and introvert in comparison to Leander Paes. Bhupathi has tremendous professional maturity as well.

Mahesh Bhupathi's full name is Mahesh Srinivas Bhupathi. He ranks number one in the doubles game. He had an excellent two-year career in the Mississippi University in 1994-95, where he won both the singles and the doubles all American title. He paired with Ali Ahmad and won the N.C.C.A. Doubles Championship in 1995. Then as a doubles player he was ranked number one and number three as a singles player.

He has been a member of the Indian Davis Cup since 1995. He was bestowed the Arjuna Award in 1996. On 26th March 2001, he was awarded the Padma Shri along with Leander Paes.

The Mahesh Bhupathi and Leander Paes duo has been breaking off and on. In the 2004 Olympics at Athens, this duo got together to play once again in the doubles event.

Mahesh Bhupathi has lost 23 matches in his entire career and won a total prize amount of $ 1,629,993. In the doubles game, he won $ 22,700 in 2004.

Mahesh Bhupathi loves to watch Bollywood movies and often carries film DVDs with him when he travels. He married model Shweta Jaishankar in 2002.

He has won a gold medal in the Asian Games in he doubles category. In 2004 he again decided to pair up with Paes for the Athens Olympics. India had a lot of hopes of winning a medal at the Athens Olympics, but the hopes were dashed when this duo stood fourth in the Olympics.

Evergreen players Mahesh Bhupathi and Leander Paes wrote a new success story at the tennis court in 2006 when they won the men's doubles in the Doha Asiad and won the love and appreciation of their fans. Mahesh Bhupathi won the mixed doubles title, pairing with Martina Hingis. This was the sixth mixed doubles title of Mahesh Bhupathi's career.

Achievements

- ☆ *Mahesh represented India in 1991 to enter the finals of the Wimbledon junior doubles. In the very same year he won the Chinese and Malaysian Satellite Tournaments as well.*
- ☆ *He won the American Collegiate Tournament in 1994 and the Indonesian open singles championship. In 1994 and 1995 he became the national champion.*

☆ *He won the Aruba Challenger doubles title with Paes in 1991.*

☆ *In the 1995 Davis Cup, he played against Hong Kong.*

☆ *He won five Challenger doubles titles in 1996.*

☆ *He started his journey for the Grand Slam after winning the French Open with Rocky Hiraki of Japan in 1997.*

☆ *During 1997, he along with Paes won six out of seven ATC doubles titles, because of which the duo qualified for the ATC world doubles tiltle. In the finals, they lost*

☆ *In 1997 he won the mixed doubles title at Rolland Garros by defeating Silberstein of Chile, and registering a 3-2 victory in the Davis Cup.*

☆ *He won the doubles championship at Los Angeles in 1998.*

☆ *In the 1998 World Group title, Bhupathi reached the singles finals with a record of 6-2 and qualified for the ATP World Singles Championship.*

☆ *The year 1999 was the best year of his career in which he won three doubles titles, including the Rolland Garros and Wimbledon. This very year the Mahesh Bhupathi and Leander Paes duo became the first ever duo to reach the finals at all the four Grand Slam tournaments. On 26th April this duo was given the number one ranking and won the Wimbledon title.*

☆ *In 1999, the Bhupathi-Paes duo entered the finals of the US Open and the Australian Open, but lost in the finals of the ATP World Championship.*

☆ *In November 1999, a surgery had to be performed on Bhupathi's shoulders. He and Paes won a total prize amount of US $ 618,004 for winning in a number of important tournaments.*

☆ *After surgery, Bhupathi won two doubles titles in May 2000. He paired with Crotzman at St. Poelton and with Paes at Tokyo to win these titles. In 2000, he reached the finals of the doubles championship at Hale.*

☆ *In the 2000 Sydney Olympics, Bhupathi had to face defeat in the second round.*

- ☆ *In 2001 he won four out of six finals of the doubles matches and in the ATP team tournament he was ranked fourth. Bhupathi reached the finals of the Indian Police Tournament.*
- ☆ *In 2001, he won the Rolland Garros title for the second time and won the third Grand Slam singles tournament. He reached the finals at Moscow, Basil and T.M.S. Paris Tournaments.*
- ☆ *In 2002, Bhupathi won five doubles titles with different partners and was ranked third in the doubles matches. He won 56 tournaments this year, producing his career's best performance. During this year Max Mirni was his partner for the maximum number of times. This duo stood fifth in the ATP doubles match.*
- ☆ *In 2002 he won the US Open and the Wimbledon Championship. He also won the championships at Chennai and Bhalorka by pairing with Paes.*
- ☆ *In 2002 he won the T.M.S. Hamburg title and the third Grand Slam Wimbledon of his career in the mixed doubles category.*
- ☆ *In 2003, Bhupathi was victorious in the Canada T.M.S., Madrid T.M.S., Monte Carlo T.M.S. and Moscow titles.*
- ☆ *He won the Rome T.M.S., Auckland and Dubai titles in 2004.*
- ☆ *In the year 2005, Bhupathi won the US Open title.*
- ☆ *In January 2006, Mahesh won the Australian Open in the mixed doubles, by pairing with Martina Hingis of Switzerland. He thus became successful in the 10th Grand Slam of his career. This was Bhupathi's sixth and third successive Grand Slam mixed doubles title.*
- ☆ *In September 2006, Mahesh won the doubles titles at Beijing Open. He won the US $ 75,000 prize in the doubles category of Beijing Open T.P.S. Tennis Tournament by pairing with Mario Evinch of Croatia.*

Tennis

Ramanathan Krishnan

Date of Birth: 11th April 1937

Ramanathan Krishnan is one of the best players of India. No other tennis player in India has managed to reach his success. He was ranked among the 10 best tennis players of the world. He became the fourth seeded player in the Wimbledon. He can be called the architect of Indian tennis in the post-independence era. He was awarded the Arjuna Award in 1961, the Padma Shri in 1962 and the Padma Bhushan in 1967.

Ramanathan Krishnan was inspired to play tennis by his father, T.K. Ramanathan who was a tennis champion himself. Krishnan mastered the game quickly under the able guidance of his father.

Krishnan was born on 11th April 1937 at Chennai, Tamil Nadu. He completed his postgraduation in economics from the University of Madras. Like any other talented player, he made a reputation for himself with his game and soon became a well-known name in the field of tennis. He won the National junior and the senior tennis championships for eight consecutive years.

He made such an indelible impression by his game that soon he came to be known as the mirror of Indian tennis. He kept demonstrating his capability for almost 13 years and retained his top slot, which no Indian player had reached before him. Even his successor, Vijay Amritraj could not match up to his achievements.

On five different occasions, Ramanathan Krishnan was placed among the 10 best players of the world. He was a fourth seeded player at the Wimbledon in 1961. At that time he had to keep away from the game because of his ankle injury.

Ramanathan started his international tennis career at the age of 16 and carved an identity for himself as a national champion. He put in an unforgettable performance, playing against Belgium in the Davis Cup tournament, even though India lost by 0-5. His powerful game thrilled the audience and left a lasting impression on their minds. In another five-set doubles match he displayed another excellent performance along with Sumant Mishra.

Among all the young players participating in the Davis Cup, each and every stroke of Krishnan was extremely impressive. His backhand stroke was his strong point. He was brimming with self-confidence and after playing the Davis Cup, it was his belief that he would participate in the Wimbledon the next year. He managed to participate in the Wimbledon tournament and defeated Ashley Cooper in the junior singles category. He was the first Indian and the first Asian to have won the tournament.

Thereafter his career showed an upper curve. Though he was never able to win the Wimbledon title, he was an extremely popular player among the spectators. He reached the semi-finals of the Wimbledon twice and at that time he was the only Indian to have reached that level. Ultimately he had to face defeat on both the fronts and in 1960 he became a Neale Fraser champion, followed by a Rod (Rocket) Laver champion in 1961. He will always be remembered for his outstanding performance in the Davis Cup. He always performed better as a team rather than in singles.

In 1966 Krishnan was instrumental in taking India to the challenge round even though the team could not win against Australia. He achieved a number of successes during his career. One such match was the one he played in the Davis Cup at Brooklyn, America in 1959, against Rod Lever of Australia when he won this match. The second was in 1966, at Kolkata, when he won the match against Thomas Koch of Brazil in the fifth rubber. This was an unbelievable win for Krishnan as he was losing in one set and in the fourth set too he was losing at 15-30. But in the five-set match, he managed to turn the game around and win it subsequently.

Krishnan was awarded with the Arjuna Award in 1961 for his sports achievements. He ws also honoured with the Padma Shri in 1962 and with the Padma Bhushan in 1967.

He remained dedicated to the game even after taking retirement from active tennis. His son Ramesh Krishnan also made a mark for himself in the game of tennis.

Achievements

- ☆ *Krishnan was one among the 10 best tennis players of the world. No other tennis player in India has managed to reach his success.*
- ☆ *He was a fourth seeded player in the Wimbledon in 1962.*

Ramesh Krishnan

Date of Birth: 5th June 1961

Ramesh Krishnan, son of the famous tennis player and veteran Ramanathan Krishnan also went to become a famous tennis player himself. In 1979, he won the Junior Wimbledon Championship and was ranked number one in the juniors' category.

Ramesh Krishnan, like his famous father, became a famous player at the international level. He was born on 5th June 1961 at Chennai. He followed his father's footsteps and went ahead to win the Junior Wimbledon Championship in 1979. After this, he won the junior French title and became the world's number one junior tennis player.

In the senior level, Ramesh Krishnan had the distinction of reaching the quarter-finals of the 1986 Wimbledon. In 1981 and 1987, he reached the quarter-finals of the US Open.

Ramesh Krishnan also holds a very impressive Davis Cup record. In 1987, India reached the Davis Cup finals for the third time due to Ramesh Krishnan's contribution. In this tournament, he defeated the experienced Wali Masoor of Australia in straight sets and took the match to a decisive position.

In the 1992 Barcelona Olympics, Ramesh paired with Leander Paes of India and took part in the men's doubles to reach the quarter-finals. Since he showed consistently good performance in the ATP Tour, he was able to reach the 23rd position in world ranking in 1985.

Achievements

- ☆ *In 1979, Ramesh won the Junior Wimbledon Championship.*
- ☆ *After winning the junior French title, he became the number one junior player in world ranking.*
- ☆ *He had the distinction of reaching the quarter-finals of the 1986 Wimbledon.*
- ☆ *In 1987, he defeated the experienced Wali Masoor of Australia in straight sets and made India reach the Davis Cup finals for the third time.*
- ☆ *In the 1992 Barcelona Olympics, he reached the quarter-finals in the men's doubles.*
- ☆ *He was ranked 23rd in the world in 1985.*

Tennis

Sania Mirza

Date of Birth: 15th November 1986

The fame that Sania Mirza enjoys not only in India but also all over the world, at the young age of 21, is a matter of immense pride for any player. She was awarded the Padma Shri in 2006. Sania is the youngest player to receive this honour. In the year 2006, she was awarded the 'Most Impressive Newcomer Award' by the WTA in the presence of veterans from the world of tennis in America. In February 2008, Sania's decision to stay away from the WTA Bangalore Open created quite a sensation in the tennis world.

Sania played her first ITF Junior Tournament at Islamabad when she was not even 14. In the year 2002, ace Indian tennis player, Leander Paes saw Sania playing before the Busan Asiad and decided to play the doubles tournament with her. This duo definitely did not disappoint India and won the bronze medal. After this, Sania won the junior doubles match at Wimbledon at the age of 17 years.

Sania's father, Imran Mirza most often accompanies her during her practice sessions. Sania is accompanied at times by her mother too if not by her father during the tournaments; so both her father and mother have not been able to spend much time together. Sania is out almost throughout the year. Imran Mirza feels that the entire family had to make a lot of sacrifices in order to make Sania a successful player. As such there are a lot of sacrifice stories behind a player who makes it to the top. In Sania's case it was her family. Her parents were determined to make Sania a tennis player and that too like Steffi Graf.

Her family background also has an important role to play in taking this teen to the peak of her career. Sania's family has always been associated with sports. Her father, Imran Mirza, is the brother of the famous cricket player, Ghulam Ahmed and he himself has been a player in the Hyderabad Senior Division League. Sania's uncle, Mirza Fayaz, was the wicket keeper of Hyderabad in the Ranji Trophy (cricket) team and is presently in the State Selection Committee. Sania hails from this very sports-rich background.

Born on 15th November 1986, she started playing tennis at the age of six years under the guidance of Mahesh Bhupathi's father, C.K. Bhupathi. After beginning her tennis from the Nizam Club of Hyderabad, she went to the Ace Tennis Academy of America. In the year 1999, she represented India for the first time at the junior level.

Sania's height is 168 cm and she is a right-handed player. Apart from tennis, she is also very fond of listening to music and loves to eat *biryani*, but tennis prevents her from having the same during her matches.

The most important aspect of her game is her first serve. She has received her training at the Senate Tennis Academy of Hyderabad. Her coach is P.A. Jain, and her sponsors are V.K. Group of Industries who bears the expenses of her air travel; Adidas supplies her shoes, clothing, tennis rackets, etc. and the companies have been sponsoring her from the age of 12.

Sania Mirza is the only Indian tennis player of the country to have won a Grand Slam title. She created a history of sports by winning the Wimbledon title. Once, on being asked in an interview as to why women had not been able to succeed in tennis so far, she said that girls get married off at a young age and also even while playing, they are unable to find good sponsors. Sania looks up to Steffi Graf as her role model.

She made a remarkable come back on 8th August 2004 when she defeated top-seeded Irena Bolikena of Russia in 1-6, 6-4, 6-1 in Rexham, Great Britain. This way, she won the US $ 10,000 ITF Women's Tennis Tournament. This was Sania's eighth professional title.

In the year 2005 Sania stayed in the headlines. Her excellent performance and success was so much in news that she was being considered a big sportstar in India, next to Sachin Tendulkar. In the beginning of the year she was ranked 166 in world ranking, which she wanted to bring down to 100. Within a gap of one year itself, she climbed the ladder of success and reached the 50th position. This achievement is not only important in the personal perspective, but in the national perspective as well.

Twenty-one-year old Sania Mirza from Hyderabad added a new chapter to the history of Indian tennis in January 2005. She became the first woman tennis player of India to reach the third round of the Grand Slam tournament after she defeated Petra Mandula of Hungary in the Australian Open.

She was to play against seventh-seeded Serena Williams when she was at 166th position. Hungary's Petra Mendula was 84th when Sania defeated her. Even though Sania could not manage to win over Serena, she received plenty of appreciation from the audience and the media for her game.

She was awarded the Padma Shri at the age of 18 and became the youngest celebrity to receive this honour.

Sania has a small family comprising her father, mother and sister Aanam. Her maternal family resides in Mumbai and most of her paternal family is in America. Sania's nose-ring has become a style statement and a part of her identity.

At the beginning of 2004, her ranking was 490, which rose to number 34 with hard work and subsequent success. Today every Indian is proud of her and wonders how far this young tennis player will go. No Indian tennis player has been able to move beyond number 50 in the last 20 years. Leander Paes too could not move beyond 73. In 1980, Vijay Amritraj was ranked 13th. Five years after that, Ramesh Krishnan reached 23rd ranking, whereas in the sixties, Ramanathan Krishnan was ranked number 3. Sania is still to come at par with Ramesh Krishnan. As of now, her ranking has gone up again, but only time will tell how far she will eventually go.

In March 2005, an apparel company launched its signature line after Sania. Thus, after becoming the brand ambassador of the company, Sania has acquired the privilege of being the fourth player after whom a signature line exists in apparels. Andre Agassi, Steffi Graf and Stephen Edberg are the three players who have signature lines named after them.

In May 2006, fifth-seeded Sania Mirza had to face defeat in the second round itself in the Istanbul Tennis Cup with a prize money of US $ 200,000. In the Doha Asiad Games held in December 2006, Sania won a gold medal in the mixed doubles with Leander Paes. She won a silver medal in the singles category too. Even the silver medal for the women's team category went to the Indian tennis team which comprised Shikha Oberoi, Ankita Bhambri and Isha Lakhani besides Sania.

Sania's best world ranking is 31, which she acquired after her excellent performance in Japan. In the year 2006, her ranking rose to number 50 as she lost a number of tournaments in second or third rounds.

As Sania hails from a Muslim background, she often has to face a lot of criticism for her attire from Muslim clerics.

Achievements

- ☆ *In November 1999, Sania Mirza won the doubles competition and reached the singles final of the Pakistan Intel G-5 Tournament.*
- ☆ *In September 2000, she won the singles final and reached the semi-finals of the doubles competition of the ITF-Mumbai G-5 Tournament.*
- ☆ *In October 2000, she won the doubles and singles competitions of the Pakistan Intel G-5 Tournament.*
- ☆ *In the doubles events, she in partnership with Zahara Umar Khan of Pakistan in January 2001, won the doubles and reached the quarter-finals of the singles competition of the ITF Junior One G F Tournament in New Delhi.*
- ☆ *In January 2001, she won the doubles and singles competition of the ITF 11 G-5 Junior Tournament in Chandigarh.*
- ☆ *In February 2001, she won the singles competition of the Calcutta G-5 tournament in Indian ITF Junior Circuit – III.*
- ☆ *She won the singles in Bangladesh Intel G-3 in February 2001;*

both the singles and doubles events in Pick Intel G-3 in July 2001 and doubles event in Smash Intel G-4 in July 2001.

☆ *She won the doubles event in Victorian Championship ITF G-2 Tournament in January 2002.*

☆ *She won the doubles event in PIC Pretoria ITF G-2 Tournament in July 2002.*

☆ *She won the doubles and singles competition of the South Central Africa Circuit Botswana ITF G-3 Tournament in August 2002.*

☆ *She won the singles competition and reached the semi-finals in the doubles event of the Asian Junior Tennis Championship ITF B-2 Tournament.*

☆ *In 2005, she won the Hyder Open title of WTA. In this year itself she made news with her excellent performance in tennis. She reached the fourth round in the US Open after defeating world-famous tennis players. Even though Sania was defeated by Maria Sharapova and could not go beyond the fourth round, she was the first ever Indian woman tennis player to reach this position.*

☆ *In the Doha Asiad Games held in December 2006, Sania won a gold medal in the mixed doubles with Leander Paes. She won a silver medal in the singles category too. Even the silver medal for the women's team category went to the Indian tennis team comprising Shikha Oberoi, Ankita Bhambri and Isha Lakhani apart from Sania Mirza.*

Tennis

Somdev Devvarman

Date of Birth: 13th February 1985

Somdev Devvarman is one of the fastest emerging tennis players who is widely seen as the successor of Leander Paes and Mahesh Bhupathi. Somdev is the first Indian to enter the final of the Chennai Open. The emergence of Somdev Devvarman has given a boost to Indian tennis. He is now India's No. 1 singles player.

Somdev Devvarman was born on 13 February 1985 at Guwahati, Assam. His father, a high ranking government official, Pravanjan Devvarman belongs to Tripura while his mother Ranjana is from Meghalaya. He received his early education in Chennai. For higher studies, he moved to the USA where he also got an opportunity to train in tennis.

Somdev started his professional career at the age of 17 in 2002. His first biggest achievement was a victory in the Kolkata F2 Championship in 2004 after which his world ranking rose to 666.

He became the first Indian to reach his first ATP Tour final at the 2009 Chennai Open, beating two time Chennai open former champion and world number 42 Carlos Moya of Spain and 25th ranked Ivo Karlovic of Croatia. However, in the final he lost to Marin Cilic of Croatia.

Somdev is a rising star on the horizon of Indian tennis. His emergence is seen to fill up the gap likely to be created by Leander Paes and Mahesh Bhupathi. He is being seen as a player who can take Indian tennis to greater heights.

Achievements

- ☆ *Somdev Devvarman beat 42 world rank holder Carlos Moya of Spain and 25th ranked Ivo Karlovic of Croatia.*
- ☆ *He is the first Indian to enter the Chennai Open final.*
- ☆ *He is presently India's No. 1 singles tennis player.*

Vijay Amritraj

Date of Birth: 14th December 1953

Vijay Prakash Amritraj, who is included among the famous sports personalities of the world, is better known as Vijay Amritraj. He is one of the best tennis players of the world. His popularity was such that he was one among the famous ABC of the tennis world — 'A' stood for (Vijay) Amritraj, 'B' for (Bjorn) Borg and 'C' for (Jimmy) Connors. Vijay Amritraj brought name and fame to India in the world of tennis.

Vijay Amritraj was born on 14th December 1953 at Chennai, Tamil Nadu. Tennis was a part and parcel of Vijay's family culture. He did not have sound health during his childhood days but he got rid of this problem as he grew due to the loving care of his parents and other family members. He was inclined towards this game right from the beginning. On coming into contact with an extremely talented player, Rama Rao, Vijay started learning the game very fast.

After this he progressed by leaps and bounds and in 1970, he got his first taste of success after he won the National junior title. In 1971, he won the Asian junior title and carved a place for himself among the four last players of Wimbledon, leaving a deep impression of his game on the minds of the tennis enthusiasts.

Amritraj, who stands at a height of 6'3", created tremors in the Indian sportsworld in 1972. He defeated players like Ramanathan Krishnan, Jaideep Mukherji and Premjit Lall. He won the National Championship for three years in 1972, 1973 and 1975 and this was time when Amritraj's game was at its peak. However, his game improved when he started playing under the guidance of Pancho Gonsalves and Ken Rosewall. This coaching added a professional touch to his game.

The year 1973 holds a special significance in his career when he made his mark at the international level. He won in the Volvo Grand Prix in Bretton Woods in USA (the international sports arena). While winning this competition, he managed to defeat many players of international repute, like Rod Lever and Jimmy Connors.

The next year, Vijay Amritraj helped India to reach the finals of the Davis Cup in Australia. He earned the reputation of an efficient player by defeating the Soviet Union.

Vijay Amritraj was always a dedicated and talented player. He used to play his strokes very casually, yet efficiently which used to enthral his spectators. He was very disappointed at not being able to play against South Africa and so started concentrating on other tennis circuits. He tried to take his game to new heights and secured a ranking of 50 among the top players of the world. He maintained this ranking for several years. His best ranking was 16.

In 1973 and 1983, Vijay Amritraj managed to reach the Wimbledon quarter-finals. In 1976, Vijay Amritraj entered the Wimbledon with his brother Anand and reached the semi-finals.

Achievements

- ☆ *In 1970, Vijay Amritraj won the National junior title.*
- ☆ *He was one among the famous ABC of the tennis world, where 'A' stood for (Vijay) Amritraj, 'B' for (Bjorn) Borg and 'C' for (Jimmy) Connors.*
- ☆ *In 1971, he won the Asian junior title.*
- ☆ *He won the National Championship for three years — in 1972, 1973 and 1975.*
- ☆ *He won the Volvo Grand Prix at Bretton Woods in America and created a name in the world.*
- ☆ *He was able to secure the ranking of 50 among the top players of the world. His best ranking was at number 16.*
- ☆ *In 1976, he entered the Wimbledon semi-finals.*

VOLLEYBALL

Volleyball is a game played between two teams of six players each, with an inflated ball which is volleyed over a high net. Each team tries to make the ball touch the court within the opposing side's playing area before it is returned. A team is allowed to touch the ball three times before returning it. The team that first scores 15 points wins the game under organised rules.

The complete rules of volleyball are extensive, but in general, play proceeds with points being scored by grounding the ball on the opponent's court, or when the opponent commits a fault. The first team to reach 25 points wins the set and the first team to win three sets wins the match. Teams can contact the ball no more than three time before the ball crosses the net, and consecutive contacts must be made by different players. The ball is usually played with the hands or arms, but players can legally strike or push (short contact) the ball with any part of the body.

Over time, volleyball developed common techniques of spiking, passing, blocking and setting as well as specialised player positions and offensive and defensive structures. Because many plays are made above the top of the net, vertical jumping is an athletic skill emphasised in volleyball.

Volleyball was invented in 1895 by William G. Morgan, a physical education director in Holyoke, Massachusetts, where he created a new game called *Mintonette* as a pastime to be played preferably indoors and by any number of players. The game took some of its characteristics from tennis and handball. It soon proved to have wide appeal for both sexes in schools, playgrounds, the armed forces and other settings.

The first rules, written down by Morgan called for a net 6' 6" high, a court measuring 25' by 50' and any number of players. A match was composed of nine innings with three serves for each team in each inning and no limit to the number of ball contacts made by each team before sending the ball to the opponent's court. In case of a serving error, a second try was allowed. Hitting the ball into the net was considered a foul (with loss of the point or a side-out) except in the case of the first-try serve.

After an observer, Alfred Halstead, noticed the volleying nature of the game at its first exhibition match in 1806, played at the Springfield YMCA, the game quickly became known as volleyball (it was originally spelled as two words — volley ball). Volleyball rules were slightly modified and the game spread around the country to other locations.

International competitions began in 1913 and volleyball became an Olympic sport in 1964.

Beach volleyball, as a variation with two players on a side, has of late grown increasingly popular and was included as a sport in the Olympics in 1996.

Volleyball

Jimmy George

Date of Birth: 8th March 1955
Died: 30th November 1987

Jimmy George was rated among the 10 best attackers of the world in 1980. He was a superb player with an eye for technical perfection. He was the first volleyball player from India to become a professional. He received the 'G.V. Raja Award' from the Kerala government in 1975. The Government of India honoured him with the Arjuna Award in 1976.

Kerala-born volleyball player Jimmy George got instant success and registered his name as a legendry player of the country. He lived for a very short span of life.

Jimmy George was born on 8th March 1955 in the tiny town of Peravoor in Cannore district of Kerala. His father, George Joseph, taught the primary lessons of volleyball to him. He gave lessons to all his other three brothers also. His father was a university-level player of his time and an advocate.

Jimmy played for St. Joseph's High School in Peravoor. He was only 16-years old when he was picked up to play for the state in the National Championship held at Jamshedpur in 1971. His playing tricks got honed when he joined the Devagiri College in Calicut. He represented Calicut University from 1970 to 1972 along with his brother Jose.

The meteoric rise of Jimmy began in 1970 when he was selected member of the Calicut University team. Jimmy's maternal uncle Prof. M.T. Emmanuel had been a source of perennial strength to him and Jimmy held him and his coach Kalavoor Gopinath in very high regard.

In 1973 Jimmy got admission in St. Thomas College, Palai and became the captain of the Kerala University team. He represented Calicut University thrice and the Kerala University four times. When he was at the Medical College at Thiruvanthapuram, he played for Kerala University. He helped the university win the Inter-University Championship from 1973 to 1976.

He captained the university team in 1973. He left his medical studies in 1976 and joined the Kerala police as a circle Inspector. He was later promoted to Assistant Commandant.

Jimmy secured a berth in the Kerala state team at the age of 16 in 1971 and thereafter he represented the state till 1979. In 1979 he took leave not only from the police but also from Kerala. He went to play for Abu Dhabi Sports Club. In 1982, he left Abu Dhabi and joined the Coletto Club at Treviso in Italy. He played there for a season before switching over to System Impiani. He played for them in 1983-84.

Jimmy George was an ambitious player and fully committed to volleyball. After playing in other countries, he returned to India and began his second phase of association with the game. He rejoined the Kerala police and played his last Nationals at Kanpur in 1985. Then he again went back to Italy to play for the Arrital team.

In 1987-88, he signed a contract with Eurostyle to play for the Euroslba team at Montchiari in Brescia. But this contract could not be completed as fate had other plans for him. He died in car crash in Italy.

Jimmy played for India in the 1974 Teheran Asian Games, the 1978 Bangkok Asian Games and 1986 Seoul Asian Games. He helped India to win a bronze medal in the Seoul Asian Games.

He played many matches against the visiting foreign teams. He captained the Indian team against Japan in 1985 and at the International Volleyball Championship in Saudi Arabia in 1985. He also captained the team in the International Volleyball Tournament in Hyderabad.

Jimmy received all major awards any Indian player could dream of. The most important of his awards was the Arjuna Award. He is the youngest volleyball player to win this award at the age of 21.

He was given 'G.V. Raja Award' in 1975 by the Kerala government. He won the 'Manorama Award' in 1976 for the best sportsman of Kerala and was adjudged the best player in the Gulf region for his association with tfhe Abu Dhabi Sports Club from 1979 to 1982. During his association with Italy (from 1982 to 1984 and from 1985 to 1987) he was rated as one of the best attackers of the world.

He died in a car crash in Italy on 30th November 1987 at the age of 33. He had got married in 1985. His son Joseph George was born just two months after his death. He had dreamt of Kerala's victory in All India Police Championship and this was achieved in 1985. He also dreamt of winning the National title for Kerala though it remained unfulfilled during his lifetime.

Following his untimely demise, his friends and relatives established a trust in his name known as the 'Jimmy George Foundation', which has instituted an award for the best sportsperson in Kerala. The Kerala government has dedicated its Indoor Stadium at Thiruvananthapuram to the memory of Jimmy George. His friends and admirers in Italy too have dedicated an indoor stadium to his memory at Montichiari, Brescia. The Jimmy George Foundation organises tournaments and coaching camps regularly.

Achievements

- ☆ *Jimmy George touched the heights of success in volleyball in a short span of time.*
- ☆ *He gave a new dimension to volleyball in India and was the first Indian player to become professional.*
- ☆ *He was known as one of the 10 best attackers of the world.*
- ☆ *The Kerala University team won the Inter-University Championship four times under his captaincy.*
- ☆ *He was adjudged the best player of the Gulf region while playing for the Abu Dhabi Sports Club.*

- ☆ *The Kerala government honoured him with the 'G.V. Raja Award' in 1975.*
- ☆ *He was given the 'Manorama Award' as the best sportsperson of Kerala in 1976.*
- ☆ *He was awarded the Arjuna Award in 1976. He was the youngest achiever of this award as a volleyball player at the age of 21.*

WEIGHTLIFTING

The term 'weightlifting' is ofen informally used to refer to weight-training. Olympic weightlifting trains the athlete for functional strength, utilising the body's major muscle groups. For this reason, the Olympic lifts (or simplified versions, such as the 'power snatch' or 'clean') are extensively used in training for the sports, such as in American football.

Weightlifting is a sport in which the competitors attempt to lift heavy weights mounted on steel bars called barbells in a competition or as an exercise. The two main events are — the snatch, in which the barbell is lifted from the floor to arm's length overhead in a single, continuous motion; and the 'clean and jerk', in which the barbell is lifted 'clean' first to the shoulders or an intermediate position, 'racking' the bar in a front squat, then standing up in the concentric portion of the front squat, and finally 'jerking' the barbell to a position above the head. In both cases, for a successful lift, competitors must hold the bar steady above their heads, with arms and legs straight and motionless.

A third lift, the 'clean and press' or simply 'press', was practiced in the Olympics until 1972. The 'clean and press' differs from the 'clean and jerk', with the weight pressed directly up from the chest with the arms only, while remaining standing, while the 'jerk' uses the leg-power to assist the arms part of the way up, followed by the body sinking downward into a split or squat to complete the extension of the arms, before once again standing. The 'press' was eliminated due to the difficulty in judging whether the lift was performed correctly; lifters used to bend so far backward as to turn it into a 'standing bench press'.

The execution of the activity is a combination of power, flexibility, concentration, skill, will power, discipline, athleticism, fitness, technique and mental and physical strength.

The origins of modern competition are to be found in the 18th- to 19th-century strongman contests in the first three Olympic Games (1896, 1900 and 1904) and which include weight-lifting, as did all the games subsequently since the 1920s.

The contestants are divided into 10 body-weight categories, ranging from flyweight to super-heavyweight. Lifts may range to over 1,000 lbs (455 kg) in the heavyweight divisions.

Three judges oversee the successful completion of the lift. Once a competitor has met the requirements in their opinion, each judge shines a white light. When at least two white lights are shown, the lift is regarded as successful and the competitor may return the bar to the platform. If the competitor fails to achieve a successful lift in the opinion of a judge, a red light is shown. The bar must be lifted to at least knee level within 60 seconds of the bar being loaded, else the lift does not count. If the competitor makes two consecutive lifts, he is permitted 135 seconds for the second lift.

Karnam Malleswari

Date of Birth: 1st June 1975

Weightlifter Karnam Malleswari created history by becoming the first Indian woman to win an Olympic medal, a bronze in the women's 69-kg category at the Sydney Olympics in September 2000.

Malleswari was rewarded with the Arjuna Award in 1995 and in the following year, she received the 'Rajiv Gandhi Khel Ratna' award. She was also awarded the Padma Shri in 1997.

Karnam Malleswari's name was in the limelight following the Sydney Olympics in September 2000. She was a much written about sports personality in Indian newspapers and magazines after she inscribed her name in golden letters in India's sports history by winning a bronze medal in the 69-kg women's tournament. No Indian woman had ever won an Olympic medal so far.

The journey to participate for the first-time in Olympic Games was undertaken by the Indian sportswoman Mary Lila Rao in 1952, but she failed to reach any height. This time it however, culminated with iron woman Karnam Malleswari's participation. She became the only Indian woman to be an Olympic medal-winner.

Ignoring the weights dangling on both sides of the rod, she stood with Herculean confidence and eyes closed. With sheer courage, she lifted the weight in an instant and a multitude of claps rent the air. Her jaws drawn inside with the weight she bore spelled her resolve of fulfilling her aspiration. Her eyes shone with pride after making a mark for her country.

Malleswari was chosen as the 'South Asian of the Year' by *Time*-Asia's web column. But all was not so rosy in 1997, the year she received the Padma Shri. She got married that year and took a 12-month leave from the sport. When she returned, her performance level was abysmally low. Though she notched up a silver medal at the 1998 Bangkok Asian Games, she drew a blank at the 1999 Athens Championship. The following year was marked by insinuations about her under-performance and how she had put on weight and become complacent.

A distraught Malleswari, determined to silence her critics, went back to training with her coach Taranenko, who firmly believed that his pupil could win a medal at the Olympics.

Malleswari was initiated into the sport in 1989 when she was just 14-years old. Her debut at Udaipur was sensational where she set six national marks and continued her spectacular progress. At the Asian Championship, Thailand, she picked up a silver medal and followed this up with three bronze medals in 1993 at the Melbourne World Weight-lifting Championship.

In the Hiroshima Asian Games, she finished second to a Chinese girl in all the three events she participated in. Again at the 1994 World Weight-lifting Championship in Istanbul, she won two gold medals and a bronze, finishing second to a Chinese girl. Though she lifted the same weight, she lost the gold on heavier body count — she was half a kilo heavier than her opponent. However, the Chinese girl failed in the dope test and the gold was given to Malleswari. At the Nationals in Pune, the same year, she shattered the world record in 'clean and jerk'. Though she stood fifth in the 52-kg category in the World Championship, Germany, she improved her position the subsequent year in the Bulgarian World Championship.

In 1995, at the World Championship in China, Malleswari set a new world record in the 'jerk' and won three gold medals in the women's 54-kg category. Her 113-kg haul beat the previous 112.5-kg world record set by China's Long Yulip in 1993. Before the start of the championship she and Kunjarani were jointly ranked number one in the world. Zhang Xiu Xiang, the Chinese who was fancied to win, was stunned when Malleswari took a 5-kg lead in the 'snatch' by lifting 90 kgs. In the 'jerk' she created a new world record by lifting 113 kg. The following year, Korea saw this gutsy lady annexing three gold medals in the 54-kg class and though her efforts were much below the Asian Games level, she ensured that she had a comfortable 10-kg margin over her nearest rival, Yuanhong Su, of China. What thrilled the crowd was her massive 90-kg heave in 'snatch' and 107.5 kg in 'clean and jerk'. This total of 197.5 kg was her personal best.

Though she won just a silver medal at the 1998 Bangkok Asian Games and drew a blank at the 1999 Athens World Championships, Malleswari's preparedness for the big day was evident when she annexed a gold at the Osaka World Weight-lifting Championship in May 2000. Her crowning glory came four months later at the Sydney Olympics, where she clinched a bronze in one of the toughest fought contests of the Games.

This 'Andhra powerhouse' became the third individual Indian – and the first woman – since India's Independence to win an Olympic medal. Before this, Indian athlete P.T. Usha had missed her bronze in one-hundredth part of a second.

Hailing from Srikakulam in Andhra Pradesh, Malleswari was born on 1st June 1975 in Voosavanipeta village, situated on the outskirts of Amadalavalasa, in a medium-class family. Her birthplace is located at a distance of 800 km to the north-east of Andhra Pradesh's capital city, Hyderabad. Amadalavalasa is a small town. Her father, Ramdass, is a constable in the Railway Security Force. Being second among four sisters in an average family, she didn't have a very comfortable childhood.

The sisters used to go to nearby railway tracks to collect coal early morning. Today she she has no dearth of money and has come a long way from the time when, as a nine-year old, she would go to the gym with her elder sister Narasamma, who was one of the 20 probables for the 1989 World Championship in Manchester and the Asian Championship in

Beijing. Her younger sister Krishnakumari is also a national-level weight-lifter.

It was when Malleswari accompanied her sister to the Bengaluru camp that she was spotted by Arjuna Award-winner and chief national coach, Shyam Lal Salwan. Her trainer advised her to take up weight-lifting. This was just the beginning. She completely gave herself to the sport and her hard work bore fruit when she was considered for the Indian team within a span of one year itself. She was successful in winning a bronze medal in the World Championship in 1992. Her zeal continued and led her to win the World Championships in 1994 and 1995. Thereon Malleswari kept climbing the ladder of success. During the selection process for Sydney Olympics in 2000, her name in the list was met with a lot of criticism as it was said that she was going as a tourist at the government's cost. This was also because Kunjarani's name had been left out to include Malleswari. Since then, there's been no looking back.

Such was the disdain for the lifter that on 19th September 2000, when her name was announced for the 69-kg event at the Sydney International Convention Centre, just seven Indians — three from the Olympic squad and four from the 42 journalists covering the Games—were present to see her make Indian sports history.

Malleswari walked to the bar, rubbed powder on her hands, bent down and adjusted her grip. Then in one clean 'snatch' she surprised the world by lifting twice her body-weight and becoming India's first-ever woman Olympic bronze-medallist. In one single sweep this lady from Voosavanipeta in the Srikakulam district of Andhra Pradesh silenced all her critics. People who had sniggered at her and called her grossly overweight and past her prime became her instant admirers after that magical moment.

Malleswari later said, "When I became victorious at the Sydney Olympics, there were numerous announcements about awards in cash and kind. When I became the world champion in 1994 and 1995, there were no such announcements." The state governments of Andhra Pradesh, Haryana and Maharashtra showered Malleswari with cash awards.

In fact weightlifting has been lucky for Malleswari in more ways than one. She met her husband, Rajesh Tyagi (who is in the CRPF), in the gym at Delhi's Jawaharlal Nehru Stadium where he too used to go for his weightlifting training. The two met and fell in love. Ignoring the protests on both sides of the family, the two got married secretly.

Rajesh Tyagi was himself a university-level weightlifter and it was at a training camp that he first met Karnam Malleswari, a shy girl from Andhra Pradesh. It was love at first 'snatch' but it wasn't 'clean and jerk' when Rajesh took Malleswari home to meet his parents. As luck would have it, his mother was suitably unimpressed with her son's choice, even though he told her that Malleswari, then weighing 54 kg, had won the world weightlifting title in her class by lifting 113 kg.

However, in 1997, Rajesh and Malleswari got married. That's when she took a break from competitive weightlifting. Subsequently, she struggled with her own weight and a job as the Deputy Manager with the Food Corporation of India only added to her woes.

Far away from Sydney, in a quiet lane of Faridabad, when the news reached the ears of Karnam Malleswari's mother-in-law, the old lady was furious. "She is bringing a bronze?" she thundered. "Doesn't she know we don't eat non-vegetarian stuff, certainly not prawns?"

But when she realised that there had been a spelling mistake, she expressed pride over her *balshali bahu's* Olympic feat. But she refused to go into a flashback and recall the days when she was fiercely opposed to her son Rajesh marrying Malleswari. The state of Haryana was jubilant over their 'daughter-in-law's successful stint'. Malleswari lifted a weight of 250 kg and the Haryana government announced a prize of 25 lakh rupees for her. The Indian flag flew at the Sydney Olympic and Haryana glowed and shone with lamps lighted. Shops were closed at Yamuna Nagar and crackers were burst everywhere. Drums and trumpets resonated on the streets.

Malleswari, who is a District Manager in the Food Corporation of India, plans to start a weight-lifting academy after she retires. "Both the

Haryana and Andhra Pradesh governments have shown a keen interest in my project," she says.

Malleswari has dedicated her Olympic medal to "my state, to my husband's state and above all, to my country. I am proud that I have brought laurels to India." With her incredible feat, Malleswari, the daughter of a railway policeman, has not just set new standards in women's sports but given hope to a nation starved of sporting icons.

The Hinduja Sports Foundation played a vital role in Malleswari's sports career. The Foundation provided her with financial assistance and other basic facilities from time to time. Her sister Narsimha also has played an equally important role in her success. When she realised that she was not cut out for international-level performances, post-marriage, she diverted her concentration towards Malleswari. Technically, Malleswari's strong physique since childhood, made her extremely suitable for weightlifting.

Malleswari's resolve and dedication have made her reach this position. She has been honoured with the highest sports honours — the Arjuna Award, the Padma Shri, the 'Rajiv Gandhi Khel Ratna' award and the 'K.K. Birla Award'.

The Food Corporation of India gave her a promotion to the post of Deputy Manager apart from gifting her a red Maruti 800. The tough days of dire poverty during her childhood fuelled the fire of resolve and dedication in her.

The Andhra Pradesh government gave her a 500-yard plot of land as a token of appreciation. However, unfortunately it took her years before she could take possession of the plot. Both the states of Haryana and Andhra Pradesh equally rejoiced at her success.

On being asked how she felt on being the woman sportsperson to win an Olympic medal, she said, "I am indeed honoured that I made my country proud by winning a medal at the first Olympic Games of the millennium." Her coaches Leonid Taranenko and Sandhu too couldn't help but comment, "Efforts have borne fruit. We will remember this day for a very long time to come."

The 26-year-old former world champion became only the third Indian since Independence to win an individual Olympic medal, emulating the third-place finishers Kashaba Jadhav, in the 52-kg Greco-Roman wrestling at Helsinki in 1952, and tennis star Leander Paes in men's singles at Atlanta in 1996. At her moment of triumph, Malleswari announced that it would be her last competition.

In her first attempt in the 69-kg category after moving up from 63 kg, the lifter hoisted a superb total 240 kg, by lifting 110 kg in 'snatch' and 130 kg in 'clean and jerk'. She finished close behind China's Lin Wei Ning and Erzsebet Markus of Hungary. Both achieved 242.5 kg but Lin, who tilted the scales at 66.74 kg against 68.52 kg of the Hungarian, ensured the gold.

"I am blessed to be the first Indian woman to win a medal. But I am unlucky not to win the gold," said an ecstatic Malleswari ensuring India's Olympic medal. She was sponsored by the Indian Olympic Union and Samsung India for the 2004 Athens Olympics, where she was confident of winning a medal. She took part in the 63-kg category instead of 69 kg. However, contrary to everyone's hopes, she was unable to lift the weight and win any medal there.

Achievements

- ☆ *Malleswari became the national champion in 52-kg category in 1990-91.*
- ☆ *She was the national champion from 1992-98 in the 54-kg. (body-weight) category.*
- ☆ *She won three gold medals in the Asian Championship in Korea in 1994.*
- ☆ *She won two gold and one silver medal in the World Championship at Istanbul in 1994.*
- ☆ *She won three gold medals in the Asian Championship in the 54-kg category in South Korea in 1995.*

☆ *She won a gold medal in the World Championship in China in 1995.*

☆ *She won a gold medal in the Asian Competition in Japan in 1996.*

☆ *She won a gold medal in the 54-kg category in the Asian Games in 1997.*

☆ *She won a silver medal in the 63-kg category in 1998 at the Bangkok Asian Games.*

☆ *In 2000 Osaka Asian Championship, she won a gold medal in the 63-kg category. However, she had to be content with a third position in the end.*

☆ *She was awarded the 'Rajiv Gandhi Khel Ratna' award in 1996.*

☆ *She was also awarded the Padma Shri.*

Weightlifting

N. Kunjarani Devi

Date of Birth: 1st March 1968

N. Kunjarani Devi is the first woman weightlifter of the country to win the Arjuna Award in 1990. She also holds the honour of being the first woman weightlifter of the country to be presented the 'Rajiv Gandhi Khel Ratna' award in 1996. N. Kunjarani Devi was also honoured with the 'K.K. Birla Sports Award' in 1996 for her distinguished performance in sports.

N. Kunjarani Devi, whose full name is Nameirakpam Kunjarani Devi, is an international weightlifter who has never failed to receive a medal in any competition that she has participated in. She became the first gold medal-winner of India in the 1995 Commonwealth Games held at Nauru. That year she was also ranked number one. However, she later slipped to the third position.

Kunjarani Devi has won more than 60 medals at the international level. She holds the important post of Assistant Commandant in the Central Reserve Police Force and has been awarded the Arjuna Award in 1990, the 'Rajiv Gandhi Khel Ratna' award in 1996 and the 'K.K. Birla Sports Award' in 1996 for her exemplary achievements.

Kunjarani was born on 1st March 1968 at Kairang Mayai Leikai in Imphal, Manipur. When she reminisces about her past she says, "People of Imphal used to mock at me when I started weightlifting. I was the laughing stock for them, but I was determined to make a name for myself and put India on an international platform in sports."

Kunjarani would have been associated with football or hockey, had she not been into weightlifting as she had been playing both these games from her childhood days. But as she grew up, she realised that both these games are team sports and she wanted to take part in an individual event where hard work and dedication would make her earn a position. Thus she decided to choose weightlifting as her career.

Choosing weightlifting was not an easy job for her. She had to face a lot of criticism from her neighbours and relatives for choosing this uncommon and 'manly' profession. People used to comment on her and say, "She has chosen a man's game despite being a woman. She will die." But such comments did not dissuade Kunjarani. They in fact strengthened her resolve to work harder. She wanted to earn a name for her country at any cost now.

After joining the Central Reserve Police Force (CRPF), Kunjarani worked harder at the Police Championship. She holds an important post of Assistant Commandant here. She led the Indian police team from 1996 to 1998. Her icon is none other than the athlete P.T. Usha. Kunjarani was highly inspired by her who had won a number of medals for India at the international level.

Kunjarani's trainer, Leonid Taranenko of Belarus has an important role in polishing Kunjarani's skills to finesse. She also believes that "whatever I have achieved in weightlifting today is a result of the efforts of Taranenko."

It is indeed an amazing sight to see Kunjarani lift the weights. She lifts the weight with such ease that it appears as if she is lifting a doll. People associated with weightlifting as also the trainers bite their nails when they see this marvellous lady in this sport. Her colleagues say this about her, "She is like a machine, almost. She feels no tiredness, no pain; she just goes on working like a machine." Her sister Pratibha Kumari could not help but remark about her sister, "She is not human at all. She never gets tired."

Kunjarani began her career in 1985 and she hasn't stopped winning medals since then and gold medals at that. She has been always a winner in the National Weightlifting Championship in 44-kg, 46-kg and 48-kg categories. Now her constant weight is of 48 kgs. She set two national records in Thiruvananthapuram in 1985. Then she changed her category in 1994 and managed to win a gold medal in the 46-kg category. After four years, she tried her hand at the 48-kg category but had to be satisfied with a silver medal only.

In the 1990 Asian Games, Kunjarani won a bronze medal but was unable to win any medal in the 1998 Bangkok Asian Games. Then she won three silver medals at in the 1994 Hiroshima Games. She again won a bronze in the 48-kg category. She was successful in retaining her second position in 1992 in Thailand and in 1993 in China. Thereafter, in 1989 Shanghai Games she won one silver and two bronze medals. Kunjarani's performance was extremely good and she won two gold and one bronze medal in the 46-kg category. In Japan, in 1996, she was unable to repeat her award-winning performance and could only manage to win one silver and one bronze medal. In the 1995 Commonwealth Games in Nauru, she won a gold medal in the 48-kg category and also set a record by becoming the first gold-medal winner in the Commonwealth Games and reaching the topmost position.

In the Commonwealth Games held at Manchester in August 2002, Kunjarani was in the limelight for being the veteran weightlifter from India to win three gold medals. Prior to this, Kunjarani had been barred from participating in any tournament for six months when she had been accused of doping. But Kunjarani proved her capability in the Manchester Games and also silenced the doping accusation forever.

In the Commonwealth Games held at Melbourne in March 2006, Kunjarani repeated her excellent performance by making a new record in the 'clean and jerk' competition and earning a gold medal for India in the 48-kg category in the 18th Commonwealth Games. This year one gold medal had been reserved for every category, which was won by Kunjarani. She clinched the title by lifting the 166-kg weight. At the age of 38 years, Kunjarani lifted the 72 kg weight in the 'snatch' and 94-kg in the 'clean and jerk' competition besides setting a new record. Even though her record was of 167 kg (75 kg in 'snatch'), she still managed to set a record despite not performing to her best capability.

Despite her growing age, Kunjarani is an icon for budding sportspersons with her indomitable spirit and that is why she is known as the 'grand old lady'. The International Weightlifting Union has declared Kunjarani as the best weightlifter of the 20th century when she held the position of being world number one.

Her golden career also witnessed a black spot when she was accused of doping (use of prohibited energy-giving drugs) in 2001 when she was barred from participating in any tournament for six months.

Achievements

- ☆ *Kunjarani established a new national record in 1987.*
- ☆ *In the 1989 Shanghai Games, she won one silver and two bronze medals.*
- ☆ *She won a bronze medal in the Beijing Asian Games in 1990.*
- ☆ *She is recipient of the Arjuna Award in 1990.*
- ☆ *She won three bronze medals in the 44-kg category.*
- ☆ *She was successful in retaining her second position in 1992 in Thailand and in 1993 in China.*
- ☆ *In the 1994 Hiroshima Games, she won a bronze medal.*
- ☆ *She won a gold medal at the National Championship at Pune.*
- ☆ *In 1994 she won two gold and one bronze medal in South Korea.*
- ☆ *In the 1995 Commonwealth Games in Nauru, she set a record of being the first gold-medal winner.*
- ☆ *In 1995, she held the position of world number one.*
- ☆ *She was awarded, the 'Rajiv Gandhi Khel Ratna' award in 1996 and is the first woman sportsperson to get this award.*
- ☆ *In Japan in 1996, she won one bronze medal.*

- ☆ *She was honoured with the 'K.K. Birla Sports Award' in 1996.*
- ☆ *In the Commonwealth Games at Manchester in August 2002, she won three gold medals.*
- ☆ *In the Commonwealth Games held at Melbourne in March 2006, she set a new record in the 'clean and jerk' competition and won a gold medal for India in the 48-kg category.*
- ☆ *She has won more than 60 medals at the international events.*

WRESTLING

Wrestling is a sport in which two competitors grapple with and strive to trip or throw each other down or off-balance. It is practiced in various styles, including freestyle wrestling in which contestants can use holds above and below the waist.

The first recorded Olympic wrestling match took place at the Olympic Games in 708 BCE. Wrestling was a highly valued form of military exercise without the use of weapons. Wrestlers oiled themselves with olive oil and dust to make themselves easier to grasp. The wrestling event took place in a *keroma*, a muddy arena. Punches, biting, tripping, and eye gouging were not permitted. No weight classes existed but boys did not wrestle with men.

There were two forms of wrestling at the Games, *orthia pale*, upright wrestling, and *kato pale*, ground wrestling, which had different holds and different ways to determine the winner. In *orthia pale*, the opponent tried to throw the other to the ground three times during a match and a match did not end until this happened. The victor was known as the *triakter*. In *kato pale*, the opponent fought until he accepted defeat by holding up his right hand with his index finger extended.

It is said that Milon of Croton won his first Olympic victory in the boys' wrestling. During his career, he won six wrestling championships at both the Olympic and Pythian Games. In total, Milon won 32 wrestling championships. Strong enough to carry an ox on his shoulders as a young man, the older Milon died a horrible death when he attempted to rip a split tree apart and one of his hands got stuck in between. Unable to free himself, wild animals attacked and killed the captive Milon during the night.

In the modern Olympics the wrestling bouts are held in different styles. In the Greco-Roman style of wrestling, holds only above the waist are allowed. In Sambo, which is Russian in origin, the judo technique is applied while Sumo wrestling is a specialised Japanese style of wrestling. The American style of wrestling today is the most popular of all spectator sports, though it principally involves mildly flamboyant showmanship, including such non-classical moves as kicking to the head, which can prove fatal or injurious, if not actually pulled away.

Wrestling

Gama Pahalwan

Date of Birth: 1882
Died : 21nd May 1960

Gama Pahalwan was fond of wrestling right since childhood itself. He managed to defeat all the national-level wrestlers by the time he was 20 years of age. He was given the title of 'Rustam-e-Hind'.

Ahmad Baksh Gama was born in Datiya, Madhya Pradesh and he used to enjoy wrestling immensely. He was known popularly as Gama Pahalwan.

He managed to get the Indian wrestling style introduced in the international games. He is solely responsible for earning international fame for this form of wrestling and was given the title of 'Rustam-e-Hind'. The nuances and tricks of the game were always at his fingertips.

A wrestling match was to be organised in 1910 and the winner of the match was to be conferred with the title of 'Rustam-e-Hind'. Gama managed to defeat all the other wrestlers easily and won the title of 'Rustam-e-Hind'. He played his last wrestling match with J.J. Peterson, whom he defeated in 45 seconds flat.

Gama Pahalwan was in the game of wrestling for years and was always a winner. His most important characteristic was his self-respect which was very strong. He had the quality of befriending people with ease. The sole credit of bringing Indian wrestling to the international platform and making it popular goes to Gama Pahalwan.

Gama Pahalwan expired on 2nd May 1960 after a fairly prolonged illness in Lahore, Pakistan. He was 80 years of age at that time.

Achievements

- ☆ *Gama Pahalwan defeated all the national-level wrestlers during his time.*
- ☆ *He brought recognition to Indian wrestling on the international platform.*
- ☆ *He managed to defeat all the other wrestlers in the wrestling matches easily and won the title of 'Rustam-e-Hind'.*
- ☆ *He was in the game of wrestling for years and was always a winner.*

Wrestling

Kashaba Dada Saheb Jadhav

Date of Birth: 15th January 1926
Died : 1988

Kashaba Dada Saheb Jadhav's name has been written in golden words in the sports history of India. He was Independent India's first individual Olympic medallist. He won a bronze medal at the 1952 Helsinki Olympic Games in wrestling, but was not given any national or state award in recognition of his prestigious achievement. He passed his life in police service.

Kashaba Dada Saheb is known by his short name K.D. Jadhav. When he won a bronze medal in wrestling at the 1952 Helsinki Olympic Games, only Norman Pritchard (an Anglo-Indian) had won two silver medals in athletics but that was before Independence. After Independence, only K.D. Jadhav could win an Olympic medal in the individual category. India had won gold medals only in hockey but that was a team sport.

For nearly half a century after K.D. Jadhav had won an individual medal in Olympics, no Indian could win an individual medal until Leander Paes won a bronze medal in the 1996 Olympics.

K.D. Jadhav was born on 15th January 1926. Hailing from a wrestling background, Jadhav was an ardent lover of sports. He was specially interested in wrestling, *kabaddi*, swimming, racing, etc. His father, Dada Saheb, was himself a good wrestler and taught Jadhav about the sport in detail. Despite being the youngest in the family, he managed to grasp the sport quickly and outclassed everyone. Though his father taught the game to all his five sons, it was only K.D. who could excel. Besides Kashaba, the four sons were Balkrishna, Jyoti Ram, Kashiram and Dinkar. He had three daughters also.

At a very tender age, Kashaba used to watch wrestling bouts, sitting on the shoulders of his father. He did his schooling at Tilak High School in Karad where he used to walk four miles briskly from his home to school daily. Gradually he began to emerge as the undisputed wrestler in the area and soon was completing in the national events.

By the time he graduated from Raja Ram College of Kolhapur, he had earned name and fame for himself all over south Maharashtra. In 1945 he came to the notice of Prof. Manik Rao who was a great patron of wrestling in the state.

Jadhav shot to national fame when he defeated the reigning national flyweight champion, Niranjan Das of Bengal, at Lucknow in 1948. This feat of Jadhav ensured for him a trip to London for the Olympics. At the London Olympics of 1948, prior to the start of the Games, Indian wrestlers were coached by Reese Gardener of the US and who was a former lightweight world champion. Jadhav managed to reach a highly credible sixth place out of 42, losing to Iranian, Mohammad Rasul Ruisi, in the third round of the flyweight category.

Four years later, in 1952 at the Helsinki Olympics, he emerged as a stronger competitor in the bantam-weight category. He defeated his opponent and finished third to earn a bronze medal in the 52-kg category. He credited his victory to his American coach Gardener, although he had coached him for only a week.

Indian wrestlers were shocked on reaching London to find a vast difference between the Indian and international rules. Fighting on a mat than in a mud pit proved unsettling to the Indian wrestlers.

Jadhav's berth in the Helsinki Olympics (1952) was sought to be sabotaged by officials who had placed him second in the national games at Chennai. Friends and neighbours helped him out with the shopkeepers of Karad by arranging to buy his kit. The principal of Raja Ram College helped him and Jadhav could move up from flyweight (52 kg) to bantam-weight (57 kg). He sailed through the first five rounds easily, winning each game in less than five minutes. The sixth round was vey tough and lasted for 15 minutes. Japan's Shohachi Ishii finally emerged triumphant by a single point. Ishii had initially been a judo player but had switched to wrestling when the US forces banned the game of judo after World War II.

Almost immediately after the tough bout of wrestling, Jadhav was ordered back on to the mat to take on the next opponent — the Soviet Union's Rashid Mamebekov—while the rules stipulated a rest of half an hour between the bouts. But no Indian official was present to press the case of an exhausted Jadhav. Finally, the Soviet player won easily to reach the final. K.D. Jadhav had to satisfy himself with the bronze medal.

On his return, many functions were organised to felicitate him. But the one function that pleased him the most was the traditional welcome by his villagers in which a procession of 151 bullock-carts with their sports hero was taken to his home village of Goleshwar, covering a distance of 40 kilometres.

Despite this unique achievement of a bronze medal in the Olympics, he was largely ignored by the Government of India. Jadhav got no national or state recognition, no Arjuna or cash award.

After this glorious moment, Jadhav slid into oblivion, though he tried to overlook the neglect shown by the sports officials and the government. He rose to be Assistant Commissioner at Naigon in Bombay. He lived in poverty until he died in 1988 in a road accident.

The modest cottage, which he built by selling the jewellery of his wife, was named 'Olympica Nivas' very aptly. His son Ranjit switched from wrestling to football. His family lives a simple life even today.

He left for heavenly abode in 1988. His widow Kusum received Rs 25,000 as compensation. Till today no other Indian wrestler has emulated his feat of standing on the Olympic podium.

Achievements

☆ *K.D. Jadhav was a player whose name is written in gold letters in the sports history of India. He was Independent India's first Olympic individual medal-winner.*

☆ *K.D. Jadhav won a bronze medal in the Helsinki Olympics in 1952.*

☆ *He excelled in wrestling,* kabaddi, *racing, swimming and gymnastics in his school at Karad in Maharashtra.*

☆ *While graduating from Raja Ram College in Kolhapur, he earned a name in wrestling for himself all over south Maharashtra.*

☆ *In 1948, he defeated the reigning national flyweight champion, Niranjan Das, at Lucknow and became the national champion. This feat ensured his trip to London Olympics (1948) where he secured a sixth place out of 42 players.*

Wrestling

Master Chandgiram

Date of Birth: 9th November 1937

Master Chandgiram was a very popular wrestler in the sixties and the seventies. He has been felicitated with a number of titles, such as the 'Hind Kesari', 'Bharat Kesari', 'Rustam-e-Hind' and 'Bharat Bhim'. He was therefore the natural first choice of the selectors for the Arjuna Award in 1969.

Master Chandgiram was one of the most outstanding wrestlers of the sixties and the seventies. He had a lot of admirers and fans all across the country during his time. He had an excellent and well-built physique and was a wrestler with a very good height. He was well known for his intelligence and sense of humour. Master Chandgiram was also popular for his tricky grip over his opponent.

Master Chandgiram was born on 9th November 1937 in Sisai village of Hissar district in Haryana. After completing his matriculation, he did his diploma in art and craft. For some time he was a soldier in the Jat regiment of the Indian Army and later he took up a job as an art teacher in a school. He also acquired the name 'Master' because of being in the teaching profession and this prefix stuck to his name forever. He came to be known as Master Chandgiram. The turban that he wore also added more grandeur to his personality.

Master Chandgiram's wrestling career started quite late in life. He entered the field of wrestling at 21 years of age. He became suddenly famous after winning the National Championship which he won in Ajmer in 1961. He then went ahead to become the national champion at Jalandhar in 1962. In the meanwhile, he also won the title of 'Hind Kesari' in Delhi in 1962.

After this he won two national competitions in 1968 at Rohtak and in 1972 in Indore. During this time, in 1968, he won the title of 'Bharat Kesari' in the championship organised at Delhi. He won this title again in 1969. In 1969 and 1970, Chandgiram won the title of 'Bharat Bhim' at Lucknow.

In 1969, he was honoured with the title of 'Rustam-e-Hind'. His most commendable performance at the international level was seen in 1970, when he participated in the 100-kg category at the Bangkok Asian Games and defeated Iran's world champion, Anwani Abulfazal to win a gold medal. Two years later Chandgiram represented India in the 1992 Olympic Games held at Munich.

He earned immense fame in the Indian-style wrestling and drew crowds by participating in the matches. The attitude he displayed towards Meherdin of Rajasthan during the 'Hind Kesari' title was commendable and people greatly appreciated his skill.

Chandgiram also worked as Additional Sports Director in Haryana. He also acted in two films in which he played the roles of Veer Ghatotkach and Tarzan. However, he did not break his ties with wrestling which had brought him name and fame.

Chandgiram opened a wrestling ring on the banks of River Yamuna in Delhi where new players are imparted training. Chandgiram has also authored a book on wrestling entitled, *The Tactics of Indian Wrestling.*

Achievements

- ☆ *Master Chandgiram has been an extremely popular wrestler of the country.*
- ☆ *He gained name after being felicitated with a number of titles such as 'Hind Kesari', 'Bharat Kesari', 'Rustam-e-Hind' and 'Bharat Bhim'.*
- ☆ *He was bestowed the Arjuna Award in 1969.*

- ☆ *He won the National Championships at Ajmer (1961), Jalandhar (1962), Rohtak (1968) and Indore (1972).*
- ☆ *He defeated Iran's world champion, Anwani Abulfazal and won a gold medal in the Bangkok Asian Games.*
- ☆ *He was awarded the Padma Shri by the Government of India.*
- ☆ *He worked as Additional Sports Director in Haryana.*
- ☆ *He has authored a book on wrestling, entitled* The Tactics of Indian Wrestling.

Sushil Kumar Solanki

Date of Birth : 26th May 1983

Sushil Kumar created history when he won the bronze medal in men's 66 kg. freestyle wrestling event on 20th August, 2008 at the Beijing Olympics. He wrote his name in golden letters in the sports history of India by winning this Olympic medal. He won the Olympic medal in wrestling for India after a gap of 56 years. This was the second medal for India in wrestling and the first since Khashaba Jadhav's bronze medal at the 1952 Helsinki Olympic Games. Sushil Kumar gave a surprise to all Indians by winning an unexpected medal.

Sushil Kumar, born on May 26, 1983, hails from the village of Baprola in the Najafgarh suburb of the national capital territory of Delhi near the Haryana-Delhi border. Sushil Kumar's father is an MTNL bus driver and mother Kamla Devi is a housewife. Sushil Kumar is employed as Chief Ticketing Inspector in Northern Railway. He was inspired to take up wrestling at an early age by his cousin and did hard work in this direction. Once he went to a Zone Wrestling Competition to represent his school and came back victorious.

Sushil Kumar started training at Chhatrasal Stadium *akhada* at the age of 14. He won a State Championship there. Sushil was trained by Arjuna Awardee Satpal Pehalwan.

His first success came at the World Cadet Games in 1998 where he won a gold medal in his weight category. He followed this up with a gold in the Asian Junior Wrestling Championship in 2000.

Moving out of the junior championship, Sushil tasted success at the Asian Wrestling Championship in 2003 by winning a Bronze medal and following that up with a gold medal at the Commonwealth Wrestling Championship.

On 20th August 2008, Sushil Kumar won a bronze medal in the 66 kg. freestyle wrestling defeating Leonid Spridonov of Kazakhastan 3-1 with a score of 2-1, 0-1, 2-0 in the three rounds. When he won the Olympic bronze medal, the whole of Najafgarh celebrated his victory with traditional dances and by distributing sweets to each other. Although Sushil Kumar was not expected to win a medal in the last rounds, yet his coach Satpal and he himself had hopes of winning the competition.

Many cash awards were given to Sushil Kumar for winning the Olympic bronze medal. The awards are as follows :-

- Rs. 55 lakh cash award and promoted to Assistant Commercial Manager from ticketing inspector by Ministry of Railway.
- Rs. 50 lakh cash award from the Delhi Government.
- Rs. 25 lakh cash award by Haryana State Government.
- Rs. 20 lakh cash award by the Steel Authority of India.
- Rs. 5 lakh cash award by R.K. Global Shares and Securities Ltd.
- Rs. 5 lakh cash award by the Maharashtra State Government.
- Rs. 25 lakh cash award by the Government of India.

Achievements

☆ *He won a gold medal at the World Cadet Games in 1998.*

☆ *He again won a gold medal at the World Cadet Games in 1999.*

☆ *He won gold medal in the Asian Junior Championship in 2001.*

☆ *Sushil Kumar got success in the Senior Asian Wrestling Championships in 2003 (London) and 2005 (Cape Town).*

☆ *He won a bronze medal in the 2006 Doha Asian Games.*

☆ *He again won the Commonwealth Wrestling Championship by getting a gold medal in London in the Men's Freestyle 66 kg. event.*

- ☆ *He won a silver medal in the 2007 Asian Wrestling Championship.*
- ☆ *He won a gold medal in 2008 Jeju Island Asian Wrestling Championship in 66 kg. category.*
- ☆ *In 2008 Beijing Olympics Sushil Kumar created history when he won the bronze medal in men's freestyle 66 kg. event.*
- ☆ *In 2009, he was honoured with the 'Rajiv Gandhi Khel Ratna' award.*

YACHTING

Yachting is a sport in which sail boats or motor-driven boats are used for racing or recreation. The sailboats, known as yachts, are usually light and comparatively small. Until the mid-19th century, yachts were designed on the lines of naval craft, such as schooners and cutters.

A modern yacht (the word is derived from the Dutch word meaning ship for 'chasing') is used usually for sailing. In the 17th century, the Dutch royalty sailed the early yachts for pleasure. Charles II introduced the sport in England. Original yacht racing began on River Thames in the mid-18th century; in North America, it began with the arrival of the Dutch in the 17th century and continued under the British. The first US yacht clubs were founded in the mid-19th century.

Sail-boat races are held over two kinds of courses — point-to-point and closed. Yacht sailing became an Olympic sport in 1900.

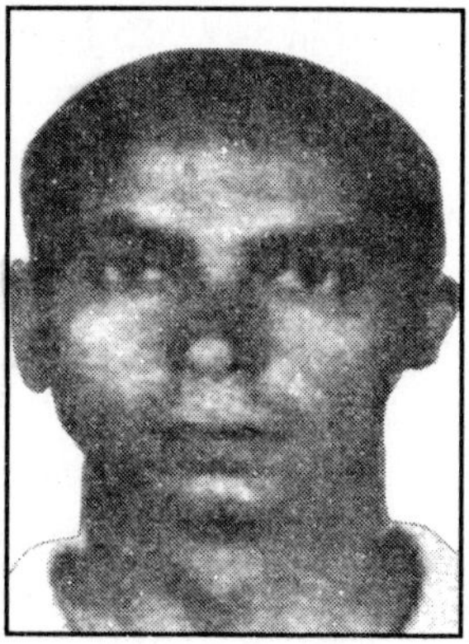

Homi Dady Motivala

Date of Birth: 18th June 1958

Homi Dady Motivala has been one of the best sportspersons in yachting. He was honoured with the Arjuna Award in 1993 and in 1994 he was awarded the 'Rajiv Gandhi Khel Ratna' award jointly with P.K. Garg. He was also awarded the 'Dronacharya Award' in 2002 for fine coaching in yachting.

Homi Dady Motivala gained success in many national and international competitions in yachting. He was the sailing master in a sailing competition from Bombay to Sydney in 1987-88.

He was born on 18th June 1958 in Mumbai. An alumnus of Scottish High School, Mumbai, he received training at the National Defence Academy, Khadakvasla. Then he joined the Indian Navy.

Motivala won his first National Championship title in 1983. He won two other National Championship title in partnership with P.K. Garg in 1986 and 1990. In 1992 he became the national champion in the Seabird class. He won the National Match Yacht Racing Championship in 1990 and 1993.

He won a gold medal at the World Enterprise Championship at Zimbabwe in 1993. He won a bronze medal each in the 1990 Beijing Asian Games and 1994 Hiroshima Asian Games.

Motivala won many competitions at the world level, bagging a gold at the South-west Area Championship in the UK in 1990 and a bronze at the North-east Area Championship the very same year. He participated in the sailing expedition of 'Tall Ships Australia' from Mumbai to Sydney.

He received the 'Shaurya Chakra' in 1983 and the 'Shivaji Chhatrapati

Award' in 1989-90 from the Maharashtra government. He won the 'Rajiv Gandhi Khel Ratna' award in 1994 jointly with P.K. Garg.

Achievements

- ☆ *Motivala won the National Team Championship of Yachting Association of India in 1983, 1984, 1986, 1987, 1990 and 1991.*
- ☆ *Motivala won his first individual title of National Championship in 1983.*
- ☆ *He won a gold medal in Zimbabwe's World Enterprise Championship.*
- ☆ *The Government of India honoured him with the Arjuna Award' in 1993.*
- ☆ *He was given 'Shaurya Chakra' in 1983. At that time he was a commander in Indian Navy.*
- ☆ *Maharashtra Government honoured him with the 'Shivaji Chhatrapati Award' in 1989-90.*
- ☆ *He was given 'Yachtsmen of the Year' trophy in 1990 and 1993.*
- ☆ *He got the highest sports honour of the country 'Rajiv Gandhi Khel Ratna' award in 1994 jointly with P.K. Garg.*

Pushpendra Kumar Garg

Date of Birth: 22nd November 1963

Pushpendra Kumar Garg is popularly known by his short name, P.K. Garg. Besides many achievements in yachting, he is the recipient of the Arjuna Award and the 'Rajiv Gandhi Khel Ratna' award.

Indian Navy Commander P.K. Garg came into limelight in sports when he won a gold medal in the National Team Championship in 1986 by pairing with Homi Dady Motivala.

Pushpendra Garg was born on 22nd November 1963 at Sasni in Aligarh district of Uttar Pradesh. He is a product of Sainik School, Lucknow before he received training at the National Defence Academy, Khadakvasla. He then joined the Indian Navy.

He won a gold medal in the National Team Championship in 1986 with Homi Motivala. Subsequently he received a silver medal in the Enterprise National Championship in 1988. In 1989, he again won gold in the National Team Championship. The year 1990 remained the most rewarding year for him as he won a gold medal in the National Team Championship and created a record.

He won the Enterprise World Championship in Zimbabwe in 1993. In the 1994 Asian Games at Hiroshima, he had to settle with a mere bronze. He was honoured with the Arjuna Award in 1990. He was the joint winner of the 'Rajiv Gandhi Khel Ratna' award in 1993-94 with Homi Motivala.

Achievements

☆ *P.K. Garg won the Enterprise National Championship four times with Homi Motivala.*

- ☆ *In 1986, he won the National Team Championship with Motivala.*
- ☆ *In 1990 Beijing Asian Games and in the 1994 Hiroshima Asian Games, he won bronze medals in the Enterprise category.*
- ☆ *He was given the Arjuna Award in 1990.*
- ☆ *He got the 'Rajiv Gandhi Khel Ratna' award in 1994 jointly with Homi Motivala. At that time he was holding the rank of Lt. Commander in the Indian Navy.*

Appendix-I

Winners of 'Rajiv Gandhi Khel Ratna' Award

Athletics	1998	Smt Jyotirmoyee Sikdar
	2002	Ms K. M. Beenamol (Joint Winner)
	2004	Ms Anju Bobby George
Badminton	2001	Shri Pullela Gopichand
Billiards and Snooker	1992	Shri Geet Sethi
Boxing	2005	Shri Pankaj Advani
	2009	M.C. Mary Kom
	2009	Shri Vijender Kumar
Chess	1991	Shri Vishwanathan Anand
Cricket	1997	Shri Sachin Ramesh Tendulkar
	2007	Shri Mahender Singh Dhoni
Hockey	1999	Shri Dhanraj Pillai
Shooting	2002	Shri Abhinav Bindra
	2003	Ms Anjali R. Bhagwat
	2004	Shri Rajyavardhan Singh Rathore
	2006	Manavjit Singh Sandhu
Tennis	1996	Shri Leander Paes (Joint Winner)
Weightlifting	1996	Ms Karnam Malleswari
	1996	Ms N. Kunjarani (Joint Winner)
	2009	Shri Sushil Kumar
Yachting	1994	Cdr. Homi D. Motivala
	1994	Lt. Cdr. P.K. Garg

Appendix-II

Winners of 'Arjuna Award'

Archery

1981 Km Krishna Das
1989 Shri Shyam Lal
1991 Shri Limba Ram
1992 Shri Sanjeev Kumar Singh
2005 Mr Tarundeep Rai
2005 Ms Dola Banerjee
2009 Shri Mangal Singh Champia

Athletics

1961 Shri G.S. Randhava
1962 Hav. Tarlok Singh
1963 Km S. D'Souza
1964 Shri Makhan Singh
1965 Shri K.L. Powel
1966 Shri Ajmer Singh
1966 Shri B.S. Barua
1967 Shri Bhim Singh
1967 Shri Praveen Kumar
1968 Capt. Joginder Singh
1968 Km Manjit Walia
1969 Hav. Harnek Singh
1970 Shri M. Singh Gill
1971 Shri Edward Sequeira
1972 Shri V. Singh Chauhan
1973 Hav. Sriram Singh
1974 Shri S.S. Rajput
1974 Shri T.C. Yohanan
1975 Inspector H. Chand
1975 Km V.A. Bai
1976 Km G. Zutshi
1976 Shri B. Singh
1978-79 Km A.M. Joseph
1978-79 Shri Suresh Babu
1979-80 Shri R. Gyanasekaran
1980-81 Shri Gopal Saini
1981 Shri Sabir Ali
1982 Km M.D. Valsamma
1982 Shri Chand Ram
1982 Shri Charles Borromeo
1983 Capt. S. Yadav
1983 Km P.T. Usha
1984 Km Shiny K. Abraham
1984 Shri Raj Kumar
1985 Km A. Agarwal
1985 Shri A.J. Sumariwala
1985 Shri R.S. Bal
1986 Km Suman Rawat
1987 Km V. Shanbagh
1987 Km Vandana Rao
1987 Shri Bagicha Singh
1987 Shri Balvinder Singh
1988 Km A. Nachappa
1989 Smt Mercy Kuttan
1990 Shri Deena Ram
1992 Shri Bahadur Prasad
1993 Km K. Saramma
1994 Ms K.C. Rosa Kutty
1995 Ms Jyotirmoyee Sikdar
1995 Shri Shakti Singh
1996 Ms Padmini Thomas
1996 Shri Ajit Bhaduria
1997 Smt Reeth Abraham
1998 Capt. Siri Chand Ram
1998 Ms N.J. Singh
1998 Ms Rachita Mistry
1998 Shri Paramjit Singh

1998	Shri S.D. Eshan
1999	Mrs Gurmit Kaur
1999	Ms Sunita Rani
1999	Parduman Singh
1999	Shri Gulab Chand
2000	Ms K.M. Beenamol
2000	Shri Joginder Singh Bedi (Posthumously) (For Life time Contribution)
2000	Shri Vijay Bhalchandra Munishwar Powerlifting (Posthumously)
2000	Shri Yadvendra Vashi-shta (Posthumously)
2002	Ms Anju Bobby George
2002	Smt Saraswat Saha
2003	Km Soma Biswas
2003	Smt Madhuri Saxena
2004	Anil Kumar
2004	Devendra (Paralympics)
2004	J.J. Shobha
2005	Ms Manjit Kaur
2005	Shri Rajinder Singh Rahelu (Posthumously)
2006	Ms K.M. Binu
2007	Ms Km Chitra Soman
2009	Shri Sinimol Paulose

Badminton

1961	Shri N.M. Natekar
1962	Km Meena Shah
1965	Shri Dinesh Khanna
1967	Shri Suresh Goel
1969	Shri Dipu Ghosh
1970	Shri J. Pitchyya
1970	Smt D.V. Tambay
1971	Ms S. Moorthy
1972	Km J. Srinivasan
1972	Shri Prakash Padukone
1973	Shri A. Kareem
1974	Shri Raman Ghosh
1975	Shri Davinder Ahuja
1975	Shri L.A. Iqbal
1976	Km Ami Ghia
1976	Shri A. Sam Christ Das
1977	Km K.T. Singh
1980	Shri Syed Modi
1982	Km M. Goswami
1982	Shri P. Ganguli
1984	Shri D. Rajaraman
1991	Shri Rajeev Bagga
1999	Shri Pullela Gopichand
2000	Shri George Thomas
2003	Shri Madasu Srinivas Rao
2004	Shri Abhinn Shyam Gupta
2005	Ms Aparna Popat
2009	Ms Sania Nehwal
2009	Shri Parul Parmar

Basketball

1961	Shri Sarbjit Singh
1967	Shri Khushi Ram
1968	Naib Sub. Gurdial Singh
1969	Hav. Hari Dutt
1970	Shri Abbas Moontasir
1971	Pilot Officer Man Mohan Singh
1973	Shri S.K. Kataria
1974	Shri A.K. Punj
1975	Shri Hanuman Singh
1977-78	Shri T. Vijayaraghawan
1979-80	Shri Om Prakash
1981	Km S. Sharma
1981	Shri Radhey Shyam
1982	Shri Ajmer Singh
1999	Shri Sajjan Singh Cheema
2001	Shri Parminder Singh

Billiards and Snooker

2003	Shri Pankaj Advani
2005	Ms Anuja Prakash Thakur

Boxing

1961	Shri L. Buddy D' Souza
1962	Hav. P. Bahadur Mal
1966	Shri Hawa Singh
1968	Hav. Dennis Swamy

1971 Hav. Muniswamy Venu
1972 Hav. Chandranarayanan
1973 Hav. Mehatab Singh
1977-78 Shri B.S. Thapa
1978-79 Shri C.C. Machaiah
1979-80 Shri B. Singh
1980-81 Shri Issac Amaldas
1981 Hav. G. Manoharan
1982 Hav. Kaur Singh
1983 Shri Jas Lal Pradhan
1986 Shri Jai Pal Singh
1987 Shri Seeva Jayaram
1989 Shri Gopal Dewang
1991 Shri D.S. Yadav
1992 Shri Rajender Prasad
1993 Shri Manoj Pingale
1993 Shri Mukund Killekar
1995 Shri V. Devarajan
1996 Shri Raj Kumar Sangwan
1998 Shri N.G. Dingko Singh
1999 Shri Gurcharan Singh
1999 Shri Jitender Kumar
2002 Mohammad Ali Qamar
2003 Km Mangte Chungneijang Marykom
2005 Shri Akhil Kumar
2009 Ms L. Sarita Devi

Chess

2003 Km Koneru Humpi
2005 Shri Surya Shekhar Ganguly
2009 Ms Tania Sachdev

Cricket

1961 Shri Saleem Durani
1964 Shri Mansur Ali Khan Pataudi
1965 Shri Vijay Manjrekar
1966 Shri Chandu G. Borde
1967 Shri Ajit Wadekar
1968 Shri E.A.S. Prasanna
1969 Shri Bishan Singh Bedi
1970 Shri Dilip N. Sardesai
1971 Shri S. Venkataraghavan
1972 Shri B.S. Chandra-shekhar
1972 Shri Eknath D. Solkar
1975 Shri Sunil Gavaskar
1976 Km S. Rangaswamy
1977-78 Shri G.R. Vishwanath
1979-80 Shri Kapil Dev Nikhanj
1980-81 Shri Chetan P.S. Chauhan
1980-81 Shri Syed M.H. Kirmani
1981 Shri Dilip Vengsarkar
1982 Shri Mohinder Amarnath
1983 Km Diana Idulji
1984 Shri Ravi Shastri
1985 Km S.D. Kulkarni
1986 Km S. Agarwal
1986 Shri Mohammad Azharuddin
1989 Shri Madan Lal
1993 Shri Kiran More
1993 Shri Manoj Prabhakar
1994 Shri Sachin Tendulkar
1995 Shri Anil Kumble
1996 Shri Javagal Srinath
1997 Shri Ajay Jadeja
1997 Shri Sourav Ganguly
1998 Shri Nayan Ramlal Mongia
1998 Shri Rahul Dravid
2000 Shri B.K. Venkatesh Prasad
2001 Shri V.V.S. Laxman
2002 Shri Virendra Sehwag
2003 Km Mithali Raj
2003 Shri Harbhajan Singh
2005 Ms Anju Jain
2009 Shri Gautam Gambhir

Cycling

1975 Shri Amar Singh
1978-79 Km M. Mahapatra
1983 Km A.R. Arthna

Equestrian

1973 Dafadar Khan M. Khan

1976 Lt. Col. H.S. Sodhi
1982 Maj. R. Singh Brar
1982 Shri Raghubir Singh
1984 Capt. G. Mohammad Khan
1987 Maj. J.S. Ahluwalia
1991 Capt. Adhiraj Singh
2003 Capt. Rajesh Pattu
2004 Deep Ahlawat

Football

1961 Shri P.K. Banerjee
1962 Shri T. Balaram
1963 Shri S.(Chuni) Goswami
1964 Shri Jarnail Singh
1965 Shri Arun Lal Ghosh
1966 Shri Yusuf Khan
1967 Shri Peter Thangaraj
1969 Shri Inder Singh
1970 Shri S. Naeemuddin
1971 Shri C.P. Singh
1973 Shri M.S. Rajvi
1978-79 Shri Gurdev Singh
1979-80 Shri Prasun Banerjee
1980-81 Shri Mohammed Habib
1981 Shri Sudhir Karmakar
1983 Km Shanti Mullick
1989 Shri S. Bhattacharjee
1997 Shri B.S.K. Shankhwalker
1998 Shri Baichung Butia
2001 Shri Bruno Coutinho
2002 Shri Inivalappil Mani Vijayan

Golf

2004 Jyoti Randhawa

Gymnastics

1961 Shri Shyam Lal
1975 Shri Montu Debnath
1985 Km S. Sharma
1989 Km Krupali Patel
2000 Dr (Ms) Kalpna Debnath

Hockey

1961 Km N. Lumsden
1961 Shri P. Singh
1963 Shri Charanjit Singh
1964 Shri S. Laxman
1965 Km E. Britto
1965 Shri Udham Singh
1966 Km Sunita Puri
1966 Shri Gurbaksh Singh
1966 Shri V.J. Peter
1967 Shri Harbinder Singh
1967 Shri Mohinder Lal
1968 Cadet Balbir Singh
1970 Shri Ajit Pal Singh
1971 Shri P. Krishnamurthy
1972 Shri Michael Kindo
1973 Dr (Km) O. Mascarenhas
1973 Shri M.P. Ganesh
1974 Km A. Kaur
1974 Shri Ashok Kumar
1975 Km R. Saini
1975 Shri B.P. Govinda
1977-78 Capt. Harcharan Singh
1977-78 Km L.L. Fernandes
1979-80 Km R.B. Mundphan
1979-80 Shri V. Bhaskaran
1980-81 Shri Mohammed Shahid
1980-81 Smt Eliza Nelson
1981 Km Versha Soni
1983 Shri Zafar Iqbal
1984 Km Rajbir Kaur
1985 Km P. Maya Sonia
1985 Shri Panda Muthanna
1985 Shri S. Maney
1986 Shri J.M. Carvalho
1988 Shri M.P. Singh
1989 Shri Pargat Singh
1990 Shri Jagbir Singh
1992 Shri Mervyn Fernandes
1994 Shri Jude Felix Sebastian
1995 Shri Dhanraj Pillai
1995 Shri Mukesh Kumar
1996 Shri A.B. Subbaiah

1996 Shri Ashish Kumar Ballal
1997 Shri Harmik Singh
1997 Shri Rajinder Singh
1997 Shri Surinder Singh Sodhi
1998 Late Shri S. Surjit Singh
1998 Lt. Col. (Retd.) Haripal Kaushik
1998 Mohammed Riyaz
1998 Ms Pritam Rani
1998 Shri B.S. Dhillon
1998 Shri Baldev Singh
1998 Shri Maharaj Krishna Kaushik
1998 Shri Ramandeep Singh
1998 Shri V.J. Phillips
1998 Smt S. Omana Kumari
1999 Shri Balbir Singh Khullar
2000 Group Capt. R.S. Bhola (Retd.)
2000 Ms Madhu Yadav
2000 Ms Tingonleima Chanu
2000 Shri Jalaluddin Rizvi
2000 Shri Baljeet Singh Saini
2000 Shri Balkishan Singh
2001 Ms Sita Gusain
2001 Shri Dilip Kumar Tirkey
2002 Ms Mamta Kharab
2002 Shri Gagan Ajit Singh
2003 Km Suraj Lata Devi
2003 Shri Devesh Chauhan
2004 Deepak Thakur
2004 Innocent Helen Mary
2005 Shri Viren Rasquinha
2009 Shri Ignatius Tirkey
2009 Ms Surinder Kaur

Judo

1992 Shri Sandeep Byala
1993 Shri Cawas Billimoria
1996 Ms Poonam Chopra
1998 Shri Narender Singh
2003 Shri Akram Shah
2004 Angom Anita Chanu

Kabaddi

2003 Shri Sanjeev Kumar
2004 Shri Sunder Singh
2005 Shri Ramesh Kumar
2009 Shri Pankaj Shirsat

Rowing

1981 Maj. Parveen Oberoy
1984 Capt. M.A. Naik
1991 Naib Subedar Dalvir Singh
1994 Major R.S. Bhanwala
1996 Shri Surender Singh Waldia
1999 Shri Jagjit Singh
2000 Shri Surender Singh Kanwasi
2001 Shri Kasam Khan
2002 Shri Inder Pal Singh
2004 Shri J. Krishnan
2009 Shri Ranjan Sodhi

Shooting

1961 Shri Karni Singh
1968 Ms Rajyashree Kumari
1969 Km Bhuvaneshwari Kumari
1971 Shri Bhim Singh
1972 Shri Udyan Chinubhai
1978-79 Shri Randhir Singh
1981 Shri S.P. Chauhan
1983 Km Soma Dutta
1983 Shri Mohinder Lal
1985 Shri A.J. Pandit
1986 Shri Bhagirath Samai
1993 Shri Mansher Singh
1994 Shri Jaspal Rana
1996 Shri Morad A. Khan
1997 Ms Shilpi Singh
1997 Shri Satendra Kumar
1998 Ms Roopa Unnikrishnan
1998 Shri Manavjit Singh
1999 Shri Vivek Singh
2000 Ms Anjali Vedpathak Bhagwat

2000	Shri Abhinav Bindra
2000	Shri Gurbir Singh
2001	Shri Samresh Jung
2002	Ms Suma Sidharth Shirur
2002	Shri Anwar Sultan
2003	Major Rajyavardhan Singh Rathore
2004	Deepali Deshpande
2005	Shri Gagan Narang

Swimming

1961	Shri Jam. Bajarangi Prasad
1966	Km Rima Datta
1967	Shri Arun Shaw
1969	Shri Baidyanath Nath
1971	Shri Bhanwar Singh
1973	Shri D.(Tingoo) Khatau
1974	Km Manjari Bhargava
1974	Shri A.B. Sarang
1975	Km Smita Desai
1975	Shri M.S. Rana
1982	Km Persis Madan
1983	Km Anita Sood
1984	Shri Khajan Singh
1988	Shri Wilson Cherian
1990	Km Bula Choudhury
1996	Master V. Kutraleeshwaran
1998	Shri Bhanu Sachdeva
1999	Ms Nisha Millet
2000	Shri J. Abhijith
2000	Shri Sebastian Xavier
2005	Ms Shikha Tandon

Table Tennis

1961	Shri J.C. Vohra
1965	Shri G.R. Deewan
1966	Km U. Sundararaj
1967	Shri F.R. Khodaiji
1969	Shri Mir Kasim Ali
1970	Shri G. Jagannath
1971	Smt K.F. Khodaiji
1973	Shri N.R. Bajaj
1976	Km S. Shailja
1979-80	Km Indu Puri
1980-81	Shri Manjit Dua
1982	Shri V. Chandrasekhar
1985	Shri K.N. Mehta
1987	Smt M.B. Mehta
1989	Smt Niyati Shah
1990	Shri M.S. Walia
1997	Shri Chetan P. Baboor
1998	Shri Subramaniam Raman
2002	Ms Montu Ghosh
2004	Achanta S Kamal
2005	Shri Soumyadeep Roy
2009	Shri Poulami Ghatak

Tennis

1961	Shri Ramesh Krishnan
1962	Shri Naresh Kumar
1966	Shri Jaideep Mukherjee
1967	Shri Premjit Lal
1974	Shri Vijay Amritraj
1978-79	Smt N. Mankad
1980-81	Shri Ramesh Krishnan
1985	Shri Anand Amritraj
1990	Shri Leander Paes
1995	Shri Mahesh Bhupathi
1996	Shri Gaurav Nandu Natekar
1997	Shri Asif Ismail
2000	Shri Akhtar Ali
2001	Shri Sandeep Kirtane
2004	Ms Sania Mirza

Volleyball

1961	Shri A. Palaniswamy
1962	Shri Nripjit Singh
1972	Shri Balwant Singh
1973	Smt G.M. Reddy
1974	Shri M.S. Rao
1975	Km K.C. Elamma
1975	Sub. Insp. R. Singh
1976	Shri Jimmi George
1977-78	Shri A. Raman Rao
1978-79	Shri Kutty Krishan

1979-80 Shri S.K. Mishra
1982 Shri G.E. Sridharan
1983 Shri R.K. Purohit
1984 Km Saley Joseph
1986 Shri Cyril C. Vallor
1989 Shri Abdul Basith
1990 Shri Dalel Singh
1991 Shri K. Udaya Kumar
1999 Shri Sukhpal Singh
2000 Shri P.V. Ramana
2001 Shri Amir Singh
2002 Shri Ravikant Reddy

Weightlifting

1961 Shri A.N. Ghosh
1962 Shri L.K. Dass
1963 Shri K.E. Rao
1965 Shri B.S. Bhatia
1966 Shri Mohan Lal Ghosh
1967 Shri S. John Gabriel
1970 Shri Arun Kumar Dass
1971 Shri S.L. Salwan
1972 Shri Anil Kumar Mandal
1974 Shri S. Vellaiswamy
1975 Shri Dalbir Singh
1976 Shri K. Balamuruganandam
1977-78 Shri M.T. Selvan
1978-79 Shri E. Karaunakaran
1981 Shri B.K. Satpathy
1982 Shri Tara Singh
1983 Shri Vispy K. Daroga
1985 Shri M.C. Bhasker
1986 Shri Jag Mohan Sapra
1987 Shri G. Devan
1989 Km Jyotsna Dutta
1990 Km N. Kunjarani
1990 Shri R. Chandra
1991 Km Chhaya Adak
1993 Smt Bharati Singh
1994 Ms Karnam Malleswari
1997 Shri Paramjit Sharma
1997 Smt N. Laxmi
1998 Shri Satish Rai
1999 Shri Dalbir Singh
2000 Ms Sanamacha Chanu Thingbaijan
2002 Shri Thandava Murthy Muthu

Wrestling

1961 Hav. Udey Chand
1962 Shri Malwa
1963 Shri G. Andalkar
1964 Shri Bishamber Singh
1966 Shri Bhim Singh
1967 Shri Mukhtiar Singh
1969 Master Chandgi Ram
1970 Shri Sudesh Kumar
1972 Shri Prem Nath
1973 Shri Jagroop Singh
1974 Shri Satpal
1978-79 Shri Rajinder Singh
1980-81 Shri Jagminder Singh
1982 Shri Kartar Singh
1985 Shri Mahabir Singh
1987 Shri Subhash
1988 Shri Rajesh Kumar
1989 Shri Satyawan
1990 Shri Ombir Singh
1992 Shri Pappu Yadav
1993 Shri Ashok Kumar
1997 Shri Jagdish Singh
1997 Shri Sanjay Kumar
1998 Shri Kaka Pawar
1998 Shri Rohtas Singh Dahiya
1999 Late Shri Khashaba Jadhav (posthomously)
1999 Shri Ashok Kumar
2000 Shri Naresh Kumar
2001 Shri Ramesh Kumar
2002 Shri Palwinder Singh Cheema
2002 Shri Sujeet Mann
2003 Shri Shokinder Tomar
2004 Shri Anuj Kumar

2005 Shri Sushil Kumar
2009 Shri Yogeshwar Dutt

Yachting

1970 Lt. Cdr. S.J. Contractor
1973 Shri Afsar Hussain
1978-79 Cdr. S.K. Mongia
1981 Shri Zarir Karanjia
1982 Shri Fali Unwalla
1982 Shri Farokh Tarapore
1982 Shri Jeeja Unwalla
1986 Lt. Dhruv Bhandari
1987 Shri C.S. Pradipak
1990 Shri P.K. Garg
1993 Cdr. Homi Motiwala
1996 Late Lt. Cdr. Kelly Subbanand Rao (posthumous)
1999 Lt. Cdr. R. Mahesh
1999 Shri Aashim Mongia
2002 Shri Nitin Mongia
2009 Shri G.L. Yadav

Appendix-III

Winners of the 'Dronacharya Award'

Athletics

1985 Shri O.M. Nambiar
1994 Mohammad Ilyas Babar
1995 Shri Karan Singh
1997 Shri Joginder Singh Saini
1998 Shri Bahadur Singh
1998 Shri Hargobind Singh Sandhu
1999 Shri Kenneth Owen Bosen
2002 Ms Renu Kohli
2002 Shri Jaswant singh
2003 Shri Robert Bobby George

Badminton

2000 Shri S. M. Arif
2009 Shri Pullela Gopichand

Billiards and Snooker

1996 Shri Wilson Jones
2001 Shri Michael Joseph Ferriera
2004 Arvind Savur

Boxing

1985 Shri Om Prakash Bhardwaj
1998 Shri G.S. Sandhu
1999 Late. Capt. Hawa Singh
2003 Shri Anoop Kumar
2005 Hony. Captain M. Venu
2009 Shri Jaidev Bisht

Chess

1986 Shri Raghunandan Vasant Gokhale

Cricket

1986 Shri Desh Prem Azad
1987 Shri Gurcharan Singh
1990 Shri Ramakant Achrekar
2004 Ms Sunita Sharma

Football

1990 Syed Naeemuddin

Hockey

2000 Shri Grudial Singh Bhangu
2002 Shri M. K. Kaushik
2003 Shri Rajinder Singh
2009 Shri Baldev Singh

Kabaddi

2002 Shri E. Prasad Rao
2005 Shri Balwan Singh

Kho Kho

2000 Shri Phadke Gopal Purshottam

Rowing

2005 Shri Ismail Baig

Shooting

2001 Prof. Sunny Thomas

Squash

2004 Cyrus Poncha

Volleyball

1990 Shri A. Ramana Rao
1995 Shri M. Shyam Sunder Rao

Weightlifting

1996 Shri Pal Singh Sandhu
1999 Shri Ajay Kumar Sirohi
2000 Smt Hansa Sharma

Wrestling

1985 Shri Bhalachandra Bhaskar Bhagat
1987 Shri Guru Hanuman
2003 Shri Sukhchain Singh Cheema
2005 Shri Maha Singh Rao
2009 Shri Satpal

Yachting

2002 Cdr. H. D. Motivala

Appendix-IV

Winners of 'Dhyan Chand Award'

Athletics

2003 Brig. (Retd.) Labh Singh
2003 Shri Mehendale Digamber Parshuram
2006 Shri Uday K. Prabhu
2009 Shri Ishar Singh Deol

Basketball

2002 Ms G. S. Randhava (Women)
2003 Shri Ram Kumar (Men)

Billiards and Snooker

2004 Manoj Kumar Kothari

Boxing

2002 Shri Shahuraj V. Birajdar (Men)

Hockey

2002 Shri Ashok Diwan (Men)
2002 Shri Charles Cornelius (Men)
2003 Shri Hardyal Singh
2003 Shri Dharm Singh Maan (Men)
2004 Shri Rajinder Singh Junior
2006 Cdr. Nandy Singh

Rowing

2003 Ms Smita Shirole Yadav (Women)

Volleyball

2003 Shri Om Prakash (Men)

Wrestling

2004 Maruti Dhyanu Mane Patil
2006 Shri Harish Chandra M. Birajdar
2009 Shri Satbir Singh Dahya

❑❑❑